ITALIA
REVISITED
THE PLAYERS' STORIES

by Harry Harris

EMPIRE
PUBLICATIONS

First published in 2020

EMPIRE PUBLICATIONS
1 Newton Street, Manchester M1 1HW
© Harry Harris 2020

ISBN: 978-1-909360-77-8

CONTENTS

Picture by David Bailey, especially commissioned by FourFourTwo magazine for an article on the movers and shakers in football.

ABOUT THE AUTHOR

Harry Harris was the Chief Sports Writer of the *Daily Mirror* throughout a turbulent period for English football. His beat soon centred on the national team as an obvious focus for the standing of the national game following the banning of English clubs from European competition following the Heysel Stadium disaster. Concurrently an escalating circulation war had developed between his paper and *The Sun* and sensational football stories were seen as a way of winning readers. It all made the job of England manager Bobby Robson that much harder. In part, this book tells the story of the media's role in the 1990 World Cup.

Harry is a Double winner of the British Sports Journalist of the Year award and was honoured by the prestigious Variety Club of Great Britain with their Silver Heart trophy for 'Contribution to Sports Journalism'. He is also a double winner of the Sports Story of the Year award, the only journalist ever to win the accolade twice. He has earned a total of 24 industry awards.

A regular football analyst on TV news and sports programmes such as Richard & Judy, Newsnight, BBC News and ITV News at Ten, Sky, Setanta, Radio 5 Live, Radio 4, and TalkSport. He has been interviewed on Football Focus, was an original guest on Hold The Back Page and Jimmy Hill's Sunday Supplement on Sky.

Arguably the most prolific writer of best selling football books of

As the article says "The sports journo they quote in the Commons"

his generation, among 80 plus books are the highly acclaimed best seller in the UK and the States *Pelé - His Life and Times*, now fully updated and even published in Vietnam. He wrote George Best's last book and best seller, *Hard Tackles and Dirty Baths*.

One of the most influential football columnists for three decades, and an acclaimed investigative journalist with the *Daily Mail, Daily Mirror, Daily Express, Daily Star, Sunday Express* and *Star on Sunday*. More recently he worked with the *Telegraph* as part of an Investigative Team that spawned the best seller *The Killing of Emiliano Sala*.

Dedicated to the memory of the Morris Men. Sadly only Colin Gibson and myself survive; Steve Curry (*Daily Express*) passed away recently, Stuart Jones (*The Times*) a while ago.

ACKNOWLEDGEMENTS

Thanks for the exclusive interviews from the players of Italia '90: John Barnes, Bryan Robson, Chris Waddle, Stuart Pearce, Peter Shilton, David Platt, Mark Wright, Des Walker, Paul Parker, Steve McMahon, Terry Butcher, Trevor Steven, Gary Stevens, Neil Webb, Tony Dorigo, Dave Beasant, Steve Bull, David Seaman, Chris Woods and Peter Beardsley. Special thanks to Katie Davies M&N Management Ltd, the new agent for Paul Gascoigne. .

Thanks for the personal contributions from the journalists who were there: Mike Ingham, Michael Hart and Steve Stammers.

Thanks to the most prominent football agents of that period who were there representing some of the biggest names in Bobby Robson's squad: Jon Holmes and Mel Stein.

Thanks to Ashley and John at Empire Publications.

FOREWORD BY PAUL GASCOIGNE

PAUL GASCOIGNE

When I see clips of Italia '90 I feel great, then immediately sad. It was the best time of my life, I loved it; I loved it from the moment I got on that plane, nothing phased me, I wanted to be in the World Cup, it's every player's dream, but it felt like I was going on holiday. I was playing tennis, table tennis, I loved every minute of it. My greatest memory of Italia '90 is getting on that plane and feeling the excitement.

It doesn't feel like 30 years ago; when those clips come up on TV it feels like yesterday. But then I'm upset, and try not to think about Italia '90. The best time of my life, yes, but how I miss it, I miss it so much, because I never got to experience it again, and that's why it makes me feel so sad after feeling so good about watching it all back on TV.

When I played against Israel for 10 minutes, they scored and I felt I was not going to the World Cup but Bobby Robson said to me that he would play me against the Czech Republic at Wembley and if I played well that he would pick me. I set up three goals and scored one, so I knew I was going to the World Cup. Bobby said that we would need two balls in our games, one for Gazza and one for the rest of the team!

Out in Italy I just loved it, but I treated it like I had treated going to a youth cup tournament; it was a holiday, I played tennis, spent time by the pool, I was on the pedal boats but the football didn't worry me, I didn't care who we were playing, what anyone said about the opposition, I knew I could get the better of them, I was full of confidence, not interested in the tactics, who their best player was, or who would be marking me, all I was interested in was in winning those games and doing my best for the team to achieve it.

Of course playing tennis at one in the morning before the World Cup semi-final didn't go down too well with the gaffer. I was on the court and I could hear this gruff voice shouting "Gazza, Gazza". I thought 'f—- I'm in trouble now'.

Bobby Robson would knock on my door if he thought I was up too late playing tennis. I would tell Chris Waddle, as I roomed with him, that if he heard a knock on the door, it was sure to be Bobby Robson and to tell him I'm asleep. Sure enough there was a knock on the door.

"Gazza, where is he?"

Chris would reply "He's sleeping, Boss".'

"Sleeping, sleeping, I've been told he's been playing tennis for the last two hours!"

Bobby Robson told me before the game with West Germany that I would be up against Lothar Matthäus who was the best midfielder in the world. I told him "Sorry, you are wrong there gaffer… I'm the best in the world." And I was determined to go out and prove it and I did.

Before that semi-final, the President of Juventus stopped me in the stadium and said he wanted to sign me after the game, that was minutes before I was about to go and get ready to play. He said I should first sign for Roma to learn the language and settle into the Italian way of life, then he would sign me from Roma, and he wanted to speak to me after the game.

As for the tears; you know I didn't touch the German, and the ref said to me that he wouldn't have booked me if he had known I'd already been booked. But I cried, not because I was missing the final as everyone thinks, I cried because I felt I had let down the fans, my team-mates, the manager, everybody.

I cried because I thought it was the end of my career, that I would never have another chance to play in a team like that, on the world stage like that, with and against such world class footballers. And, of course, I was right to have that feeling.

In '94 I broke my arm, and, in any case, we didn't qualify for the States, I had a good Euros in '96, but Glenn Hoddle left me out in '98. He said he'd found God - must have been a great pass! So, it was my first and also my last World Cup but I don't have any regrets that Glenn Hoddle left me out in 98, because no one can take away from me what I did in Italia '90.

When I got back to the north east my dad threw a party for me at our usual local working men's club, but half way through I told him I had to nip out for a while. I went round to the park where I would spend virtually all night kicking the ball around as a kid. In that park I cried, thinking about the kid kicking the ball around there, who had made it all the way to the World Cup semi-final and nearly made the

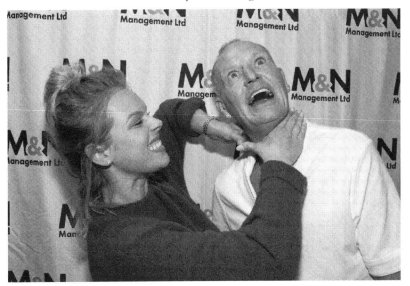

Paul and his new agemt Kate Davies;
we've all wanted to throttle him from time to time!

final.

If I do have a regret it is that I became an alcoholic, and that I now have pellets in my stomach. It's okay if I can have a glass of beer or even a glass of wine, but if I have too much beer or wine, any vodka or spirits or any drugs, then I just spew it all out.

If I have regrets, I keeping thinking: why in, say, America if you are famous that's it you are treated with respect. In our country if you are famous you become a target, you get so much stick.

But, look, don't worry, they can't hurt me any more, they've hurt me far too often, they can't hurt me any more now. I'm happy going fishing. If anyone contacts me to say that I am in the papers, I tell them I don't care, I don't read it any more, I'm not interested.

Pelé would always say, "There's only one Pelé and there will only ever be one Pelé".

Well, there will never be another Paul Gascoigne. And if there is another they will need to be in rehab nine times!

PREFACE

I have been credited with inventing the phrase 'GazzaMania' after the England midfielder's world class exploits in Italia '90, his infamous Tears of Turin, ridiculous false boobs, and a hero's homecoming.

England World Cup Campaign
· Media Accreditation ·

Harry HARRIS

Daily Mirror

Written Press Journalist

The 1990 World Cup lingers in the memory with the image of Gazza's tears, the haunting music of the BBC coverage and the drama if not the quality of the football.

It is hard to believe it all happened 30 years ago but this book brings it all back to life and attempts to bring some perspective to all the hooliganism, racism, humour and edge of the seat football, that has become clouded in the myth that Italia '90 changed football in this country. The 1980s had been very bad for football but the national team's performance and the sudden likeability of the characters in the team has been said to have opened the sport up to people who had hitherto regarded it with disdain but did it?

I was one of the accredited journalists at the tournament as the chief football writer for the *Daily Mirror* and knew exactly what went on behind the scenes, in the training camp and in the team hotel. Few had such privileged access, or knew the key participants better to rekindle the true inside story of Italia '90, and to debunk a few myths.

There was the (widely accepted at the time) drinking culture of the England superstars, their hysterical behind closed door antics, and how they fooled their manager when out on the booze, and made him the target of some amazing practical jokes. In essence it seemed like a long lads holiday and at the centre of it all was Paul Gascoigne who only just scraped into the squad but whose personality and footballing ability dominated. Then there was the role the media played during the tournament, and the bitter rows that went on between the press on one side and the manager and his players on the other.

Certain questions linger 30 years on: was Sir Bobby Robson a tactical genius or did his players dictate the successful switch to the sweeper system? What were the fans really like? How bad was the hooliganism, and the outright blatant racism and why did captain Bryan Robson really leave after only playing two games?

I was there and saw it all, heard it all, and for the first time I'm prepared to tell it all. The book delves into untold stories and insights from players and those behind the team that were privy to what really went on and it's a vastly different England set up to the one led now by Gareth Southgate.

I was at the heart of an ongoing tabloid war between *The Sun* and *The Mirror*. I stayed at the Forte Village hotel where the incident involving captain Bryan Robson and his broken toe took place, and where Gary Lineker's wife Michelle was staying with some friends, and where he even played in front of a watching crowd a game of doubles on Centre Court of the resort's plush tennis centre, with global superstar violinist and Aston Villa fan Nigel Kennedy against then Villa manager 'Big' Ron Atkinson and England's star striker Lineker on one of the players' days off where Gary came to see Michelle.

I spent many evenings dining with BBC Radio 5's outstanding broadcasters Mike Ingham, Alan Green and their future star analyst Terry Butcher, as well as many of the Italia '90 stars such as Lineker, Bryan Robson, Chris Waddle, Paul Parker, Mark Wright, Peter Beardsley, and Peter Shilton. I have subsequently written the autobiography of Steve McMahon. The inside stories of Bobby Robson alone are worth a read!

This then is the story of Italia '90; about how Sir Bobby guided England to their best World Cup finish since '66 and should have won the World Cup, but this was an era when England always seemed to be in awe of Germany and always lost to them and couldn't win a penalty shoot-out to save their lives. Yet while they may not have quite been the good enough to win the biggest prize in football they were still top of the world's drinking league.

I set about tracking down the entire 22 man squad, plus David Seaman who started but didn't finish, tracing Gary Stevens to Western Australia, and having been told Terry Butcher was stranded in China, I thought the big centre-half would be the one totally unreachable. Terry had returned from a Caribbean cruise a day before the USA announced it was closing its borders to residents of the UK, but this was not his biggest scrape with the deadly coronavirus. He was working in China as a defensive coach at Guangzhou having been hired by manager Dragan Stojkovic and in November they played in Wuhan, the origin of the Covid-19 outbreak. Butcher says: "Yes, I had a very lucky escape. We played in Wuhan last November, just days before the outbreak, in our third last game of the season. There was no sign or talk of the virus then. We were based just outside of Wuhan two days before the game, and then flew into the city, trained, came back to the hotel and slept there for the night. Everyone was wearing face masks, but that didn't alert us to anything, because they wear face masks out there anyway, to protect against colds and the like and they protect others from catching things, the Chinese tend to wear face masks as much for other people's protection, so I didn't think anything of it, and it was nothing different than you would see in any other Chinese city."

Having returned to the UK, Butcher was due to fly back to China when his manager was surprisingly replaced by Giovanni van Bronckhorst in January. He continued: "The season finished at the start of December, and I was all set to go back, and I spoke to Dragan and we were working on an exciting pre-season schedule, talking about doing a camp in Thailand or Israel, and I flew home to Suffolk. Then news came at the start of January that Dragan had got the sack, and, as usual, that means all the backroom staff go as well. So I didn't go back out to China but had I done as scheduled then lockdown would have started straight away and it would have been quite bleak out there. Guangzhou is the third largest city in China and it's been one of the worst affected by the coronavirus. If I'd gone back out there as planned then what would have happened to me? I was watching the news seeing all these Brits desperately trying to get home. It was like 'wow, that could have been me'."

Butcher's account of Italia '90 is among so many insightful interviews with so many stories being told for the first time as the stars of the England camp reveal secrets they have kept for the past 30 years. There is plenty of interesting new material about the penalty shoot-out. Penalty kicks may have been invented in 1891 and penalty shoot-outs had been around since 1970 but it was only when the semi-final finished in a draw that England found themselves in their first shoot-out. West Germany by contrast were old hands, having won shoot-outs in both the 1982 and 1986 World Cups. Chris Waddle and Stuart Pearce missed their spot kicks, and the stigma lives on 30 years later. Pearce for one is still clearly haunted by it.

Both cashed in on their notoriety with a Pizza Hut advert, and while it seemed they were self deprecating, the reality was vastly different. It had a profound effect on them; Waddle chose not to take a penalty when his Marseille side lost a shoot-out in the European Cup final a year later, while Pearce famously erupted with relief and emotion when he scored in England's first-ever shoot-out win against Spain at Euro 96.

As of 2020, England had been knocked out of six major tournaments on penalties, with some of the best players to pull on the three lions among those to have missed including David Beckham, Frank Lampard and Steven Gerrard - and the very mention of a penalty shoot-out lead to assumptions of defeat, failure and panic, until Gareth Southgate finally laid that ghost to rest with World Cup penalty shoot-out success against Colombia in 2018.

England's obsession with penalty shoot-outs extended to psychological study as Professor Matt Taylor went as far as to suggest that successive penalty shoot-out failures showed the country's weaknesses whereas other countries saw it as a chance to show their strengths.

Besides the football, there was the music. New Order's *World in Motion* was England's official World Cup song and it seemed to usher in a new football culture with John Barnes providing the memorable rap and becoming a pop star in the process. All of a sudden football went from cheesy sing-a-longs to 'cool' thanks to the Manchester band.

Barnes recalls: "It helped that the team did well and the nation had an empathy with the team. Everything came together; it was iconic. It was a fantastic song and the relationship the fans had with the England team at that time meant they adopted the song. Even now, people still talk about it. I was on the radio with Ed Sheeran the other day and we did a little rendition of my rap."

Written by New Order and comedian Keith Allen, the song famously featured a rap segment by Barnes and a number of other players contributed vocals, while also appearing on the official music video as well as clips of the team in action during the qualification phase. *World in Motion* was the band's only UK No 1.

The first image at the start of the video is Barnes spinning a ball on his finger. He appeared throughout, doing tricks in the background as lead vocalist Bernard Sumner - wearing a T-shirt with the words *World in Motion* on it - sang. Paul Gascoigne, Peter Beardsley, Des Walker and Steve McMahon also featured in the video.

JOHN BARNES

ENGLAND
JOHN BARNES

We had recorded a World Cup album in 1986 for the Mexico World Cup. You must remember it, *The World Cup Party, We've Got The Whole World At Our Feet* and *When We Are Far From Home*. It was so bad that when Bobby Robson told us we would be recording a new record for Italia '90, some of the lads from '86 recalled the last attempt and didn't want to know. We all thought it was going to be another Cup final song; arms around each other, swaying a lot, pretending to sing lousy lyrics to a terrible tune.

Bobby knew how much we disliked meeting up at the hotel on a Sunday for a friendly in the build up to the World Cup finals, as most of the lads preferred to pop into the pub on a Sunday lunch time, so Bobby told us we didn't have to report on the Sunday, they could all go straight to the recording studio in Marlow but they all went to the pub, and only a handful turned up; Peter Beardsley, Steve McMahon, Gazza, Chris Waddle, Des Walker and myself. But when we got there something different was happening. For a start it was New Order, Keith Allen was there, and Craig Johnson was also there as he loved his music as well as his football. With New Order we knew it was going to be a decent song.

We all had a great time, there was plenty to drink and we all had a laugh, a few jokes, and at the end of the song Keith Allen and Craig suggested we should write a rap and add it to the song. That's what we did and I was the one who did the rap. I had recorded the *Anfield Rap* a couple of years earlier but that was a joke really – I had actually been rapping since I was 13 or 14 and I'd write my own. Oddly enough when it came to the video, it looked as though Bobby and the entire team were signing on it, but of course it was just a few of us.

At the time of the World Cup the two most senior players were Bryan Robson and Peter Shilton and they headed up the England players' committee, and the 'brains trust' were told they had two options; settle for royalties only or accept £5,000 for the players' pool. They were told that if the record didn't sell then, of course, there might not even be £5,000 for the pool. In 1986, for example, I can't imagine many were sold despite us getting to the quarter-finals and it was thought that if we didn't do very well in this tournament that song might go the same way, so the brains trust opted for the fee rather than the royalties. You can guess the rest...

Because it was New Order and we did so well out in Italy, the song captured the imagination of the nation and of course it went to number 1 in the UK charts! It was a perfect storm of success, and just about every other week I'm asked to do the rap from *World In Motion* and there was even talk of re-releasing it a few years ago. Then you wonder how much the royalties would have fetched...

My memories of Italia '90 are strange really, mostly clouded by my injuries and also the siege mentality we endured as a result on intrusive media coverage. I was injured going into the tournament and then injured against Belgium and shouldn't have started against Cameroon so missed the semi-final. It was disappointing for me that I wasn't able to perform as I would have like because of those injuries.

England's performances were similar to 1986 in Mexico, not very good to start with but growing into it and having a siege mentality against the media. Some of the tricks they pulled included them bringing women into our team hotel trying to set us up, and I had once experienced the press going to my mother's home in Jamaica, there was so much being reported about us as the media tried to find out what we were up to.

Then again we got up to all sorts without the media trying to set us up! The lads would sneak out to a bar in Puli they used to call their Working Men's Social Club, they'd have a few drinks but not if it was a few days before a game.

The media weren't against us, but they created a bad atmosphere which brought all the players closer together, supporting each other, so that we all pulled together no matter what was being reported. We had strong individuals, strong senior players, and we could cope with it. These days the media are a lot more supportive of the team, there is a more harmonious relationship, even if the team doesn't play well at times.

There are numerous stories about Gazza, far too many, throwing soap at chickens in Albania comes to mind, his tennis in the middle of the night before the semi-final; he was just hyperactive, it was like having a little child running around who couldn't sleep, but it was all high jinks, nothing sinister, and when you are away for so long in tournaments, he kept you entertained, that's for sure, he was great entertainment.

THE ENGLISH DISEASE

Did Italia '90 really change football in England? In reliving the tournament 30 years on I have tried to look back without rose-tinted glasses, as most assessments have done in the past, but in the harsh reality of a tournament in the context of a tabloid circulation war and the low expectations of Bobby Robson's squad in May 1990.

There is no doubt that to some degree it had a profound effect on the country and transformed football. The national game has come a awful long way since then and it acted as a catalyst for the country to rediscover the game after a decade of tragedies when the sport was seen as the preserve of the worst elements in society. Almost overnight it became fashionable once more and Margaret Thatcher, perhaps the biggest critic of the game, couldn't wait to be photographed with Gazza at No 10 on his triumphant return. On the 30th anniversary of the semi-final defeat to West Germany, the summer of Gazza's tears, *World In Motion*, and *Nessun Dorma*, it still remains one of the defining episodes in the post-war history of English football and continues to resonate to this day... but would all this have happened anyway had England gone out meekly in the group stages?

There's no doubt that the 1980s were dark for English football. Fans were dying in stadiums, hooliganism was rife, clubs were banned from playing in European competitions, attendances had fallen, racism was deemed acceptable and even Bobby Robson's black players in his World Cup squad, John Barnes and Paul Parker, were racially abused by England supporters invited to an open training session in Sardinia ahead of the tournament.

The government's response to the Hillsborough tragedy seemed to be to ban the sport. After the Heysel and Hillsborough disasters Margaret Thatcher had tried to introduce an ID card system that would have meant only registered fans could attend matches. Papers released in 2012 revealed the government briefly considered withdrawing from the 1990 World Cup amid fears that it would provide a "natural focus" for hooliganism. In a letter to Mrs Thatcher in September 1989, the then Deputy Prime Minister Geoffrey Howe said it would be "premature to reach a firm view" on the team's participation but he wrote that should England pull out "the likelihood is that the determined hooligans will make their way to Italy anyway and find a different cause to champion". A deep concern for the FA hierarchy was that serious disturbances at the tournament would provoke the Government into swift action in recommending that the England team returns home.

Against that backdrop it was almost unthinkable that football would soon become a sport enjoyed by 'respectable' people and attended by families but as England progressed through the tournament, an increasingly gripped nation watched on TV against a soundtrack of Luciano Pavarotti singing *Nessun Dorma*, originating from a 1926 opera, which became one of the hits of the summer as the theme for the BBC's coverage.

The BBC's choice to introduce opera into its titles proved to be just as enduring as the tournament itself. Pavarotti reached number two in the UK singles chart. John Barnes rapping on New Order's *World In Motion* reached number one, and both songs reverberated around the pubs long after the tournament ended. Originally *World In Motion* was going to be called *E for England* but the Football Association vetoed the name in fear that it would be taken as a reference to the drug ecstasy.

As Colin Irwin, editor of *Number One* magazine at the time, says: "Italia '90 was when they had *Nessun Dorma* and I think that changed things. People started calling it 'the beautiful game' and opera was associated with it. People began to think of football as an art form. It had been damaged by that horrible period of hooliganism, racism and horrible football but then you had opera, Paul Gascoigne and Gary Lineker, and women started taking an interest. Stadiums became much safer and the whole culture of football changed really.

"Before 1990 football team songs tended to mean one thing - players standing in a group singing in various levels of embarrassment out of their comfort zone, often dressed in casual knitwear - or even dinner suits. Singing? Well, it could be loosely described as such. Yet, England had reached number one in 1970 with *Back Home* and number two in 1982 with the over-ambitiously-titled *This Time (We'll Get It Right)*, so, the FA took everyone by surprise by collaborating with Manchester band New Order.

"Because it was a band of real credibility at the time it was extraordinary. People wondered what New Order were doing, they thought they had gone mad. Before then it had been all these cheesy songs with self-conscious footballers giggling."

"*World In Motion* was not especially a football song. It had footballing connotations but they could be applied to life in general. It had the line in it 'express yourself' - meaning show your talent - but you could interpret it in other ways. It was quite clever that they didn't go totally committed to a football song, an anthem. It was a very clever piece of music, and people do regard it as the best football song."

Six years later, Baddiel and Skinner joined forces with the Lightning Seeds to record *Three Lions* - an England team song with no footballers on it. Irwin, whose book *Sing When You're Winning* examines the history of terrace chants, said: "*Three Lions* was brilliant also because of the video and the sentiments expressed by all football fans - 30 years of hurt. It just caught the imagination of people so well, and it's very good lyrically. It was clearly written by football enthusiasts."

It is the peripherals of the tournament, rather than the games themselves, that have made an indelible mark on the memory. Much of the football played at the tournament was dull and defensive and there was no outstanding team in the role of a Brazil 1970 or Holland in 1974.

Of course Gazza's Tears in Turin is probably the moment that brings back the most poignant memories but this book sets out to look back in search of the real story, and concludes that all was not as it seemed.

The nation was soon engulfed in the heroics of England's bid for glory before the heartbreak of yet another penalty shoot-out defeat but it ended in the unashamed weeping of hardened sportsman which some have said made men crying in public acceptable, even sexy. However, it masked the real intent of Gazza's tears, not that of any noble sense of the pursuit of England's glory, but selfishness as he contemplated suspension as a reckless tackle brought a yellow card that eliminated from the final should England get there.

At 23 Gascoigne's talent had reached a global stage, the kid I had seen blossom from the England under-20s team at Toulon, before his big money move to Spurs catapulted him into the glamour of the London scene after turbulent times in his home town up in Newcastle.

At the time, Gazza looked a talent to join the pantheon of greats. A potential world beater, as Bobby Robson said before the tournament, he could have been England's match winner like Diego Maradona had been for Argentina. Instead, it was to be his only World Cup as he self-destructed with great recklessness and then headed off to Lazio as his £5 million transfer underpinned an ill-conceived Terry Venables takeover at Spurs.

Off the pitch all was not sweetness and light. The hooliganism that I witnessed on the shores of Cagliari during the tournament was later suppressed only to return more recently, and it left me wondering whether it ever really went away. It bubbled away hidden under the surface like a sickening and contemptuous disease ready to catch you by surprise and spread its evil intent. Worse still, the '90s was still rife with the ugly face of racism in football, and for a while Kick It Out and Show Racism The Red Card and the multitude of good causes to attempt to eradicate racism were spawned, but again did it really ever go away? Arguably it is as bad now as it has ever been.

In the light of England's progress to the last four, it was easy to forget how poorly the team had began the tournament. The opening game against the Republic of Ireland was so poor that some sections of the media called for the team to be sent home! A few weeks later and we all had this romantic notion that this was the dawn of a new era, and led by Gazza we would be back winning the World Cup next time!

It was a romantic vision all too quickly shattered. Gazza soon became a cause for derision and pity for his obsessive nature that turned a Geordie who liked a pint into an abusive alcoholic, yet even to this day many continue to revere him and overlook those excesses.

Graham Taylor succeeded Bobby Robson who had announced in advance of the tournament that he would be stepping down. I liked Graham as a manager at Watford but the feeling upon his appointment was that he was not cut out to be an international coach and so it proved. After a poor campaign in the Euros in Sweden in 1992, England were placed in a qualification group with Holland, Norway, Poland (yet again of course), San Marino and Turkey - it was hard to see how they could not make one of the top two places to qualify for the tournament in the States. Yet having drawn with Norway at home and Poland away and having thrown away a two-goal lead at Wembley against the Dutch, they succumbed to a Ronald Koeman free-kick in Rotterdam and so faced San Marino in their final qualifying game needing to score seven goals, which they did, but conceded after just 8.3 seconds after a kamikaze back pass from Stuart Pearce - this time the full-back didn't succumb to the added pressure of a World Cup penalty shoot-out but to Davide Galtieri, a San Marino computer salesman. The other side of that equation was England needing the Dutch to lose in Poland but they won 3-1 and took the runners-up spot and Taylor resigned the following week. Taylor had dubbed Gazza's growing alcoholism as 'refuelling' but he soon lost patience with the star of 1990 and so what should have been a crusade towards winning the World Cup in the USA became something of a car crash campaign, later turned into a feature length documentary called *The Impossible Job,* a title that ignored the fact that Bobby Robson had coped admirably with similar criticism for most of the previous decade.

Paul Gascoigne, reborn as football cartoon character 'Gazza', was transformed into a heart-on-the sleeve role model who overnight bonded with the common man as the flag bearer at Italia '90. Tricky, witty and committed, he was the symbol of England's failed bid for glory. The reality was that the pressure of overnight stardom quickly turned him into fodder for the tabloids who revelled in his fall from grace. Within the England camp he had been indulged by fellow Geordies Bobby Robson and Chris Waddle and cocooned by the siege mentality of England's progress through the tournament, but once that protection disappeared his tendency towards being easily bored and his excessive drinking was a gift to the newspapers fighting a bitter tabloid war.

In any case the tackle that preceded the tears was, in truth, a desperate lunge on Thomas Berthold. In a few years it would be seen as a typical 'Gazza Tackle'; out of control, desperate, and bound to end in trouble both for him and his victim. Ask Gary Charles who was fortunate not to have suffered a career-ending injury following Gazza's moment of madness just seconds into the following season's FA Cup final. In Italy Gazza lost control of the ball with a poor touch, his determination to make amends was typical of the cartoon caricature as Paul Gascoigne now transformed into Gazza. He had no chance of winning the ball, didn't even get near his opponent to actually kick him and was yellow carded when he should have stayed on his feet as he was on the half way line so such a challenge was unnecessary.

As tackling became more sophisticated, the mantra of the coaching manual became 'stay on your feet', something that defenders in the modern game have become used to, although there are many midfielders and forwards who still tackle like Gazza and end up with the same punishment.

That yellow card meant automatic suspension from the final if England defeated West Germany - and so the tears rolled, and that wise old pro Gary Lineker signalled to the 'bench' to watch him, as anything reaction was possible. That came from a team-mate of Gazza's at White Hart Lane who knew him better than most. He could see a red card looming and Robson must have pondered whether to haul him off.

Lineker was deeply concerned because he wanted to get to that final with or without Gazza. As it turned out Gazza did his job for the team and performed creditably in his attempt to get his team-mates to the final, once the realisation that he wouldn't be there had been superseded by his desire to go out in a blaze of glory, even if he then turned down the chance to take a spot kick in the shoot-out which meant his room-mate Chris Waddle took the ill-fated fifth penalty.

All was quickly forgotten back home as the nation fell in love with Gazza, their hearts broke as they watch transfixed at the drama unfolding on TV. It was one of those rare events when you will always say "I remember where I was when Gazza cried". Not difficult really as the vast majority of the nation were sitting at home in their lounges watching on television or watching in the pubs.

Yet those tears were a cataract covering the reality of the entire tournament, hiding the truth of something far less uplifting for a nation welcoming back the England team as if they had won the World Cup, and Gazza being Gazza wearing false boobs to perpetuate the myth that he was a jokey, fun-loving, Jack the lad Geordie with a heart of gold.

The tournament was actually typical of England at that time. Abysmal to start with, then pulling themselves together, suddenly winning a couple of relatively easy games that they should really have won and excelling in the most difficult match against the best team in the tournament, only to fall at the final hurdle when it really mattered.

Overall the tournament was disappointing, averaging fewer goals per match than any other previous World Cup and was criticised for negative tactics, yet Italia '90 continues to shine like a beacon for England fans because it represented the closest the nation has come to matching the fabled boys of 1966 in over half a century until Gareth Southgate took a similar route to near-failure by getting England to the semis in Russia in 2018.

Now, don't get me wrong. Italia '90 lives on in my memory as one of the greatest all-time England tournaments but not perhaps for the same reasons as the vast majority of England followers. One of the highlights of the tournament was watching Cameroon humbling the world's elite and almost toppling a contemptuous England who thought they could swat them aside – to me they were the real stars of the show.

John Motson has been a good friend of mine for some time, and has seen more World Cups than most, so it is worth noting what the man in the sheepskin had to say about Italia '90 in his book *Motty,* "Gazza's tears are an iconic image of Italia '90 , and there is a theory that his and England's performances in that World Cup - when they lost on a penalty shoot-out to the eventual winners - turned the game in this country around after the dismal decade that had gone before. Forgive me, but having covered the 1990 World Cup from start to finish, I consider this a load of tosh. But don't just take my word for that. Gerald Sinstadt, the senior commentator of my generation, who was covering World Cups when I was at primary school, is in agreement with me on this. Sinstadt's World Cup portfolio goes back to 1954, when he worked for British Forces Broadcasting in Switzerland. When Gerald was the Granada commentator in my early days with the BBC, he lived in London, and many was the time I sat at his home in Highgate and marvelled at the meticulous way he kept his records. So I sat up and paid attention when he described the 1990 World Cup as the poorest he had covered. With my more limited experience, I have to agree with him. Leaving England on one side for a moment, there was too much negative football, too many teams playing for extra time and penalties, and precious little pleasure travelling around Italy. The legacy of hooliganism hanging over the eighties meant no alcohol was served in the city on the day of a game. That summed up the austere atmosphere in which this World Cup was played."

Many years later, after Motty hung up that famous sheepskin, he had a much more rose-tinted memory of Italia '90. The mind plays tricks over time and nostalgia kicks in. Yet for me it was an experience more memorable for what went on off the field rather than on it and this book looks to unravel the incredible inside story of this mythologised tournament.

STEVE McMAHON

"I got a gold disc for World in Motion"

Whenever you went off to a major tournament whether with England, or if you are involved in a Cup final, one of the gimmicks back in the 80s and 90s was to release a song, and in the case of Italia '90 it was *World In Motion* but this time there was a big difference - it was actually quite a good song, and I've got a Gold Disc, and I don't think many footballers can lay claim to that distinction!

We recorded *World In Motion* one Sunday afternoon when we joined up for an England game, but most of the lads couldn't be bothered with yet another football song and opted to go off to the pub, the White Hart where they would normally meet up when it came to England get-togethers. Only six of us turned up for the recording; me, Chris Waddle, Peter Beardsley, John Barnes of course, Gazza and Des Walker, so only those six received the Gold Disc. You had to sell 400,000 copies to hit gold, and as we progressed through the tournament sales soared. It also helped that New Order did the song, and they were a legitimate band. Usually it's a gimmick, and the media try to make you look a fool when these songs are recorded. For a change the song was taken seriously and did well.

Barnsie did the rap but I was also on the *Anfield Rap* and that got a Silver Disc, so I've got gold and silver. The truth is, of course, I can't sing, but do a bit of karaoke, that's about it!

It is hard to believe Italia '90 was 30 years ago, it really still seems like yesterday. You are never far away from recalling what happened. It was such an iconic tournament for England that it pops up from time to time. It occurs to me that it is thirty years since Italia '90 and thirty years since Liverpool last won the title!

THE TABLOID WAR

T here was no better time to be one of the elite football writers than the 1980s and 90s. There were no emails, mobiles, Instagram or any form of social media. Newspaper circulations were thriving, for many the Margaret Thatcher era was a successful time of excess and expenses flowed and, as the *Daily Mirror*'s chief football writer, the influence that I carried was put into perspective when respected football magazine *FourFourTwo* published the most powerful men in sport and I was only a few places behind Tottenham Chairman Alan Sugar!

The FA's top brass would even consult the big name football writers when it came to choosing a new England manager; there was direct access to the England manager and some of the top stars, and any campaign to unseat an England manager put the FA's hierarchy under real pressure. Having tasted the incredible experience of the World Cup in Mexico, the prospect of Italia '90 seemed even better. The World Cup committee spared no expense in making the world's media welcome.

Straight after the Euros in Germany, a select group of the world's leading football writers, two or three from each country, depending on the standing of that country, were invited to Capri for a pre-tournament seminar as the Italia '90 World Cup organisers wanted to know what the world's media requirements would be, and it seemed that they would be bending over backwards to accommodate us.

Aside from England's abysmal showing at the Euros, the tournament had been perfectly organised, and the media enjoyed some exceptional German hospitality. The Italians had been there making notes, and wanted their World Cup to be the best ever in every conceivable way, including how the media would report it, reflect the country, and the tournament.

We got a flight from Germany to Naples, then a ferry to Capri, then a coach up a steep mountain to one of the world's loveliest spots and most picturesque hotels at Anacapri. The Island of Capri has two towns, Capri and Anacapri. Anacapri is located on the slopes of Mount Solaro at a higher elevation than Capri town and has about 7,000 residents. The room had a balcony that could fit two sun beds and a table and four chairs, the room was clearly a suite, and on the king size bed was a fashionable branded Valentino holdall. Inside were an array of World

most cash
their team in the
league in
coughing up an
£1,248. Everton
at the least (£526)

or,
ns
all

...rope last season and to the top of the
...emier League this year with a team
...English players.

Power ■■   **Wilkinson:**
Influence ■■■   **long coat.**
Money ■

33 Brian Woolnough
■ Job: Sun chief football writer

Although *The Sun* sells 3.6 million copies a day
compared to *The Mirror's* UK circulation of 2.24
million, Woolnough has slightly less influence within
the inner corridors of the game than Harry Harris.

Power ■■■■
Influence ■■■
es at   **Money**
ie

32

31 Harry Harris
■ Job: Daily Mirror chief football writer

If Harris did not exist he would have to be
created – the epitome of the Fleet Street
football writer. Harris has the ear of the game's
movers and shakers. Campaigned energetically
to discredit Terry Venables over his dodgy business
dealings when the rest of the national press
seemed to be closing ranks.

Power ■■■■
Influence ■■■■
Money

30 John and Phil Smith
■ Job: Football Agents

Historically they have been Mr 10 per centers for Diego

"If Harry Harris didn't exist, you'd have to invent him!"

Cup goodies, samples of just about everything that would be part of Italia '90, plus one or two items that could easily have formed part of a *Sunday Times* Investigation if they had been handed out by the Qatar World Cup Committee!

There was a champagne welcoming committee, a lavish welcoming dinner (more presents), and the Italia '90 hostesses were assigned, virtually one per journalist. All of them had clearly been hand-picked for their intelligence, their age, and their beauty. Not one was much older than 25, and they all looked like models.

At least two top football writers that I know of brought new wives back from the Mexico World Cup, even though they were already married! The thought crossed my mind that there would be mayhem when the English media were hooked up with these hostesses. We also discovered that the hostesses would be assigned to each of the competing nations. There was trouble ahead. However we were informed, right from the word go, that all the hostesses had agreed to contracts, which specified that they were not allowed, under any circumstances, to become 'involved' when we discreetly made this point when the opportunity arose but the organisers were comforted by the contracts signed by the hostesses. A few of us remained unconvinced.

Although there was a daily timetable of talks and interaction with the organisers about various aspects of media relations that would affect the World Cup tournament itself, there were some days off, and in reality it felt like a lovely ten-day holiday. There were trips to Capri for shopping, sight-seeing, late-night clubbing for the younger ones, and on the penultimate night, a no expenses sparred banquet at a hotel in Capri, with Italy's top pop group of the time. The two girl singers took a shine to my colleague Stuart Jones - no change there. He was single and enjoyed the late night partying that went with the job, and asked me to accompany him with the pop group. Some of the hostesses were keen to join in, but it was clear that those chaperoning them had ordered them not to. The World Cup organisers must have learned an awful lot from this seminar, but judging by what happened within the England camp, they didn't heed our warnings about the hostesses!

It was a short break from the intensity of my job back home where Bobby Robson was at the centre of a circulation war between *The Mirror* (Robert Maxwell) and *The Sun* (Rupert Murdoch) for some time leading up to Italia '90. As the tabloids devoted ever more space to football in their bid to attract readers, so the manager of England became an easy target. *The Sun* had handed out badges demanding that Robson be sacked as early as 1984, but it was in the period following a disappointing European Championship in 1988 that the newspaper campaign to oust him became most heated.

During its "Super Soaraway" Kelvin MacKenzie era, when circulation was soaring, *The Sun* was a law unto itself. Libel writs were laughed at and the belief at the newspaper's base in Wapping was that the man on the street had the right to read whatever *The Sun* deemed to believe it could get away with, so they published stories with a healthy disregard for whoever might get hurt along the way. *The Sun's* staff carried through this mission with an almost religious zeal and a tenacious self-righteous fury.

Robson wasn't alone, as everyone in the public eye was a potential target, but football was special, as it carried millions of fans so the England team were constantly under the media spotlight in the tabloids; back then they were either world beaters or they should hold their heads in shame - there was no grey area, it was black or white, all or nothing, and the manager carried the can. Bobby was a hero when the national team won and the man who should be kicked out on his arse when they lost.

It was during the Robson era that the England manager's role started being referred to as "The Impossible Job", and as events unfolded around Robson it was easy to see why yet the mild-mannered Geordie steadfastly refused to let the press or the pressures of the job get to him. Nevertheless there were occasional flashes of anger and frustration from the normally phlegmatic manager which were the inevitable consequences of the extra pressure applied by the media.

The villification of Robson began the tabloid trend that continued with Graham 'Turnip' Taylor, Terry Venables and his questionable business dealings, Glenn Hoddle and his 'spiritaulism', Sven's many misadventures and ended with the vilification of the "wally with the brolly" Steve McClaren following a rain-drenched defeat to Croatia which cost England qualification for the 2008 Euros. The debate has raged about whether the press should back or barrack the man in the hot seat. In truth, the media's duty is to have a balanced view. Fair criticism is one thing, victimization another. The dawn of the social media era and the decline in the influence of the tabloids has made Gareth Southgate's job far easier, his success has obviously helped as well.

In the run-up to the 1990 World Cup the attacks on the England boss became more vicious and personal. They had begun after the European Championships in 1988 when the media were split about whether he was actually fit for purpose to be England manager. After the brutal exit at the Hand of God in Mexico, expectations were running high that Robson had developed a team to be proud of and one that might finally compete for major honours at the Euros two years later. They had sailed through a potentially tricky looking qualification group containing Yugoslavia, Northern Ireland and Turkey by dropping just 2 points, so hopes were sky-high heading into the tournament with their group opponents the Netherlands, the Republic of Ireland, making their debut at a major tournament and the USSR. So the shock of England's abysmal performance in Germany, where they lost all three games, and in particular the humiliating final game when England capitulated to Russia, led to a torrent of negative back page headlines. There was now a justification to bring the debate about whether Robson was the right man for the job to the forefront of the agenda. The tabloid attacks became vindictive as they fought to outdo each other in the way they could attack the England manager; sometimes it was humorous, often it was not.

Robson was suffering enough anyway as Mike Ingham in his recently published memoirs *After Extra Time and Penalties*, points out: "I sat long into the night in the bar at our Frankfurt hotel with Bobby Robson. I was admitted to his inner sanctum only because I was with his predecessor Ron Greenwood and Bobby wanted to pour his heart out to him. He was distraught and very emotional, not so much because of the performance but more from the sound of his players letting their hair down in an adjoining room. I vividly remember his saying: 'Listen to that Ron; they just don't feel defeat like we do. It just doesn't seem to matter as much these days.'"

Both *The Sun* and *The Mirror* used a 1-1 draw away to Saudi Arabia in November 1988 as a chance to come up with memorable headlines telling Robson he should leave, but arguably the stance of *The Mirror* was more spiteful following it up a day later by listing 20 reasons why he should not be manager. There is no question that England's record in the Euros had been very poor and merited both concern and criticism, but the vitriol Robson had to contend with seemed to go well beyond what was both justifiable and decent.

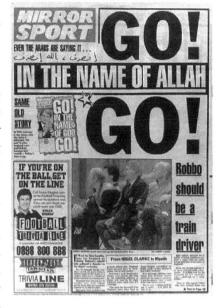

"When the Italia '90 campaign began, there were some weird and wonderful trips," Mike Ingham recalls, "There was a bizarre midweek friendly for commercial reasons in Saudi Arabia. No wonder some clubs were becoming reticent about releasing their top players. In the heat of Riyadh, it was cold turkey for us all. We had to endure three days without booze, although staff at a British embassy reception did assure us that from time to time they were in receipt of a 'special cargo'. So what does the press corps do when deprived of alcohol and fun for three days? Obviously, we piled into someone's room and played Trivial Pursuit."

British Airways was part of the commercial package sponsoring England's World Cup campaign, and facilitated the journey to Saudi Arabia by Concorde. With space at a premium, and in any case Robson was sick of the media entourage by then, the press were not invited. Even broadcast representatives such as Trevor Brooking were carded.

Persuading Robert Maxwell that it would be a coup for *The Mirror* to be part of the England/FA party on Concorde, a meeting was set up by Maxwell, *The Mirror's* proprietor and Oxford United chairman, at his club's boardroom where he invited me along with the BA chairman at the time, Lord King of Wartnaby, for a pre-match lunch. Lord King had been appointed Chairman of British Airways by Margaret

Thatcher in 1981. Maxwell's influence was at a peak at this time. It later emerged that he had attempted to secure a $20 billion loan from the British government to prop up the collapsing USSR. A letter released by Margaret Thatcher's private secretary, Charles Powell, revealed that Captain Bob claimed to be acting on behalf of Mikhail Gorbachev's closest advisers when he visited the 'Iron Lady' at 10 Downing Street in March 1990. In that meeting, the owner of the *Daily Mirror* allegedly asked Thatcher to provide a massive state loan to the Soviet government to ensure that *perestroika* reforms would continue. So in comparison to that, trying to get his paper's chief football writer on a flight to Riyadh seemed like a doddle!

All went well over a convivial lunch and the BA chief said he would do all he could to facilitate a place aboard England's Concorde flight. The usual travel agent handling the media 'tour' to Saudi Arabia, to coincide with the FA party, had booked my place on a club class flight with the rest of the chief football writers, although they were usually in economy. I contacted Maxwell's office as the date for the trip neared requesting my ticket information.

Now, whenever Maxwell had issues fulfilling his promises he would usually go quiet on me, and this was one of those occasions; a few days before the flight I was beginning to have a gut feeling that this wasn't going to happen. I then received a message from Maxwell's office that his son Kevin was dealing with it. I tried to contact Kevin, but again with no luck. Finally, the day before I was due to fly, I was given a message from Maxwell's office to turn up at Heathrow and let the BA staff know that their Chairman had authorised my place and everything would be okay. I was not so sure about that, but I did as I was requested, and was greeted with a lot of blank expressions and shrugs of the shoulder. Clearly the Chairman had made no such notification, probably forgot all about it, or thought better of interfering in the hope it would all go away!

Finally, with about half an hour before Concorde was due to take off, I was taken to a room and it was explained to me that the final word rested with manager Bobby Robson. The England manager felt it was unfair for just one journalist to be given preferential treatment and he vetoed it. Back home I went, and contacted the travel agent who booked me on the same flight I was already booked on but 24 hours later. So I trooped back to Heathrow the next day to make the flight on my own. The resulting 1-1 draw produced one of the more memorable headlines during Robson's tenure.

The flak continued in February 1989, when a low-key friendly away to Greece saw *The Mirror*'s No 2 Nigel Clarke declare that "Robson will be fired" if England came unstuck. Nigel was more at the sharp end than myself as he was the mouth piece for Sports Editor Keith Fisher's more fanciful and increasingly extravagant excesses aimed at Robson.

England won 2-1 but Robson would recount this episode many times in the years that followed. Amid all this, it was easy to overlook the fact that England were actually in decent form. They completed the 1988-89 season without defeat and a 3-0 win over Poland left them on course to qualify for Italia '90 and they qualified without conceding a goal, yet so nearly missed out after the Poles hit the crossbar in the dying seconds of the goalless return game. Once again the knives were out following an uninspiring display, the critics believing England had demonstrated why they would not come close to glory in Italy the following summer. "Under the deeply uninspiring, cautious and mediocre management of Bobby Robson and Don Howe I really don't give them a chance," declared the eminent Brian Glanville in the video *England: The World Cup Story* ahead of the finals.

England's route to Italia '90 had begun in December 1987 when the qualifying draw was made. At that point Robson's side were still celebrating qualifying with an unbeaten record for the European Championships and being one of the favourites to win it. They had no reason to fear other sides in the World Cup qualifying draw and were one of the seeded teams. The draw, not unlike the eventual qualifying process as a whole for England, would prove to be a case of 'could have been better, could have been worse'.

They crucially avoided the Dutch from pot two, landing Poland who had reached the past four World Cups but were entering a period of decline. They could have drawn an easier side from pot three than Sweden, but the Swedes had not qualified for a major tournament for a decade and Albania were a candidate for the weakest team in pot four, being something of an unknown quantity to the English. The Three Lions were favourites to progress, but being drawn in one of the groups with just four teams meant they would have to finish top to be sure of a World Cup spot. In an era before play-offs became the norm for second place sides, if they had the poorest of the runners–up records from the three groups with four teams in, then they would miss out.

Thoughts of the World Cup were put on hold as England focused on their Euro '88 preparations. Gradually, things began to go wrong with Terry Butcher ruled out with a broken leg and the goals drying up as the finals approached. Losing all three games resulted in a clamour for Robson to go.

'Plonker' screamed the headlines but the FA stood by him after Robson appeared set for the axe. "Those who demanded my resignation – and I am thinking in particular about specific newspapers – will be disappointed to hear me reinforce my decision not to quit. It might have crossed my mind, fleetingly, when I wondered if my family could cope with almost intolerable strain, that I should step down. But I am not a quitter and will not back down," Bobby Robson stated in his first programme notes after the European Championship.

Robson stayed on at the Euros as one of TV's panelists of top analysts, no doubt raking in a sizeable fee for his services, but he also remained to see some of the games, as he was a student of the game. However, even a routine decision to give his expert views on TV became a subject for derision by the tabloids as he had been so inept as the England manager in the tournament that it was considered a contradiction in terms that he could be an expert on anything to do with football!

The usual small select group of chief football writers from the mainstream newspapers remained behind with him to continue to report on the rest of the tournament and to interview the England manager on his summing up once the final was over. It was the 'done' thing, which England managers in the past had tolerated.

It was probably more for a dare than anything else, but the group nominated me to seek out Robson in his hotel room soon after breakfast to chat to him about the tournament and to pass on his comments to the group for our following day's editions. It was a tradition among the now small contingent from the English press to work in this way, and it just happened to be my turn, and there was no persuading the group otherwise, even though they knew full well that I had been the most vociferous in calling for Robson's head at this time.

Steve Curry was very close to Bobby Robson, but that did not impair his journalistic opinions; when push came to shove, he wasn't for pushing Robson out of the England door. *The Express*, therefore, very much sat on the fence, with Curry giving a very balanced opinion of the situation and his conclusion was that Robson should be kept on but the next tournament should be, and would be, his last chance to prove himself in the biggest managerial job in English football. My assessment in the *Daily Mirror* was very much that he had had his chance and, after expectations had risen appreciably following the exploits in Mexico, the Euros had been an unmitigated disaster, and that the confidence-sapping final game against Russia meant that his time was up. Curry would have been, therefore, the ideal man for this task, but no, they were not for budging. It was my turn and that was that.

I took up the challenge the only way I knew, head on, and so with a large degree of trepidation I knocked on Bobby Robson's hotel door hoping he was out! Bobby opened the door, and at first he was his usual charming self, then he must have realised that I had been one of the media at the forefront of the 'anti' section of the media and his mood suddenly swung. There was a worrying aggressive look on his face as he pinned me up against the wall by my collar. Fortunately he calmed down very quickly and put me down! It wasn't long before he apologised for his behaviour and took me into his room and gave me the interview I was seeking, albeit a touch begrudgingly, after I made him fully aware I would be sharing the quotes with my colleagues as I had arranged. Bobby rode out the storm, but after the shockingly inept performances he was vilified for most of the time he managed England. He was even "Booby Robson" according to one paper.

Looking back it was a strange time in domestic football; Luton Town and Wimbledon had just won the two main domestic cups while modern day giants Chelsea and Manchester City were still in the Second Division. English football remained under a huge cloud because of the Heysel ban which showed no sign of being lifted and the best English players were looking to get out of elite First Division clubs with the likes of Gary Lineker, Ian Rush and Mark Hughes heading to the continent while a large English contingent arrived at Ibrox to spearhead Rangers domination north of the border. The quality of football in the top flight wasn't the best as proved by the success of Wimbledon's direct tactics. We seemed to be light years behind the continent and falling further behind.

All of which placed more pressure on the England team and specifically its manager. There was no other outlet for the English to prove themselves. Qualifying campaigns operated on a two points for a win basis and this was still the era of the old Eastern Block powerhouses with the likes of Czechoslovakia, USSR and Yugoslavia having very good, state-funded teams. The Berlin Wall had yet to fall and the 1990 World Cup would be the final qualification campaign featuring both East Germany and West Germany.

Hopes that the ban on English clubs competing in Europe would end had been severely damaged by further hooliganism in recent months, most notably at the European Championships. It was a widely

I always had the ear of Mirror supremo Robert Maxwell and it ended up getting me in some trouble during the World Cup.

held belief that the national team would also pay the price for the continued spread of the 'English disease' and would be banned from major tournaments if there was further serious disorder.

Meanwhile domestic football continued to provide our bread and butter headlines during the summer of 1989 with several big money transfers, including Paul Gascoigne's £2.2 million switch from Newcastle United to Tottenham. ITV splashed out to secure exclusive coverage of the Football League and their new deal would have particular emphasis on the 'Big Five' who were then Arsenal, Everton, Liverpool, Manchester United and Spurs and the First Division title race. The BBC countered, striking a deal for exclusive terrestrial rights of the FA Cup and England matches. England fans would be hearing a lot from Jimmy Hill in the coming years.

Bobby Robson was forced into several tough decisions. He dispensed with several members of his core squad; Kenny Sansom, Glenn Hoddle, Mark Hateley and Dave Watson played for Robson for the last time in Germany while Viv Anderson and Peter Reid were never recalled after winning their final caps shortly before the tournament. Tony Adams played the first three games after Euro '88 but was never picked again by Robson while fellow central defender Mark Wright was discarded until April 1990 before returning to prominence at Italia '90. In their place emerged an abundance of new players who were gradually phased in with 17 new caps awarded between September 1988 and December 1989. Key call ups included Paul Gascoigne, Paul Parker, David Platt and Des Walker, who would all start the 1990 World Cup semi-final, while players such as Steve Bull and David Rocastle would also establish themselves in the squad. For several others such as Brian Marwood, Mike Phelan and Mel Sterland, it would be a very short international road. Robson gave several players from the under-21s their chance at full level and also utilised the England 'B' squad as a means of assessing talent.

The threat of hooliganism meant England seldom ventured abroad for friendlies and they played six successive matches at Wembley after qualifying for the finals. England's road to recovery began with a clash with fellow Euro '88 flops Denmark in a friendly at Wembley in September. Old campaigners such as Peter Shilton, Bryan Robson and Terry Butcher were joined by three debutants; Gascoigne and Walker came off the bench, on a night when Rocastle also made his first appearance. Luton Town's powerful striker Mick Harford won his second and final cap as Robson tried to find an alternative big man to Hateley, while Stuart Pearce was now first choice left-back after previously being Sansom's understudy. Neil Webb scored the winner in a low-key atmosphere before just 25,837 supporters.

Five weeks later came a more important test as Sweden visited Wembley in the opening World Cup qualifier. It proved to be a night of frustration as England were unable to break down their opponents, for whom defender Glenn Hysen ran the show. Gary Lineker, who had been hospitalised with hepatitis shortly after the Euro finals, lacked the sharpness that had previously made him so deadly. The goalless draw was not a good start as Robson faced a long five-month wait before the next qualifier.

Things would get worse before 1988 was out; that 1-1 draw in Saudi Arabia attracted the infamous 'In the name of Allah, Go!' headline. Robson wouldn't be leaving and would justifiably point out how the Saudis had managed draws with several other established football nations, but that would not wash with many critics. The match saw Robson experiment and recognise Arsenal's strong start to the season with first caps for Michael Thomas, Alan Smith and Brian Marwood along with David Seaman (QPR) and Mel Sterland (Sheffield Wednesday). It was clear Robson was feeling the strain and was increasingly on the defensive telling BBC commentator Barry Davies he was "impertinent" the following day over his line of questioning in his post-match interview.

England began 1989 with an away friendly in Greece, but mercifully Robson's side came from behind to win 2-1 and kept their unbeaten run going. Come March, the World Cup campaign resumed with a trip into the unknown as England travelled to Albania.

England had never played in Albania before, and at this time it was a nation that few, if any, foreign visitors were allowed into and few probably wished to. Such were the mysteries of this country that I pitched a feature revealing what the England players and fans could expect. I thought it would be a journalistic coup to get inside the country ahead of the World Cup tie and I had an ace card; Robert Maxwell's eastern European connections. His son Kevin had an office in Paris, the venue to apply for an Albanian visa. Having put in my request to first Robert, and then Kevin, and through their diplomatic connections, Monte Fresco, our No. 1 sports photographer, and myself, travelled to Paris to apply for a visa at the Albanian Embassy. We found this tiny embassy building in the back streets of the French capital that looked like something from a James Bond thriller. As we entered the dark, dingy rooms we were met by the Consul who went through our documents and asked a number of questions before stamping our passports with the appropriate visitor's visa. Monte took some pictures of me near the Champs-Élysées with the documentation to illustrate the story about how we planned to infiltrate Albania, as part of a series of articles.

We discreetly made our travel arrangements and I didn't even tell any of my close friends on the media circuit what I was up to. Everything was very hush-hush. On arriving in Tirana we were shocked by the size of the airport and its facilities, it clearly hadn't welcomed very many visitors and had the capacity for about a dozen at a time, I don't think I had seen an airport quite like it. As you can imagine there were no shops or duty free! We had been warned not to bring any glossy magazines into the country that might be construed as western decadence, and we were told it would be unwise to take any pictures unless they were authorised.

We were met by a driver, and it was easy to spot him, as he had

Photographer Monte Fresco and I made it to Albania's capital Tirana, few western journalists were allowed in.

the only car outside the airport! It didn't take long to work out that he was part of the Albanian Government's Secret Service. His mission was clearly to make sure these two western European journalists didn't get up to any mischief. He hardly left our side during the entire three-day trip, and it was clear that he had the authority to take us where his Government had preordained we could go; which pictures we could take, and which we could not.

Monte took some incredible pictures at the national stadium where England were due to play, featuring the less than basic facilities and conditions in the dressing rooms, where the hot water rarely worked.

We discovered that star Albanian internationals travelled to the games by bike. We sampled the England team hotel and tried the food. There was an extensive 20-page menu with just about everything on it. We eagerly ordered a chicken dish but no, they didn't have that. We tried ordering a fish dish but again there was no fish at all that day. Unfortunately they didn't seem to be serving any of the long list of alternatives. There seemed to be only one waiter, and we were the only ones dining in the restaurant apart from one table of two in the far corner who we assumed were Secret Police, as, presumably, none of the locals could afford the hotel restaurant, even though the prices were cheap. It was little wonder there was hardly any food from the menu, as no one ever ate there.

Eventually the waiter suggested chicken and chips, we had a basic starter of sliced egg, and he also asked us if we could also order our dessert, which, as it happened, there was only one - ice cream and jelly! We waited for some considerable time, wondering what the delay could possibly be, although we imagined there was only one chef. Finally the food arrived, and we were pretty hungry by then and all three courses arrived at the same time!

It was much different when the England team arrived, as the FA brought their own chef and packed their own food supplies. They had stayed at the same hotel Monte and I stayed in, the media had the only other hotel across the main square. If the team hotel was pretty basic, you can imagine what the other hotel was like!

In pre-internet days our stories were filed via telephone. On this trip I shared a room with *The Telegraph*'s Colin Gibson, as there was insufficient accommodation for each journalist to have their own room as usual. We had an old fashioned black phone in our room, but it wasn't connected to the outside world. You had to contact reception, who would then connect you, and the telephone bills were clearly going to be hiked way beyond the rates the locals might be charged, if indeed any Albanians were ever allowed to be connected by phone outside of the country. The connections worked okay but one time I had to rush down to reception as the connection from there to the room kept cutting out, and I had to file my story from the front desk.

On another occasion the phone rang in our room, so it was bound to be a call coming in from either the *Daily Mirror* or the *Daily Telegraph*. Colin wasn't in the room at the time, and I was in the shower. I dashed out of the shower, slipped on the rug, and ended up in the wardrobe upside down. I wasn't a pretty sight as Colin came into the room and I explained that the phone rang but I failed to reach it in time, but as he could see form my unusual position upside down in the wardrobe I had made a valiant attempt!

As for the match itself; England could have fallen behind in Albania, but the watching audience back home on a Wednesday afternoon could at least enjoy a 2-0 win thanks to goals from John Barnes and Bryan Robson. Lineker's ongoing poor form prompted concern, Jimmy Hill in the London studio calling for him to be dropped for the return at Wembley later that month. Initially the fixture had been overshadowed by a row over the scheduling as the crunch Liverpool against Arsenal clash for TV purposes, being due to be played just three days beforehand on the Sunday afternoon, much to Bobby Robson's annoyance. But this dispute was put into perspective by the horrific events at Hillsborough on April 15th at which I was present, and which became all consuming as *The Mirror*'s campaigned to support the Liverpool fans against lurid accusations from our rivals *The Sun*. So the Liverpool-Arsenal match was postponed and John Barnes withdrew from the squad, but Liverpool team-mate Peter Beardsley would play.

Wembley fell silent before kick-off 11 days on from the tragedy as English football paid its respects, with the team then turning in a committed display to win 5-0 and boost their goal difference and qualification hopes. Lineker kept his place and scored his first England goal for 10 months and the night was capped by Gascoigne coming off the bench to round off the scoring with his first international goal. Robson was still not satisfied as he told Sportsnight interviewer Tony Gubba that Gascoigne had "played in every position of the pitch except the position I told him to play in".

The Hillsborough Disaster meant that there would be a prolonged end to the league season which limited England's squad for the Rous Cup, with Liverpool and Arsenal players all absent. The three-cornered tournament was the bastard child of the century-old Home International Championship. Chile had been added to the tournament but failed to excite the public imagination in England and Scotland and the tournament clearly didn't have much life left. Its success was not helped by a tube strike, a record low Wembley crowd for England of 15,628 witnessed a 0-0 draw that saw Wimbledon's John Fashanu and Nottingham Forest's Nigel Clough win their debuts in a new-look attack. The selection of the forceful but technically limited Fashanu was not universally approved and his international career lasted two matches.

Four days later, the night after Robson had been at Anfield to witness Arsenal dramatically clinch the league title, what turned out to be the last annual Scotland against England fixture brought a 2-0 win for the visitors at Hampden Park, with arguably the manager's biggest selection gamble of his reign paying off. The powerful Steve Bull was still technically a Third Division player with Wolves, for whom he had been scoring goals for fun for the past couple of years but came off the bench to seal a 2-0 win.

On June 3rd England took a big step towards the World Cup finals by beating Poland 3-0 at Wembley. For all the talk in the build-up of the Poles infamous visit in 1973 when they qualified at England's expense, this was a comfortable win as Lineker, Barnes and Webb all scored. After four games England led the table by two points from Sweden, who had played a game less, with Poland cut adrift. The season ended with a 1-1 draw away to Denmark, Lineker again scoring on a night when Peter Shilton became England's most capped player. England hadn't actually met any real world class opposition, but the statistics showed it was their first unbeaten campaign since 1974-75.

England's World Cup qualifying programme resumed in early September 1989. For many years the Three Lions had been hit by 'Septemberitis', bad results in their first international of the season, so it was not an ideal time to be facing a crucial qualifier in Stockholm. A draw would edge England towards the finals, although it would not make certain of their place there. Reports of trouble involving fans did not lift the mood as the side prepared for a vital clash. It was a night mainly remembered for injuries: captain Bryan Robson sat it out and watched from the BBC studio with Des Lynam, Jimmy Hill and Terry Venables while Neil Webb was carried off just weeks after joining Manchester United having made a superb start at Old Trafford while Terry Butcher took the back page headlines by refusing to let the fact he split his head open and was covered in blood put him off, as he played on as his white England shirt which became increasingly red.

It was another 0-0 draw. Lineker, now back playing in England with Spurs, again spurned chances and Waddle fired wide after doing the hard work with a jinking run towards goal. The draw meant England still had to get something in Poland a month later. A win would ensure they topped the group, a draw would take them through as one of the best second place sides. It was a big game, with an international break the weekend before, *Saint & Greavsie* came live from the England team hotel. Poland had to win all three remaining games and overturn a fairly substantial goal difference to finish ahead of England.

In the event Robson's men were fortunate to get the draw they needed to make it through to Italy. Shilton gave a vintage display to keep the Poles out and lay the ghost of 16 years earlier to rest when his error had cost his side but England were ultra-cautious at times in the hostile Katowice atmosphere. In the dying seconds Shilton was beaten from 30 yards by Ryszard Tarasiewicz, but the ball struck the bar.

Nevertheless England had qualified without conceding a goal and had now not lost a qualifying match for a major tournament since September 1983. Later it became clear just how close England came to not making the finals. Had they conceded that last-gasp goal to Poland, they would have been reliant on any of three results going in their favour and none did. They saw Sweden leapfrog them to top spot winning in Poland while Denmark's defeat to Romania and West Germany's win over Wales would have seen England finish as the poorest of the second-place teams by virtue of having scored fewer goals than Denmark. As it was, they finished a point ahead of them and the Danes missed out.

Almost immediately England started planning for Italy and did so with a friendly against the World Cup hosts at Wembley in November. The game once more ended 0-0 but was perhaps most significant for the emergence of another new face, David Platt, who made his international debut. New caps were also handed out to Dave Beasant, Nigel Winterburn and Mike Phelan. Gascoigne, who was yet to fully establish himself, played in the B international against the Italians at Brighton.

Before the year was out England would ominously be placed in a World Cup group with European Championship opponents Netherlands and Republic of Ireland, along with Egypt.

It felt like *deja vu* as the Netherlands and the Republic of Ireland had both beaten Robson's men at Euro '88 but crucially England drew unfancied Egypt in place of the Soviet Union. The tournament format also meant that England would have a chance of progressing if they finished third.

A rare December friendly at home to Yugoslavia brought the curtain down on the 1980s, with Tony Dorigo becoming the 17th new cap since the summer of 1988. In a decade when the Robsons symbolised the England set-up, it was perhaps appropriate it would be captain Bryan who scored twice, one in the first minute, to give England a 2-1 victory. England went into the new decade off the back of a 14-match unbeaten run, having qualified for the World Cup finals and started to lay the Euro '88 mishaps to rest. A momentous and memorable year was in store.

Their long unbeaten record finally went in the last of the friendlies against Uruguay in May 1990, shortly before leaving for their World Cup base of Sardinia. But that setback would seem very minor for Robson compared to what the rest of the week had in store.

Bobby described Gazza as "daft as a brush" before Italia '90, but he had many little sayings that live on as some of the most amusing *Coleman Balls* in the history of the game. Bobby confused players names, couldn't tell his captain and namesake Bryan from his own name, mixed up his Waddles with his Hoddles, asked Kenny Sansom who that guy was he talking to at the suitcase carousel, only to discover it was Derek Statham who he had selected for one of his squads, on another occasion he thought Paul Parker was Danny Thomas - but Bobby was a genuine, lovely footballing man who didn't deserve the treatment he endured from the media of his time.

Yet Robson was caught in the cross fire of open warfare that summer between the team and a British media then in the throes of Robert Maxwell's circulation war with Rupert Murdoch. Before he became a national treasure Sir Bobby was a tabloid target and savaged by lurid and derogatory back page headlines. He was not the first football manager to feel that he had been subjected to the full glare of the media spotlight, but he handled the intensity and sometimes vicious nature of the attacks with huge dignity and restraint as I know from first-hand experience.

When Sir Bobby Robson passed away there was an outpouring of emotion, quite rightly, for one of the last remaining gentlemen in the game. Hindsight is supposed to provide 20-20 vision, but often it fails to do so and Sir Bobby was portrayed as being part of a more decent age. That was just not the case. In reality he was one of the first of many to become football manager of the modern media era and to suffer the consequences. If anything the vitriol he endured has all but disappeared from the new generation, as social media has superseded newspapers as the main line of communication through which anonymous personal abuse can be directed by anyone with a phone and a Twitter account.

In the '80s and '90s, the England boss became a figure of fun and outright abuse by the red tops, notably *The Sun* and my paper *The Mirror*. During this war it was a case of a 'race to the bottom' as the two rivals attempted to out-strip each other by lowering their journalistic standards. Let me stress that I was bitterly opposed to this sort of journalism and made my feelings clear at the time yet although I held the lofty position of Chief Football Writer, the real power was in the hands of the editors. However, I did have the ear of Robert Maxwell and that power and influence meant I was sometimes in direct confrontation with the editor.

Italia '90 changed the perception of Robson overnight. If anyone came out of that tournament smelling of English roses it was the manager while the likes of Gazza, the hero of the hour, quickly became the pantomime villain. Robson's treatment at the hands of the nastier elements of the media disappeared as in his later years when Sir Bobby was recast as a national treasure but during his eight years as England manager he suffered the unsympathetic and invasive pressure of an increasingly demanding press. In the 1980s that had its ugly side, and the personal attacks affected Robson because he felt the impact on his family and friends.

I got to know Bobby extremely well when I started out in Fleet Street with the *Daily Mail* working alongside Brian Scovell and their chief football writer at that time Jeff Powell. I was very much the junior and was given the Ipswich 'beat' covering many of their league games during one of the most exciting periods in the club's history but it was when travelling abroad on their pursuit of European glory that I became much closer to the players and manager than reporters can today. While highly paid by contemporary standards, they were not the mega-rich footballers of today who communicate via their PR teams over social media, so they were much closer to the media.

I got to know the Cobbolds, Ipswich's convivial owners, and was welcomed into their inner sanctum after matches and I was given the opportunity to chat with the manager and chairman in a relaxed 'off the record' atmosphere. I enjoyed my overnight stays in Ipswich and those long evenings with the Cobbolds and Robson, and some of his team's performances in Europe were breathtaking. However by the time I progressed to become Chief Football Writer for *The Mirror* Robson had stepped up to become England manager and the dynamic changed dramatically. My relationship with Bobby was often fraught through no fault of mine. However it ended up unimpaired despite the fact that he suffered so many unjustified attacks from my paper.

Everyone has their favourite Bobby Robson story. The trouble is, it's so tough to pick the best one! For example, I was sitting on a sun-lounger by the outdoor pool in the team hotel in the centre of Mexico City where the England party and media were staying together in preparation a year before the 1986 World Cup Finals. I was relaxing after filing my copy to *The Mirror* offices back in Holborn from my lofty room on the 17th floor of this giant hotel right in the centre of the city I saw Bobby lead the entire England squad down to the pool area, and they found themselves sun-loungers, Bobby sat close by with a stopwatch in his hand. I was in the corner with only a couple of hotel guests and went totally unnoticed by the entire entourage who were all concentrating on their manager's strict instructions. Every fifteen minutes Bobby blew the whistle and all the players simultaneously turned from their backs to their sides, like some sort of organised training session. Fifteen minutes later Bobby blew the whistle again and the players made another turn from their sides to their backs, then to their side, then to their front, in a perfect rotation – every quarter of an hour! Bobby had been told about the damage caused by, as he called them 'ultra ray violets', because of the weak ozone layer in Mexico City and wanted to ensure that on the first few days that none of his players got sun burnt and had a base tan but his methods caused some amusement.

Arguably the most re-told of all the Bobby Robson tales goes likes this: Bobby was the manager, Bryan Robson his captain. Bryan is walking down the stairs of the England team hotel with his manager at the foot of the stairs ready to greet him.

"Hi Bobby", says the England manager.

"No", replied Bryan, "I'm Bryan, you're Bobby!"

The football industry never ceases to laugh at the story, because it was far from a one-off, Bobby could hardly remember anyone's name. However, all these comical tales mask the fact that he was full of passion, pride and commitment and was deeply patriotic, he wanted nothing more than to win for his country and beneath that friendly exterior lay a tactical brain as good as any in world football even if his absent mindedness got him into all sorts of trouble, and on one notable occasion I was caught up along with it.

As mentioned, Bobby had problems with his Waddles and Hoddles, and later called Paul Parker Danny Thomas and sometimes even called him Danny Wallace which generated laughter even when it was not intended. As Parker recalled in his 2006 autobiography in his chapter on "The magic of the World Cup" he wrote, "Bobby Robson was notoriously forgetful about names and he used to call me Danny Thomas. Danny was built like me and had a good career at Coventry and Tottenham and, had he not already retired three years previously, he might even have been called into the World Cup squad by mistake. Bobby didn't mean it as an insult, he forgot the names of bigger and better players than me, it was all part of his eccentricity and extended to not remembering the name of the country we were playing or individual opponents. There were always prompters on hand. If I could have hand-picked a club manager it would have been him, certainly until Alex Ferguson came along. At that stage he was the best I had come across. Both had this colossal appetite for the game and both had every quality you, as a player, would want in a manager although there was an element of Robson the good cop and Fergie the bad cop in their approach. Both also had this fantastic desire to win and if you had anything about you as a player it would be bound to improve you. Robson was a lovely bloke and he had this capacity to get the best out of every player through building us up as individuals. His team talks were great orations and while he gave everything of himself in those, he expected and got the same from his players."

I already had first-hand experience of Bobby's capacity for forgiveness. In 1985 the FA had accepted an invitation to a mini-tournament warm-up in Mexico City for the England team alongside Italy, West Germany and the host country. A couple of days before departure had England played their traditional fixture at Hampden Park against Scotland. There was talk of the manager's peculiar decision to substitute Glenn Hoddle because it later emerged he had given the official the incorrect number on the substitutions board. This brought Robson's frailties to a wider audience and word soon reached none other than the *Daily Mirror* proprietor of the time Robert Maxwell, whose ownership of football clubs gave him what he thought was an insight into football management. What he didn't know is that everyone in the game knew how badly the England manager mixed up names, and there was a 'so what' attitude to this incident as it happened so often.

However this was clearly the first Maxwell had heard of it. 'Cap'n Bob' was flying back from an Eastern European summit, one of many he was prone to attend, accompanied by his usual entourage when he read about Robson's cock-up in the *Sunday Express*, the only paper that devoted a single column item about it on their back page. I was interviewing Chelsea striker Kerry Dixon for an exclusive prior to my departure the next day along with the rest of the media corps on a fact-finding acclimatisation visit to Mexico City to prepare for the finals in 12 months time, when I received a rather strange call from the office. It was not from the usual sports desk staff but from one of Maxwell's offices. This was not a good sign. It usually spelt trouble, usually for me. Whenever Maxwell was involved there would be something special, complex, out of the ordinary, bizarre, or just plain complicated involved. Invariably he would come to me first for any advice on football affairs. I was wondering what he might want as the instruction came through to see whether I was free and if so to make my way to Heathrow to meet Maxwell when his flight landed. It's always a good idea to be there when the boss calls, so I set off immediately. I had not long since been recruited by Maxwell himself but calls out of the blue to see him on football topics had become quite frequent, so I imagined it must be about my impending trip to Mexico and with the World Cup so close, alarm bells began to sound and I feared it might have something to do with *The Mirror*'s coverage of the impending tournament.

I arrived at Heathrow as quickly as I could and awaited Maxwell's arrival and was told that a private conference room had been hired by him and that he had been escorted directly to the room, he had not, as far as I could tell, gone through the usual passport control checks, at least not the public ones. As I entered the room Maxwell was sat with half a dozen or so of those he had travelled with and as soon as he struck up a conversation with me most swiftly left, perhaps sensing the growing tension and feeling it advisable to be out the way in case sparks flew as there might be some collateral damage! That left Bob and myself, and a couple of flunkies remaining to take notes.

Maxwell had already begun to relate how he had read the *Sunday Express* on the journey back and spotted a small item on the back page relating to the substitution of Hoddle who was having an outstanding match when Robson really wanted to take someone else off. "This bumbling buffoon is not the man to manage our national team, we need someone who knows what he's doing to take us to the World Cup Finals", boomed Maxwell in Churchillian tones, as if his pronouncement was indeed precisely what was going to happen, and indeed what the entire nation wanted to happen. Bob must have noticed how my jaw dropped as I knew what was coming next… a *Daily Mirror* campaign, and my first words had his entourage, who had no doubt been agreeing with his every word on matters of the national team and their idiot manager, rushing for the exit doors.

"I don't agree" was all I could mutter.

While his travelling entourage might have agreed with him, anyone with a smidgen of football knowledge would not. And here I was, the 'go to' man for Maxwell's football advice, contradicting him. I was thinking this wasn't going to end well for me, and wondered when I would be collecting my P45.

Normally Maxwell would take my advice on board and not always act on it, and I wouldn't have expected him to, but he always respected it. This time, I felt he had dug himself in far too deep with his entourage, didn't want to lose face, and didn't want to back down. As our 'chat' became more intense, his tone indicated that there was no persuading him. I soon discovered why there was no turning back. Maxwell had instructed his Editor and Sports Editor to leave the front and back pages open for his blockbuster campaign under the headline 'Robson Must Go'. And, of course, yours truly would be giving it authenticity and credibility by writing it. I had to find a way out of this, but I was struggling.

One of my arguments, if you can call it that, was that I wasn't actually at the game as I was preparing to leave with the squad for Mexico City and secondly, from what I could tell, it was just another of Bobby's blunders and most people in the trade were familiar with the manager's propensity for making laughable mistakes in muddling names and faces. Furthermore I argued Bobby was a genuine football man and still the one capable of leading the England team in the World Cup Finals. I also made the point that at this stage of preparation, so far down the line, there wasn't a single football writer, commentator, player or manager who would say otherwise. Perhaps most importantly of all, the fans were backing Bobby and the boys, there was no dissent at all among the supporters or indeed anyone else that I knew of. Taking all these things into consideration we would be making a lone stand and it wouldn't go down well. It had all the ingredients of backfiring terribly.

Then I tried a slightly different tack; maybe Bobby Robson *would* prove to be the wrong man for the job, but the timing of this campaign to unseat him was all wrong. The England team were just about to depart for Mexico for a couple of weeks of acclimatisation, and it wasn't feasible to find a replacement overnight. My argument must have eventually hit home with Maxwell, as I could tell he felt he had made a mistake but wasn't going to back down and admit it.

He asked me if I would write the article, but that he would ensure that someone else's name was on it when it appeared in the paper. I told him it was a reasonable compromise, but that I was very uneasy about this solution, but there was no time to brief another journalist. I was handed a pen and paper, and ushered to a corner where I began to scribble some words of *The Mirror* campaign to oust Robson. I told Maxwell I still remained very uneasy if only for the reputation of the newspaper, but also for the rest of the media and the England camp would want to know who really wrote the article if there was a fictional name on it.

"What would make it easier for you to accept?" Maxwell asked.

"I would like your permission to inform Bobby Robson about it in advance of publication, he is a decent man whatever you think about him as the England manager, and that's the least he deserves."

Never one to flinch from a face to face confrontation, I knew he wouldn't worry about that. "Fine", he said. "And tell him that there will be a front page and two more pages available to him for his first hand response - should he wish to make it".

It was a *fait accompli*, I knew Maxwell wasn't backing down, it was happening, I had pushed the newspaper owner as far as I could, if I had gone any further then my job would have been under serious threat. No-one stood up to Maxwell, and while I may have had a strong relationship with him, you can only push that so far. A typewriter miraculously appeared and I began to knock out the article that in essence Maxwell dictated to me. I then filed the 'copy' back to Holborn and left to find the nearest telephone inside the airport.

So now I had to do a bit of damage limitation if I was to continue to have a very difficult, if not impossible, on-going relationship with the England manager at such an important time during the build up to the World Cup finals. I liked Bobby and felt it was the right thing to do to tip him off about the impending onslaught he was about to face in this *Mirror* campaign, which I knew would be relentless and not just a one-off.

I left the private room, and headed for the nearest telephone in the airport and rang him. I knew it wasn't going to be an easy conversation, but I came straight to the point, I explained all the circumstances as accurately and as honestly as I could, plus my own recommendation about the campaign, which had not been accepted. *The Mirror* was going ahead with this front page "Robson Must Go", and my only advice was that whatever comments he made would counter-balance the articles, and might even supersede some of the headlines, or at least mitigate them. I also promised him that whatever he said wouldn't be taken out of context, and would be published precisely as he said it, and in its entirety.

Robson said he would go away and think about whether he would take up my offer of a right of reply, he appreciated that I had contacted him, but clearly he was furious, if a little baffled by it all; all of these emotions were hardly unexpected. I later discovered that he had rung one of his journalistic confidantes, of which he had a few, to seek his advice. Firstly he contacted the late Joe Melling, who was on the *Daily Express* at the time. He might also have asked Steve Curry, but the England manager probably thought he was too close to me and might have been swayed but that; knowing Steve, that would not have been the case, he would have, if anything, swayed on the side of Robson, and quite rightly so. However Curry might have thought differently about the right of reply, we shall never know.

Geordie Joe Melling advised Robson to ignore it and not to respond. I called Bobby back after about half an hour as deadlines were pressing and I couldn't leave it any longer. He told me that he had decided not to respond. He thanked me for all my efforts and that I had the guts to contact him ahead of publication, and I truly believe that he accepted my version of events but overall he remained extremely angry and upset by it all.

The next morning's *Mirror* screamed 'ROBSON MUST GO' in the biggest possible type on the front page. As for my name being left off the article, both the Editor and the Sports Editor suggested that it needed the name of an authoritative football writer to hold weight, and so it needed the name of the Chief Football Writer. My name therefore appeared on it. No one had the courage to let me know, not even Maxwell, as anyone who had told me would have known my reaction and how hard I would have fought to have kept Maxwell to his word. I feared it would turn out like this...

The following morning I arrived at the England team hotel near Gatwick airport where the media were gathering to travel with the FA party, as they used to at the time when there was a closer travelling group between the England party and the media, it was Glenn Hoddle in the World Cup in France 98 who stopped the joint travel arrangements, Hoddle's logic being that the media were always the last to leave the stadium waiting usually for the photographers to dispatch their pictures, or the last writer to file his copy before the advent of new technology. It meant the plane sitting on the tarmac waiting, as the flight was invariably held up until the media party was complete. Hoddle's view was that sitting in such cramped conditions added unnecessarily to player fatigue and was likely to aggravate any injuries. The FA used to accept the inconvenience because the media paid a premium to travel with the team group and stay at the same hotels, which greatly offset the FA's travelling budgets.

Anyway, back to 1985 and the long flight to Mexico. This was not to be a pleasant trip for me. Normally I would relish such journeys but one of Robson's back room staff spotted me arriving at the reception desk at the hotel at Gatwick and launched into a tirade of abuse. I thought I would encounter hostilities, but didn't expect it to be quite so forthright! I tried to explain the circumstances and was determined to give him a full account of events, of which I was quite sure he was not fully aware, but it was clear he wasn't listening and was not really interested in any explanation. Within the football industry, those on the receiving end of ugly tabloid headlines were almost immune to the journalists concerned coming up with their excuses. I shouldn't have been surprised that this guy was not interested in what he perceived as excuses.

Interestingly, though, my fellow journalists took an unexpected stance. On the flight I sat alone. None of the other journalists felt it wise to even sit next to me. Clearly I was pretty toxic all round that day. Inside the hotel in Mexico City the atmosphere was equally not a good one for me, so I asked to see Bobby to try to clear the air. He invited me to his hotel room, so this was my first opportunity to explain the circumstances face-to-face with the England manager, although, of course, Bobby knew the circumstances, and I related the story perhaps with a few more details I was unable to give him or he was unable to take in, while it was all a bit frantic the previous night. Examining the morning's *Mirror*, it was every bit as hard-hitting as I had expected. It was certainly the major talking point for just about everyone connected with that England party that day.

Thankfully Bobby was not a man to hold a grudge, but this was different, it couldn't have been more personal, more damaging, more hurtful, and may even have triggered the personal abuse that would came his way over the next few years and that would go on to dog future England managers.

Back home the story escalated into a frenzy of media activity, as it was perceived to be an escalation in the tabloid war, with Maxwell stepping up his campaign to gain sales on his main rival, Rupert Murdoch's *Sun*. To achieve his aim, Maxwell had targeted the England manager and used the England team as a front line weapon.

The truth is that, though it might well have evolved into one of the many facets of the cut-throat struggle for circulation supremacy, Maxwell kicked it all off on a whim having reading about one of Bobby's boobs. Knowing Maxwell as I did, he was actually very tough to read. He could be very childish, act on a whim, and I believe that this is what happened in this case. However, he could also be devious and it might well have been a plot to use the England World Cup profile as a vehicle to wage war on *The Sun*. Would he have confided in me that his motives were to engage in a circulation battle with *The Sun* using the England team? I don't know the answer to that one. Either way it made for an uncomfortable few days for me as Enemy Number One among both the squad and my journalistic colleagues.

Five years later and we were on the eve of another World Cup. While Paul Gascoigne had burst onto the scene with Spurs with impeccable timing, Bobby still wasn't sure whether it was too early for him to hold down a place in his final squad. To pile pressure on the manager, FA chairman Bert Millichip briefed journalists that unless England won the 1990 World Cup the manager would not have his contract renewed. The FA's then secretary, Graham Kelly, later recalled how over the previous few years each media attack after the Euros disaster had only redoubled the FA's determination to stand behind its man. Now the FA had broken ranks and cracked with typically inexpert timing. "The irony was that just before the 1990 World Cup, the chairman, Bert Millichip finally lost patience, let his tongue run away with him, and said Robson either had to win the World Cup or go, and Bobby reacted by approaching PSV Eindhoven. Had this not happened, he would have served another four years, believe me," Kelly later admitted. It would prove to be a disastrous moment for the future of the national team.

Robson thought the FA were putting him on trial. The speculation intensified. What would be considered a 'success' in Italia '90, a quarter-final place, a semi-final, losing the final on penalties? No one at the FA had an answer and Robson wasn't waiting to find out. He could have, hypothetically, reached the semi-finals, lost on penalties to Germany and it would have been considered failure. Who knows? So Bobby reacted by seeking alternative employment. He agreed to join PSV Eindhoven after the World Cup – when the news leaked the same papers that had castigated him for 8 years now condemned him as a traitor!

When it was clear that the news was about to be leaked, Robson decided he better confess to the arrangement. The announcement that he would leave after the 1990 World Cup provoked the expected outrage in some newspaper columns. Robson was accused of being unpatriotic for lining up a job abroad. He was hardly alone among the Italia '90 bosses in planning for another job after the tournament, with West Germany's coach Franz Beckenbauer also moving on.

The headlines were uncomfortable for such a proud patriot as Robson; it was particularly hurtful given he was hardly giving up the job voluntarily and had stuck it out previously when a lesser man would have walked away. Robson noted in the 1990 edition of his autobiography, "The very same papers which had been demanding for so long that I quit were now taking me to task for accepting another job, even though they had told their readers that I would not be kept on." He must have felt like he couldn't win.

All was forgiven in the wake of Turin as the open-top bus, adorned by Gazza's comedy breasts, made its way from Luton airport surrounded by thousands of adoring fans. Inevitably, the media alighted on English football's new era and its new clown prince with huge enthusiasm. England's stumbling but exhilarating charge to the last four brought one of the game's all-time dramas; the epic semi-final against West Germany that brought Paul Gascoigne's tears, defeat on penalties and a dignified exit. It was only then that the nation he adored began to reinvent Bobby Robson as a brilliant, if absent-minded, football sage, who needed to be ring-fenced as England boss, but who instead was already on his way out. His subsequent career in Holland and at Barcelona would further gild Bobby's image before he returned to England to take the Newcastle job.

HOW I GOT GAZZA HIS ENGLAND BREAKTHROUGH

Gazza became a firm favourite of mine, as indeed he had done with many Spurs fans who had witnessed some of his inventiveness and wizardry, dribbling into the opponent's box, getting to the by-line and dribbling his way back out of the box past the same defenders, before turning to face the goal, and shooting into the corner. Such impishness had endeared him to the Spurs faithful right from the start, ever since chairman Irving Scholar managed to pull off the coup of signing him from Newcastle United from under the noses of Manchester United.

I first came across Gazza and his phenomenal talents when he turned out for England's under-20s in the Toulon Tournament. People knew of the raw talents in this young Geordie in the black and white of Newcastle United, but it was at this tournament, actually being there for its entire duration, when you discovered that, along with his genius on the field there was his sheer cheek off it. Cheekiness was probably the right description back then; his was an impertinence, a natural rebelliousness of youth and *joie de vivre*. It quickly emerged that he was the comic of the group. He was never able to stand or sit still for a second and always wanted to make people laugh. It bore the classic signs of wanting to be accepted.

As a wannabe top football writer on the *Daily Mail* you would cut your teeth on the Toulon tournament where you would get to know the best of the nation's young talents many of whom would develop into future superstars of the game. It was a good way to forge relationships before they became big stars. Gazza was clearly going to be one of those. The stadium where England played had concrete steps to sit on, and precious few facilities to speak of, and one side was open to a motorway with only a wire mesh fence and a stretch of grass between the players and the cars hurtling along clearly visible. It made for an unusual back drop to international games. As an example of his exuberance; after scoring a spectacular goal Gazza ran across to that side of the stadium looking out to nobody, as the motorway side was devoid of spectators for obvious reasons, to begin his wild celebrations to an imaginary crowd!

Back at the team hotel, where a handful of Fleet Street's junior journalists had gathered for a daily briefing, Gazza didn't simply look out of his window way above us in his hotel room, but decided to urinate down in our direction. Talk about taking the piss out of the press! We all dived for cover, but his aim was pretty poor, bearing in mind he was some distance above us that was hardly surprising, but it wasn't that funny at first.

At Toulon airport after 10 days away surviving all of Gazza's tricks, the players managed to wander off in groups to board the buses that took them to the plane. Not Gazza. He managed to get himself a little lost, and ended up on a bus full of journalists who tended to stick together in a group, along with assorted FA officials who tended to steer clear of the young players as much as they could. He was a bag of laughs, always smiling, laughing, playing the fool, and you knew here was a boy in love with the game and loving every minute of being involved in it at this level. No one imagined he would turn into a man with such dark moods and deep personal problems, yet it was understandable that if reports filtered back to the England manager, that Bobby Robson knew his fellow Geordie was "as daft as a brush" and there was great reluctance to trust him in the World Cup squad for Italia '90.

A measure of my admiration for Paul's talents is that when I received my first PC at *The Mirror* offices and had to use a password for the first time, I chose G-A-Z-Z-A, and used it throughout my 18 years at the newspaper, and used the same password for just about everything else I needed one for.

Mel Stein and Len Lazarus were Gazza's agents at the time, and both became firm friends of mine. Mel was a specialist sports lawyer, and there was a mutual trust. If he told me anything off the record about Gazza's antics, and there were many, they remained off the record but often Mel would confide in me when there was a need for me to write about some of his more unsavoury episodes.

Briefings with Bobby Robson were a joy and worth looking forward to, as not only did they guarantee a few stories, they were extremely fun and informative. Invariably he would grant the senior football writers a separate audience following the main media conference, sometimes we would enjoy a leisurely lunch or dinner with him, where much was off the record, but it was wonderful background material for use at a later date when appropriate.

The more informal smaller groups of chief football writers gave me the opportunity to bang on about Gazza, and why he should be given a chance to prove himself before Robson selected his World Cup squad. Robson, though completely convinced about his gifts on the field, knew only too well his disruptive influence off it and was wary of whether it was a good idea to subject his squad to weeks and weeks of Gazza nonsense. More important for the England manager, he was still young and untested at such a high level. My argument was that there was no harm in using one of the build-up games to give him a full run out to see what he can do. Robson didn't seemed convinced.

He brought Gazza on for his England debut against Albania at Wembley in a World Cup qualifier, which England won comfortably enough 5-0, and Gazza scored but from the very second he raced eagerly onto the Wembley turn he had forgotten everything Robson had instructed him to do [play wide on the right hand side] as his natural instincts instantly took over and he played wherever he fancied. Robson gave him a rollicking after the match when Gazza told him he was not a right-sided midfield. Robson told him: "When you are picked for England you bloody well play where you are told." So while the Wembley crowd might have loved his 23 minutes against Albania, his manager was berating him for his lack of positional discipline.

By the turn of the year my persistent rallying cry to 'give Gazza a chance' had not only bored Robson, but also my colleagues on rival papers, who suggested that I give it a rest because it just wasn't going to happen! Robson continued to agonise and as late as February at a Football Writers' Association lunch that he told us that 22-year-old Gascoigne and 23-year-old Platt were fighting over one place at the finals. But Robson couldn't ignore calls for him forever as his form at Spurs seemed irresistible and the clamour for him to be given a chance become so strong and to Robson's credit he always insisted that he had planned to give Gazza one big chance and that would be against the Czechs at Wembley.

Later, in response to publicly being called "daft as a brush" by the England manager, the midfielder turned up for training ahead of the friendly against Czechoslovakia with a hairbrush sticking out of his sock. After turning it on against the Czechs, the joke was on those who considered Gazza too much of a risk. "The England manager may still consider Paul Gascoigne to be 'as daft as a brush', but last night the brush was in the hand of a man who did not need artistic licence to make his point," wrote David Lacey of *The Guardian*.

As Paul recalls in the introduction to this book, "Going into the match against Czechoslovakia, I was terrified I wouldn't make the World Cup squad. We'd gone to Israel and Bobby Robson had said 'this is your chance', but I had a crap game. Plenty in the press were saying I wasn't ready – I knew this was my last chance to prove them wrong. I just thought: 'What have I got to lose?' It was magic. Everything I did came off. I walked off the pitch pretty sure I'd be in the squad. To play a faultless game, to score, to set up two goals for Steve Bull and to get the press boys screaming for me to play made it a great night."

Outwardly at least Robson let it be known that he was taking a calculated risk with Gazza. On the morning of April 25, 1990, with the World Cup only 45 days away, the nation's back pages once again reported that Bobby was agonising over whether Gascoigne was sensible enough to make his Italia '90 squad but in the end the manager went with his gut feeling. Gazza had been the star of the show against the Czechs, and it was clear that he had to be picked.

After a worrying start, in which he might have been booked for a clumsy challenge and then patted the ref on the cheek, Gascoigne took control. A glorious 25-yard pass for Steve Bull to open the scoring, a corner on the head of Terry Butcher, who knocked down for Stuart Pearce to score, then another put on a plate for Bull before he strode onto a ball from Tony Dorigo and finished. In the dressing room afterwards, Robson and Gascoigne jokingly squabbled, the manager claiming he couldn't count the corner as an assist if it had been flicked on. Robson told reporters: "He passed the test, but you're not a player after one match."

When Gascoigne got back to his hotel room, he wanted to see his performance and in particular his late goal again. "I watched the highlights, and as the ball hit the net Bobby Robson turned to Don Howe and said, 'That's fantastic'. When I saw what he said I knew I'd made it." And after that performance the manager even said that Gazza could be England's Diego Maradona!

"I thought it was a bit of mind games because he was such a Bobby-type player," says Peter Shilton. "He'd brought in Arnold Muhren and Frans Thijssen at Ipswich and he loved players who could pass the ball and dribble. I thought there was an element of kidology to it. It would have been very difficult for him to have left a player like Paul Gascoigne at home.

"He'd made an instant impression on me from when he first played against Derby. In the England camp he scored some brilliant goals against me and did some funny things to keep the atmosphere going. He would score from distance, pass well and get up and down the pitch. We had some good players but not many could do that. Bobby was great at handling Gazza. We had Waddle and Butcher and Bryan

Robson – so there were enough players to keep their eye on him. At times he would be a bit childish; most times it was funny."

Today journalist Rob Shepherd agrees, "there was a bit of psychology to make him focus; to let him know he couldn't be a circus act. At the same time, Bobby did have a concern that despite all his talent he could not be trusted." 'Shep' added: "Bryan Robson and Chris Waddle, who were very influential, wanted him in the squad. Everybody liked him, partly because he'd do these things. Once, at an airport, we were waiting for the baggage carousel and he emerged from the hole the bags come through, riding a suitcase."

Gazza always seemed to be an accident waiting to happen, and the first 'accident' occurred even before he joined up with the World Cup squad. He travelled to Newcastle to say his goodbyes, a routine enough idea, wanting to share his excitement with friends and family but where Gazza is concerned trouble lurks round every corner. He doesn't so much look for trouble, trouble looks for him, and finds him all too easily.

As he was leaving a bar he was accosted by a young man in the car park, who he had never seen before, although the guy seemed to know him. Well, in Newcastle it would have been hard to find a single soul who didn't 'know' Paul Gascoigne. Clearly, Gazza in a bar again might sound like reasonable behaviour for such a young footballer, but the fear is that he might not have downed just the one Newcastle Brown Ale! A quiet meal in with his mates might have been more sensible.

It turned out that Gazza was a target for someone wanting to show off and this guy said he was going "to get" him. Paul tried to lighten the confrontation and joke with him but the lad was having none of it. Gazza said he wouldn't hurt anyone with glasses, so the bloke took off his glasses and placed them carefully on the bonnet of Gazza's car, and shaped up to strike him. Gazza turned round and landed the first blow, punching him once on the nose, and the boy ran off in tears. It seemed 'tears' would be a theme of Paul Gascoigne's World Cup, but this time he had made someone else weep!

Gazza thought that was the end of the matter. Unforturnately it wasn't. Under a banner headline in *The Sun* "World Cup Wallies" there was a picture of Gazza and Bobby Robson side by side, as the England manager had just hit the news when an alleged mistress was threatening to write a book about their affair and news broke of the England boss's decision to sign up for PSV Eindhoven just weeks before the tournament.

Here I am as a stand-in for Gazza at the launch of England's 1990 World Cup kit.

In Gazza's authorised biography Mel Stein, his friend, lawyer and agent, wrote that the story had the affect of "bonding the team together, placing them firmly behind their comic genius and their forgetful manager." Stein added: "It also drove Bobby and Paul further into a father-son relationship that was to be so vital in getting the best out of Paul." But Stein admitted it was not "the most auspicious start to the campaign".

I experienced Gazza's unreliability at first hand when the player had been commissioned by some of my friends at Umbro, the England kit sponsors, to attend a photo shoot at *The Mirror* building in Holborn along with Gary Lineker, David Seaman and Paul Parker. It was quite a coup for *The Mirror* to have such England superstars turning out to model the new Umbro kit. Such a picture shoot would never happen these days, with players earning vast fortunes, they no longer need publicity or the profile generated by newspapers and they soon graduated to the millions on offer from celebrity magazines such as *OK* and *Hello*, and more recently still they have been content to manage their own social media profiles with back up team on hand to tweet about and Instagram every moment of their lives. But back then even the highest paid players in England earned nowhere near the vast sums in a career that the top players can now command in a week, and a few extra pounds for such personal appearances was always something they would consider, but it would need to be compelling and this was something organised by the kit suppliers who paid handsomely.

Despite the carrot of a substantial fee it came as no surprise when everyone turned up except Gazza. The then Sports Editor Keith Fisher thought it would be a laugh if I stood in for Gazza in the picture shoot, and so there I was wearing the England kit alongside Lineker, Seaman, and Parker. However, that was not the first time I had worn the England kit, as I turned out regularly for the England press team and in my time played alongside and against the likes of Bobby Charlton, Paul Mariner, Ron Atkinson, Trevor Brooking, Arsene Wenger and Michel Platini.

STEVE BULL

"The biggest thrill was standing on the steps of the plane ready to depart for the World Cup"

I enjoyed every single minute of my experience in Italia '90, but the memory I treasure is standing on the steps of the plane about to begin the journey of my football life. I was there next to Gazza, Beardsley, Waddle, Lineker, Shilton, Butcher, it was surreal. Yes, Steve Bull from Tipton. Wolves had just finished 10th in the old Second Division, it was our first season back at that level following promotion, and Bobby Robson had picked me, but I don't believe that will ever happen again, that an England manager will look down at the lower divisions for a World Cup player.

Surreal is the only way to describe standing on those steps ready to embark for the World Cup, so my greatest moment was the mere fact I was playing in it. I was one of the lucky ones, perhaps the luckiest of all time, to have been scoring goals in the lower divisions and got picked for a World Cup.

Bobby Robson was a great manager and a great bloke, and he managed to get a united squad together, and for someone like me who wasn't first choice it was about supporting everyone, and everyone supported each other; it was never a question of "I should play" or "he should play".

He picked me for a few of the games and I got to spend six weeks with David Platt who was also from the Midlands and he's a great lad. My worst moment was when I was about to come on against the Germans in the semi-final for the final 15 minutes, I was warming up along the touchline when Gary Lineker scored and Bobby Robson told me to sit down for a while, but I never got on. I tell you this, had I come on I would have been like a Tasmanian Devil, I'd have run all over the place in an effort to have got us to the final.

The home coming was something else. When we flew into Luton we had no idea that we would be greeted by such a welcome home, and I was stood next to Gazza, false boobs and all, at the front of the bus!

DAVID SEAMAN

I can recall the night we qualified for the World Cup, I was sitting on the bench, so was Gazza, and on the final whistle we jumped up together, hugging, shouting, dancing, and singing 'We Are going to The World Cup', neither of had ever been to a World Cup and it was so exciting.

It was a pretty special feeling getting on that plane with the squad, even as the No. 3 goalkeeper, with Peter Shilton the No 1 and Chris Woods the No 2. I was on the bench for the Ireland game, and then it happened in training, a broken thumb. We were doing the usual training routine with the players firing shots at me, and I'd just saved one from Paul Parker and was focusing on the next one, when this ball came at me, which I didn't see coming, from an 80 degree angle, and I thought "What was that?" and then felt the pain.

Dr Crane was the Arsenal doctor and also the England doctor, and I had just signed for Arsenal. He took me to hospital where they confirmed it was a fracture. "Oh shit, doc, what does that mean?"

"It means you are going home," said Dr Crane.

He contacted the England camp to let them know the bad news, about then he made a call to George Graham, my new manager, as George and the Arsenal vice-chairman David Dein were on a boat in the harbour, and we had to make a detour to see them before returning to the England hotel. Naturally they were worried as they had just bought me, and were concerned how bad it would be. But once they knew it wouldn't need an operation, and would just need three or four weeks to repair, they were more relaxed about it.

Naturally, I was pretty upset about going home, it was such an amazing journey to have got to the World Cup and when I got back home I watched every game. Being in the eye of the storm, you didn't realise how much excitement had been generated back home but I got to see it from both sides and it was more exciting back home then it was out there.

The excitement was built up so much, I couldn't take it any more and had to go back out there as a fan to watch the semi-final. I wanted to be there. I got my ticket through the FA and was sitting with a few people from the FA up in the Gods. That night I went back to the team hotel, and stayed with the lads, it was an odd feeling being with them again, I didn't quite feel like a spare part, but it was a weird feeling. They were low as you would expect them to be as they had just been knocked out so close to the final, but I kept on telling them what an amazing feat they had achieved and that it had had such an effect on everyone back home and they only really believed me when we all arrived back at Luton to witness that welcome.

While it was a huge disappointment missing out on so much of the World Cup through injury, it was still a big time in my career and it was huge thrill to look forward to my first season with Arsenal.

Everyone has their favourite Gazza story, but mine was actually Euro '96 when we were fishing together with Ian Walker before the Spain game, and a photographer took pictures and Gazza chased him, and the guy locked himself in his car. But Paul was determined to get the film off him, and somehow got his mobile and said he'd give him his mobile back for the film, but the guy sped off crashing through some gates. I told Gazza to redial his phone, and he got straight through to Piers Morgan! *The Mirror* ran some silly story about the Spanish Armada next day instead of the pictures!

BUILD UP

As England made the journey to Italy, they would also be joined by Scotland and the Republic of Ireland for a tournament that existed in an age before social media and players lived without selfies. Bobby Robson had much to prove with the media always on his case. Robson had his favourites, and some of them backed him to the hilt, but the vast majority had already set the agenda, that the England manager was very much under pressure.

Having already decided to leave his post after the tournament, Robson seemed more relaxed. He still got angry at times, but he was never a man to bear a grudge, even against his most vociferous detractors. But he put up the barricades at the team's lavish Is Molas Golf Hotel, and conducted his media briefings at the training complex, or on the odd occasion went to the media centre at the Forte Village resort where the press were billeted.

The Is Molas Resort is 43 km from Cagliari airport and offers a magnificent panoramic view over the sea, embracing the ancient watch tower of Nora. The resort is recommended to those wishing to enjoy the golf, with a splendid 27-hole course, while they can also enjoy the beaches and coast, and the lively nightlife of Pula, all accessible with a short drive. Even though it was only a four star hotel and down at heel in comparison to the five star luxury of the Forte Village, it suited Robson's requirements; it was remote, but gave the players the opportunity for golf and other sporting past times, as well as the games they brought with them.

There was a lot of media pessimism towards the England team before the tournament as John Barnes recalls, "I was used to it, because it was a feature of being an England player back in the 1980s and 1990s. Every time we went to a tournament, there was a lot of negativity surrounding England for a lot of things which went on off the field, especially with Gazza in the squad and different bits. It made us stronger, we had good togetherness, a good spirit and a never-say-die spirit, we understood how to deal with that. We had a bit of a siege mentality because we were having a hard time with the newspapers and stories coming out.

"I think the press are much kinder now to the England team in terms of their support and wanting them to do well. That's why I say negative influences can affect a very young team, but generally speaking

I think the press in recent times have been very supportive, so they're not going to have the problems we had. That's why tournament experience counts for a lot, knowing how to handle the situation.

"The press were giving Bobby a hard time, giving the team a hard time and we probably didn't help ourselves by sneaking out late at night. It's a bit different now in terms of the support the press give the team, but back then it was different. The adversity I was talking about was not just on the pitch, but off it as well, and we really had to come together as a team.

"One of the sad aspects of modern football at club and international level, and it's much more apparent now than it was in my day, is that individual players put themselves above their teammates. They see themselves as better than their teammates, either in terms of prestige or social media, and this makes individual players much more important, so it's even more necessary to stick together as a team. Because if players aren't playing well or scoring, other players will think 'I should be in the team because I have more followers on social media, my fans think I'm better than him, I think I'm better than him'. That's a modern phenomenon, but in my day we had a strong mentality as a team and it was forged through adversity.

"In both '86 and '90 we did not start well. So then we had to beat Belgium to qualify — that's when you need togetherness. Individual players, me being one, might have been going through a hard time but everybody got behind me and supported me. It's different from how it is now. We were very close. I do not think there were the egos there are now. Back then, you had players like Bryan Robson, although he got injured, who was the best player in England but he was just one of the lads. That was the way football was."

There were fun and games during England's stay at the golf resort, according to Barnes, "We had a horse racing evening when Gary Lineker and Peter Shilton were the bookmakers but the most important thing was that we were there to play football. To alleviate the boredom, we had things like the racing day as light-hearted relief but that was not that important, as far as I was concerned. You were there to play in a World Cup.

"Normally, when you play on Saturday, you get together with England on the Sunday, train Monday and Tuesday, to be back Thursday — it's three days away. Having to be away for five to six weeks takes some getting used to and the experience actually helps. So they will have to try and alleviate boredom and get the players focussed on matches, but once the games start they'll be fully focussed."

Barnes felt he had matured since 1986, and was reinvigorated by emerging young talent, including the precocious Paul Gascoigne. "When you have characters like Paul Gascoigne everything just goes out the window because Gazza, really, with his youth and his naivety just pulled us through and it was just a marvel watching what he was doing. His character around the dressing room and around the place, of course, he took the attention of the press from us.

"He was a lunatic! He was always making you laugh by doing crazy things. It was probably not the best preparation to be doing crazy things, jumping out of windows, sneaking out and doing whatever he did but Gazza was a young boy then. Gazza emerged out of that World Cup. Was he one of the main players in the early rounds? No, not necessarily, but he was a happy chap."

Italia '90 would be Bobby Robson's last tournament in charge of England yet Barnes was loyal to his manager. "He was a fantastic manager, because you wanted to play for him. Not only did he have a respect but he had a real empathy and love for everybody. He was a lovely man. I do not think managers and players have that relationship anymore. Bobby was just a humble man who wanted you to do well."

Trevor Steven observed: "At that time Serie A was the best league and Italy was set up to host a great event. Hooliganism was an issue, though, so all our group games were held in Cagliari to restrict England fans to Sardinia. It was a turbulent time for Sir Bobby Robson. Our manager was under fire and, having announced that he'd be stepping down after the tournament, we were written off before getting there."

Robson's press conferences were always a treat as Mike Ingham explained in his recently published memoirs "I fondly remember him with the media occasionally straight batting a question by saying, 'I'm not getting into that' but then, like a dog with a bone, he would keep gnawing away at it, returning to it and by the end would have more than comprehensively answered it."

Mike also recalled how, after Gary Lineker's two penalties against Cameroon rescued England from a humiliating exit, he was denied access by security officials to the area where Robson was waiting for our a BBC radio sports interview. Gary Lineker spotted the problem and rescued Mike by pushing his microphone through a barbed wire fence to record the England manager's thoughts. Mike considered that he was a manager with an awareness of the media's needs and he was only too willing to accommodate them. Some managers would have had nothing to do with the media after all the barbs Robson had suffered, but here he was going through barbed wire for a journalist!

The FA were at pains to run a PR exercise on the Sardinian island to get the locals onside, and also to engage with the England supporters. When the media arrived at Cagliari to journey on to the tranquility of the Forte Village, the arrival of English fans was clearly visible and it wasn't a pleasant sight. They were herded together by the police who had been awaiting their arrival with well rehearsed policing methods – to treat them all like potential hooligans.

The travelling army of England fans were a stigma on the tournament, and a blight on the country. Hooliganism was at its peak back home, and attempts at restraining the export of our hooligan fans was never quite effective. There were plenty of misleading images of these fans in *All Played Out* by Pete Davies, soon to be followed by more romantic books and plays about supporters that masked the reality of the times.

The secretary of the local World Cup organising committee, Roberto Papalardo, whose family owned most of the cinemas on the island, had known for some time that England's opening games would be in Calglairi, Sardinia's capital, and that the venue for England's first round games was not going to be left to chance at the World Cup draw. The plan was to isolate the most notorious travelling fans in the history of football, the English disease as it was known at the time, that had spread like a modern day virus throughout the football world. Copycat hooligan gangs had started following all the biggest European teams while every large city in Italy had its own groups of Ultras who would be waiting for a chance to take on the English.

England's reputation abroad was hard for the rest of the world to fathom. There was still an image of the British as the bowler hatted, brolly carrying, sharp suit wearing stockbroker type. Yet the more England played abroad, the more that image began to change alarmingly into the pot belly, topless, tattooed, beer swilling thug. Of course they remained a minority but the law-abiding fan was becoming concerned about following the national team and fearful of falling into the wrong category.

"You have to say it was nice to get out of our country that summer," Terry Butcher reflects. "If you think about the Poll Tax riots, hooliganism and football's dreadful reputation, it wasn't a particularly nice place to be and that's why they put us on the island of Sardinia to get us out of the way."

Robson led his squad from the Sardinian island to a final friendly warm up game in Tunisia. Yet again his planning went pear-shaped and the tabloids sharpened their knives yet again as allegations concerning Robson's previous romantic dalliances made front page news.

Paul Parker takes up the story: "Bobby got off to a bad start before a ball had even been kicked. After talks over a new contract with the Football Association had broken down, he announced that once the finals were over he would be going to manage the crack Dutch side, PSV Eindhoven. This did not go down at all well with the press or public. Not many years previously Don Revie had walked out of the England manager's job and fled to the Middle East to fill his boots with gold (and sand). Some of the criticism of Robson was a bit hysterical, along the lines that he was deserting his country in its hour of need and that his mind would inevitably be elsewhere as the competition was unfolding. As a result, there was an air of tension between him and there was a danger of a siege mentality developing."

Parker described how the tension mounted with places at stake in Tunisia, and the change of location didn't go down well with the players. "The players' wives, who had accompanied us to Sardinia, went home and we swapped a glorious hotel for a much poorer one in Tunisia which I found to be an awful place and I was a spectator at an awful match, which we drew 1-1. Any complacency we had as a team was shattered, but it did not stop the press criticising us and I suppose we deserved it.

"It was also a time when a woman revealed an affair with our manager in a tabloid newspaper and while it must have embarrassed him, he did not show it but there was a by-product. We always had the English papers at our hotel, partly to see what the reporters were saying about is, but also to keep in touch with what was going on at home. These were now banned."

The achievement of selection for three World Cup squads while making a total of 77 appearances for England gives Butcher a perfect insight into Robson's management, and Italia '90 stands out most vividly. "I started out wondering whether I would get into the team," he said. "I didn't seem to fit into the sweeper system Bobby Robson had in mind and then I behaved stupidly at the end of a warm-up match in Tunisia, taking off my shirt and throwing it on the floor. It was reported as a protest but in fact I was angry with myself for playing so poorly."

As Mel Stein wrote in the authorised biography of Gazza, "If the Tunisia match had been arranged to restore the team's confidence it failed miserably. Firstly it poured with rain, which rather ruined the acclimatisation aspect. Then Tunisia scored and it took Steve Bull, coming on as a substitute for Lineker, to grab an equaliser. Paul played the whole 90 minutes, but was to blame for the goal. 'It was strange. It wasn't that I wasn't trying. I just didn't feel motivated' he said. Paul Parker summed it up when he called Tunisia the 'worst country in the world' but then he'd not played in Albania!'"

The stories relating to alleged past matters in Robson's personal life would further antagonise the manager and it all made for a particularly stormy press conference. "Garbage" was how he described much of the coverage, before castigating sections of the media for their conduct as he told them they had "ruined" what the team was trying to achieve. It was certainly far from the way England would have wanted to depart for the World Cup. As if to add to the fractious game in North Africa, Terry Butcher was accused of head butting an opponent. Robson now had to contend with calls for Butcher to be sent home, which he resisted.

On 27 May Gazza turned 23. Stein wrote, "It was incredible to think he was still the baby of the party. Some baby! But at least his youth put a lot of other things into perspective. At an impromptu, belated birthday dinner in Italy he rose to give a speech. 'I was great at seven...' There were cheers and he signalled for silence, 'by the time I was ten I was brilliant, at seventeen I went to Newcastle and showed them how to play... They offered me a grand a week and I said I wasn't going to take a drop in salary for them.... at twenty I was the greatest player in the league... at twenty-one I was earning £7,000-a-week. Now I'm a millionaire. What have I got?' Waddle muttered, 'Loads of money - and a big mouth.'"

Fellow Geordie Waddle drew the short straw, he'd be Gazza's room-mate. However that pairing was inevitable. Waddle told Mel Stein for his book on Gazza, "He'd be up before eight, off to the pool, have a game of table tennis, take a sauna and then be raring to go for training. Even when that was finished he'd be down to the beach for a pedalo race, or dragging somebody out of bed to play tennis with him. He couldn't sit still for a minute."

Stein revealed how Gazza gave shirts away, not just his own, but his team-mates, to everyone he came across, wanting to be friendly and accommodating, but had to be stopped before the squad ran out of kit for their games! "Nobody could get on the table-tennis table while Paul was about, and if anybody had the temerity to beat him he'd simply play them again and again until he finally won. He had to have the last word, had to end up on top. It was his way of life."

Senior football writers grilling Bobby Robson. Nothing like the more formal, regimented FA organised press conferences of today.

Eager to show a friendlier face of the homeland, the FA embarked on a charm offensive. How much Robson bought in to this is debatable as he wanted to focus totally on preparing his team. One of the FA's bright ideas was to have an open training session to invite the England fans, the locals, and the media to report on how friendly and accommodating the England team can be.

Paul Parker's autobiography published in 2006 recalls how the whole episode backfired. Tony Adams, David Beasant, and David Rocastle, who was Paul's England room-mate, had been the unlucky ones to be left out of the final World Cup squad and sent packing from Bisham Abbey shortly before departure for Sardinia. 'Rocky' was in tears and couldn't wait to get out of the hotel with Paul helping him pack and loading his gear into the boot of his car. In contrast Paul was elated to be told he was going "I felt like he [Robson] was my dad, even if her did call me Danny!"

But the open training session was typical of England's build-up to the tournament; it was an unmitigated disaster. The England manager knew what he was doing in galvanising his players, as Parker revealed that on the eve of the big internationals the manager would evoke a battle of cry that opponents feared England because we were England. "That always struck a chord with me and I think it did the rest of the squad, it made us feel proud and I know there was not a player in Italy who did not love and respect him."

Relations with players were generally cordial until the 'hostess' story broke.

However, off the field, Robson was an accident waiting to happen. Parker writes: "We were at our training camp in Sardinia and the manager decided to have an open day for the press and to allow our session to be watched by our many fans who had followed us out. It was supposed to be a public relations afternoon, but it went horribly wrong for David Seaman and me.

"Sure enough, the invitation to let in the fans meant abuse for me and John Barnes as the two black players, but we had learned not to let it affect us and got on with what we were told was going to be an easy session. The problem was that many of us took it too easily for Robson's liking and he stepped in to administer a rollicking, making the reasonable point that the press and a whole swathe of supporters would be getting the wrong impression our preparations.

"Robson singled me out for special condemnation and I had a go back at him because I felt we were all a bit lackadaisical, not just me. In a sort of fit of indignation I swung wildly at the next ball which came my way and I can say now, I have never struck a shot as sweetly in my life. It flew at great speed towards Seaman who was not looking. The next thing I heard was a cry of pain from our goalkeeper and worried medical men were soon surrounding him with looks of concern. Verdict:

one broken thumb. Culprit: a contrite Paul Parker. We needed a special sanction form from FIFA to allow Seaman, whose World Cup was over, to be replaced by a reprieved and relieved Dave Beasant."

Inside the camp, though, Gascoigne lightened the mood with his constant capers - driving golf buggies through bunkers on one of the players' days off before having a chocolate cake delivered flat into his face on what someone seemingly thought was his birthday. The players' race-night at the Sardinia team base which did not end well for 'bookies' Lineker and Peter Shilton. The players had been given advance sight of the race videos. "The lads trusted each other," recalled Terry Butcher. "We loved each other. There's a common bond and I think that's everything."

Mel Stein described Gazza's golfing antics: "Golf has never been his strongest or favourite sport. It takes far too long and involved walking long distances before anything actually happens. In the tournament organised amongst the players, there were some serious scratch golfers and nobody wanted to pair up with Paul. Waddle finally volunteered, but because of the numbers a third was needed, and the dubious honour fell to the tournament favourite, Tony Dorigo. Paul believes it was engineered by the bookmakers in the team, usually Lineker, Robson and Butcher, who thought Paul might be the downfall of a good thing.

"Paul actually controlled himself and got through to the last six, but once the TV cameras arrived on the scene he went wild, lying flat on his stomach and pushing the ball along with his nose, dancing and signing with Chris, swinging the club upside down. Give Paul an audience and he simply cannot help performing."

STEVE McMAHON

How Bookies Lineker And Shilton Were Taken To The Cleaners

When we got to Sardinia to prepare for the Finals we were in lockdown for weeks, with this remote hotel booked out just for us, all we had was a week with our wives otherwise we got on with the job of concentrating on the World Cup. It was surreal having the hotel and the beach to ourselves, but the hotel was luxurious enough. But I agree with the new way of thinking that players should be more in the centre of things, experiencing the country, the culture, seeing some of the sights, filling their time more profitably, rather than glorious isolation.

I didn't mind being locked away, though, because all I wanted to do was to ensure England had a good World Cup, but it did become monotonous at times, but I didn't worry about the no drink regime.

The manager gave the boys a day off a few days before the opening game against Ireland after being penned in for so long, and Robbo said "come on, let's go down the pub". Quite a few went for a drink, and the only mishap was Robbo coming back and unfortunately damaging his toe in the shower. The whole toe nail lifted and there was blood everywhere, the doctor had to be called at midnight, and Robbo had to have pain killers either side of his toe and even at half time to get him through that opening game, but he would still have been in pain at the end because there are only so many injections you can have before it becomes dangerous. I came on for Robbo in the opening game after about 65 minutes.

Gazza was one of the players who got more upset with the press than anyone else when there was a fabricated story about one of the Italian hostesses. Newspapers go looking for things at times, but it's not good to wake up to a story that caused so much anger in the camp, that upset so many people, not just with us, but also back home. Over the years I've come to the conclusion that football should embrace the media more, as it plays such an important part of the game, but at that time, especially coming from Liverpool, the attitude was all for one, one for all and to keep in house anything that could hurt any of us.

We had a race night and somehow everyone got to know the outcome of the races beforehand and Gazza and a few others took the bookies Shilts and Lineker to the cleaners. Gazza isn't really into his golf, so it was wasted on him being at a golf hotel resort, and on our departure we were given some new Japanese clubs, and I told Gazza that as he didn't need them, I'd be happy to take them off his hands, which I did. He still reminds me I've got his golf clubs!

DES WALKER

I mistrusted the media and never gave interviews

I'm nothing but truthful, that's how I view myself, and I have always felt that talking to the media there was an issue about how those views would be construed. I've always been concerned about the political nature of the press, why they write certain things in certain ways to suit the nature of their publication. For me, though, facts are facts, and when I played for England or even when I watch England play, it's the facts that are of importance. I am my own biggest critic and always have  been, and that is all I need. I don't need to say anything or do anything with the media.

I roomed with Stuart Pearce at Italia '90, and I am sure no one to this day really knows what Stuart is really like, probably they don't know what I am really like either, and I am more than happy for it to stay that way.

I never enjoyed giving interviews, I wasn't paid to give interviews, I was paid to play, so I never did give interviews. The best place to do your talking is on the park, the rest is all bull. You get questions that are designed by the journalists to get the answers they are looking for. I did an interview once, it was before I played against Gary Lineker when he played for Everton, but it was pointless because I knew what they wanted me to say about him and I refused to be part of it all, it was all bull because you say something and the next day when you read it, it doesn't reflect what you were trying to say, it's all politically motivated as the papers choose to use only what they want to use, rather than airing my views the way I want them to be aired. Then you heard the excuses, "I didn't write it", or "I didn't write the headline". And you think "Oh really?" I see so many TV and newspaper interviews these days and they talk a lot of shit, the pundits especially are not telling you the truth, they are all playing a political game. I grew up in a world where you dealt with things face-to-face, now it's the internet, something I have nothing to do with, as, for me, it's used by cowards who do not deal with things face-to-face, it's a forum for bullying and it's easy to hide behind social media. The modern day person doesn't value honesty.

As a player, I gave everything there was to give on the field, and hopefully that was good enough. It didn't matter what I said, so I didn't say anything, and I thought it was best to keep my views to myself, it was the safest way, and that's what I did throughout my career.

Every time I put on the England jersey, every time I played for England, I thought it was a game we could win, especially when I looked round the dressing room in Italia '90 and saw the likes of John Barnes, Chris Waddle, Peter Beardsley, Gary Lineker, Paul Gascoigne, Terry Butcher and Stuart Pearce, they were the best group of players I had ever played with.

I never enjoyed losing, regardless of what the media thought, and so I never went into a game without thinking I could be on the winning side, I'd go out to win the game and do my job the best I could, and I must have played 800 games and that was my approach in every single one of them. That is why losing to Germany in that semi-final was a massive disappointment. Every game we played in that tournament took us a step closer to winning it, we had the confidence we could win the World Cup. We felt we could beat every team in it, and more to the point every team in it knew we could beat them. But I don't look back in life with any regrets, I would give it my best shot, and that's all you can do. I don't look back with any regrets about not qualifying for the next World Cup, it was a massive disappointment, but there is no point in self evaluation, I don't think that way, all I ever thought about was the next game, and winning the next game, and that didn't always go to plan, and you have to accept it. France won the World Cup and didn't get through the first round in the next one, so it can happen to anyone at the highest level.

We have to earn that respect and I feel that we did that as the tournament progressed, but you always need a few ingredients to end up winning, a little bit of luck and a fantastic team. But with that amount of talent in that England team how could you not feel confident and I cannot believe that there were such low expectations of us when we started out.

Take Bryan Robson, for instance, there is no way someone with his attitude and mentality would go into a tournament with little expectation of winning it, and then you look around at the other enormously talented players; Waddle, Barnes, Butcher is a born winner, and Lineker would be thinking he's going to be the tournament's top scorer. There were so many established top players with only Stuart Pearce and myself as the younger players in the team. This was the best group of players I ever had the pleasure of playing with, and in addition they were all so mentally strong and to win the World Cup mental strength would be vitally important.

For instance, how many club captains did we have? Virtually all of them had been throughout their careers, those captains had moral courage, and it's courage above all qualities that makes you a winner, and they all had to be mentally strong to overcome all that negativity by the press, but the negativity came from the press, not from the players. Eventually the players were brave enough to turn it all around

England teams are always, it seems, fighting against the press negativity that surrounds them, and especially when it comes to going into big tournament, whereas in other countries the press support the national team going into major tournaments. The hostility at Italia '90 was not created by the players, but the players had to be brave enough to overcome it, to look beyond it, and that's where the courage came in, you don't want people who are scared or worried about that negativity, you need players who have a lot of courage to battle against it, and that's what we possessed.

Gazza was one of the best, if not the best, player I had ever played with or indeed have ever seen, he could do things others couldn't do. He was a great footballer, and for me that was all that was important. That was all he needed to be. What he did off the park was his business. What he did on the field was unreal. But we all know he tended to do some silly things off the pitch, but he was one of the world's best. You need all 11 players with all their different ingredients to make a good team and while Gazza was the icing on the cake, for me Robbo was the most important player, not just as captain, but a special captain, respected by everyone, as he made everyone's job that much easier, the captain who would drive everyone on, get the best out of everyone. If Robbo had been fit all the way through I am convinced we would have won the World Cup. If Gazza was the best footballer, then Robbo was the most influential, and so much of this game is about character as much as it is about talent. Robbo understood how a game was won or lost, understood how the team as a unit must do their job, and if need be, make them do it. He was also incredibly consistent, and you could see him doing it in every game.

OFFICE POLITICS

While the England party were billeted in a luxurious golf village complex about three miles from the media contingent, we were luxuriating at the Forte Village. It has been expanded since those days, but for a couple of years after the tournament I returned there as it is one of the world's loveliest locations. There was a hotel at the resort's entrance adjacent to a magnificent Spa complex, and the hotel overlooked the main restaurant and the sea close to the beach, with a variety of villas, in different sizes scattered through the resort which contained numerous restaurants and bars, some of the villas were much more affordable than the inflated prices for the beach side hotel.

The *Daily Star*'s chief football writer at that time, Bob Driscoll, had been assigned the reconnaissance job along with *The Sun*'s Alex Montgomery, and they booked themselves and their fellow chief football writers into a section of the costliest rooms in the beach side hotel; the top floor was simply palatial, and the second floor wasn't too shabby either, but the top floor was booked every summer by the German World Cup winning team of 1974.

Gary Lineker wasn't on mega bucks in those days, but his Spurs salary was hefty enough to afford to put his wife Michelle up there, where Bobby Moore's daughter, Roberta, was also staying. As one of the younger of the chief reporters of that generation, I would like to pass the late evenings at the resort's disco, a term that would now date me with the younger fraternity, but the place was near deserted apart from Roberta, her friend Dave Smith, who worked for *Shoot* magazine, and is now sadly departed. Michelle would often pop in too, as it was okay during the day with so many spa amenities, but a bit lonely in the late evenings waiting for the World Cup show to start. Coincidently, I bump into Michelle quite often these days as we both live in Sunningdale! Small world.

I loved my tennis, having spent a year covering the sport for the *Daily Mail*, so took advantage of the resort's impressive tennis club, where on one occasion I played a doubles that included Ron Atkinson, Gary Lineker and my partner, Aston Villa nut Nigel Kennedy, who was much more comfortable with the strings of his violin than those of a tennis racket, it would be fair to say. Big Ron was a bit top heavy, so not so nimble around the court, but was devastating at the net with his wonderful drop shots, while Gary carried their team being the natural athlete.

All the excitement of covering a World Cup and staying at the plush Forte Village complex was soon eroded by the total disconnect between Bobby Robson, his squad and the media. Yet, it shouldn't have been like that, as Robson actually had developed a wonderful rapport with the elite press corps assigned to following England; a group of in the main, highly accomplished and experienced journalists. The perception was of the media at Robson's throat, the reality was vastly different. The media assigned to the England team adored Robson, and I was among them, and saw for myself the way the England manager fostered harmonious relationships with the aid of the FA's mushrooming media team.

Robson was wonderfully entertaining on the numerous occasions I shared the same table with him, along with my chief football writer colleagues, in our 'off the record' briefings over a convivial lunch. Invariably the gatherings would culminate in Robson grabbing the salt and pepper pots, some cups and whatever he could find to make a tactical point about his team, certain players, or the opponent he was about to face. It was hugely entertaining and informative but most importantly provided relaxed insights into his thinking about tactics, certain individuals and the opposition.

We all wanted England to do well and actually win the World Cup – we are all fans after all! So it would pain us to have to report the consequences when things went wrong for England, and it was even more painful to have to call Robson out for anything we might think he did wrong. We liked the man.

Naturally, Robson had his favourites and he gravitated toward the *Daily Express* chief football writer Steve Curry, sadly now departed, along with *The Times* Stuart Jones, the pair going way back to when Curry covered the England youth team as a junior and their relationship blossomed when Robson was Ipswich Town manager. Generally speaking Robson trusted most of us, but trusted Curry more than most.

Therefore it was quite a shock to see Robson and Curry exchanging heated words and shouting at each other in front of all the other writers during an England training session. Robson was livid with the media coverage, and the games had not even kicked off yet and unfortunately I was at the centre of it all, as Robson took greatest offence to a *Daily Mirror*'s article on the back page with my name on it. So I was the one putting Steve's long association and friendship with Robson at risk as he came to my defence – this is how it happened...

The tensions and pressures always intensify the closer a tournament gets, and there is usually an uneasy peace between the England camp and the media, particularly when there is something of a news vacuum before the opening game, when injury updates become tiresome, and the Sports Editors are demanding something a touch more juicy to fill their back page headlines. With less and less to write about at the long preparation stage, the wilder and more extreme become the headlines, often for no other particular reason than to drum up a bit of interest and controversy, as the tabloid wars began to bite.

One long hot evening the media were given the night off because Robson was attending a local league match and none of the journalists were invited. We had the normal press briefing, and had filed whatever emerged from it, probably nothing more than an injury update, very routine. The photographers were allowed access to Robson's night out but not the reporters. It was a peculiar decision, however a night in the Forte Village was perfect, the food was excellent, the entertainment, the bars, the media hospitality centre set up there, it was all very idyllic, so no one was complaining about what we all thought was a rather strange PR decision on behalf of the FA – some thought it might have been a joint decision with the local World Cup organisers, no one was really that bothered.

So with our work seemingly over we were all enjoying a relaxing night in one of the Forte Village's finest restaurants, which was the main restaurant beach side, with accompanying string quartet and the most exquisite seafood buffet. No one was complaining at this point!

Just after the main course I received a message from the hotel. My office wanted to speak to me urgently. That didn't sound great, but I assumed they were panicking over a minor thing and they just wanted to check it with me. The worst case scenario was that the first editions were dropping back in London and one of our rivals had a story they wanted to run past me.

When I found the nearest phone in the hotel, the reception put me through to my office back in Holborn, on the other end of the line was Michael Bowen the deputy sports editor and a very nice guy. He informed me that *The Mirror* were going to carry a back page story about how Robson had been booed by local fans when he was paraded on the pitch before the game played that evening. The FA's carefully planned charm offensive to woo the local support, away from the prying eyes of Fleet Street's finest, seemed to have backfired terribly. It would have actually been far better to have the chief football writers there, instead only the Press Association were accredited to attend as well as the photographers.

The story being run was the Press Association's version, and the office were curiously informing me that my name was on it and that I should be forewarned as it was clearly anti-Robson. I asked Mike the source of PA's story, and he said it was a photographer who was present and who had filed pictures of Robson being paraded on the pitch. Mike was an excellent journalist and he asked me to check the authenticity of the story. I did so and was told by the FA's public relations guys that photographers were indeed at the game, but the story they had returned was bogus. Instead, the FA insisted that the local fans had showed their appreciation of Robson, not booed him. The whistling when Robson came onto the pitch had been wrongly interpreted, as it was actually the custom on Sardinia for whistling to show appreciation, and so was actually pro-Robson, not against him or the England team.

I hastily called Mike back and told him that I doubted very much the validity of this story having checked it out thoroughly, but was told that I was too late and the paper was committed to running it. Worse still, my name was still on it! "Here we go again," I thought to myself, I was set for yet another confrontation with the England manager.

Being so far away from the office on this type of drawn out tournament and with little to report, it was actually helpful not to see the newspapers, and I tried to avoid them whenever possible, unfortunately they always seemed to be available in the media room and worse still the England players had access to them as the FA shipped over the English papers to keep players and staff occupied. The logic was that the players would get to know about the back page headlines, good or bad, from whoever they were calling back home.

So Bobby Robson was far from amused next morning when he was informed of *The Mirror*'s back page story, long before any delivery of the newspapers. As usual a coach was waiting to ferry the media group to the training camp, but it was a far from a sunny day in Sardinia, in fact the mood was notably overcast, if not thundery! In keeping with the dark mood that had descended over the England manager, it started to rain quite heavily and the storm clouds were most definitely gathering and there were about to be a few bolts of lightning from Robson. But Steve Curry, being a close friend of mine at the time, and part of our little circle of chief football writers who would travel together, dine together, and enjoy the evenings socialising, knew the ins and outs of the entire episode as within the small media community there are few secrets, and within our group of four there were none.

Curry knew that the England boss was not in command of all the facts, and had only had one side of the story which painted me in a very poor light - I was very firmly in the frame. Although it seemed that the previous night I had been told by my office that this story was on general release, the other papers had done their background research and the vast majority had either opted not to use it or relegated it to a filler. Not *The Mirror!* For my paper it was back page news - look out!

Robson was clearly going to blame me for this episode and no doubt anything else he might want to get off his chest. I knew I was about to get the old fashioned 'hair-dryer' treatment but I had been on the receiving end before, and it was not something that fazed me. However, it wasn't something I felt I deserved under the circumstances and that made it a vastly different issue. If I was responsible for an article in my paper I would stand by it and argue my corner but it's not easy if you disagreed with the article in the first place. From his point of view he probably assumed I was just making excuses and hiding behind the "desk" back at HQ.

So it was that Steve Curry boldly marched out to the centre circle before training began and stood toe-to-toe with Bobby Robson to put my side of the story about that day's article in *The Mirror* and explain to him what had happened. He added that I shared the England manager's feelings of being let down and had tried my damnedest to stop the article being published. You couldn't exactly hear what they were saying but the body language was pretty clear, they were shouting at each other and gesticulating furiously. It didn't look good, but you couldn't hear them over the general din of training ground chatter.

Curry reported back that the England manager was in a foul mood and that, while he had accepted the version of events that led to *The Mirror* article, he was still fuming about the way the English media were turning on their own team and manager so close to the tournament and he wanted to thrash it out with all of us.

Once training was over Robson had calmed down substantially, at least toward me but his fury in general had not subsided because he was particularly angry about alleged scandals involving one or two of the players and a gorgeous young Italian hostess assigned to look after the squad. So, as it turned out, Robson was going to hit the roof with the media anyway, it just meant that I was not directly in the line of fire.

The latest incident, though, guaranteed a Robson rocket for the press.

Mike Langley was an award-winning sports writer for *The Sunday People* at this time and later became a colleague on *The Mirror*. Poor Mike was oblivious to all these ramifications with the media rattling around behind the scenes; being a weekly journalist he was not involved in the daily cut and thrust. At this point Mike's wife had flown out to Sardinia during this pre-tournament break and he decided to bring his wife along to the training ground along with what looked like representatives from just about every media outlet in the world.

As the World Cup grew closer, so the world's media began to descend on each of the major nations in ever increasing numbers. Before the proper media conference, Robson invited the English press into the England dressing room for what can only be described as a bollocking. By now it had just started to rain heavily, so rather than leave his wife out in the rain, Mike brought her into the changing rooms, completely unaware of the reason for this impromptu conference. Just as Robson was about to round on the gathered writers and lay into us all, he spotted a lady in his midst. With no female football writers at this time at the World Cup, she stuck out like a sore thumb.

"Mike", Robson enquired. "Who is that lady with you?"

"It's my wife, Bobby," Mike responded as he was still swishing the folded up brolly to remove the excess water.

"Why is she in here?" continued the England manager, pretty sure that everyone had already been aware as to why he had called us all into the dressing rooms.

"Well, Bobby, it's because it's raining outside", explained Mike. What followed made for another golden Bobby Robson moment as he tried in vain not to swear in female company!

"Give her your f——— umbrella and get her out of here, Mike, I've got a few things to say, and I don't think a lady should be present, and oh pardon my language," Robson replied his fire slightly dampened by the presence of Mike's wife.

Once Mrs Langley had departed, the England boss laid into us but refrained from turning his venom on me alone, in fact he never mentioned *The Mirror* article at all, and I think he was far more concerned about the lurid Sunday paper stories which had named John Barnes in a compromising sexual liaison with the hostess. During Robson's attack on the English media he told us precisely what he thought of us all, and he also announced that the players had decided that they would no longer give press interviews, something they had decided among themselves. Robson admitted that as England manager he felt contractually obliged to continue as it was an FA requirement but he quickly added that he felt like joining his players in their media boycott.

It had been the custom that a couple of players, usually selected by the media, would attend the press conference alongside the manager. Now there was no opportunity for that this time as the players were already leaving the training ground when we all emerged from the dressing room. The players had made their decision and they were off, without even bothering to listen to any mitigating circumstances to persuade them to change their minds. A couple of the younger journalists gave chase to the coach as it was just about pulling out through the exit gates and Paul Gascoigne leaned out of the window and spat on them! They pretty much got the message about how the players felt about Her Majesty's press.

It was a watershed incident in the relationship between the media and the players, and I am not sure it was ever the same again, it was the beginning of outright distrust and antagonism between the two. The straw that broke the camel's back was a lurid article alleging that three England players had been involved in a bedroom 'romp' with 'hostess' Isabella Ciaravolo who had been expelled from England's base amid rumours of what were euphemistically described as 'hi-jinks'. The cliche 'what goes on tour stays on tour' had long been sacrosanct in the football dressing room and among the sports writers. The fact that this kind of episode hit the headlines was the calling card of tabloid news journalists, nicknamed 'The Rotters' by us sporting journalists, who went looking for any unsavoury activities which had traditionally been kept under wraps by the sporting section of the media. So we had effectively been shot by our own side.

In his biography of Gazza, Mel Stein gives the players' version of events, "The official line was that she [the hostess] had been removed because her English was not good enough, but the players for their part had genuinely liked her friendly smile and helpful attitude. A delegation, Paul amongst them, sought to get her reinstated. It never occurred to him not to meddle, that it might give some strength to the lies; he just felt sorry for a young Italian girl with a nice smile. It was naïve but it was Paul."

"Things had changed a lot during my time in the game," Terry Butcher has said subsequently. "With Ipswich and England I had got on well with sportswriters, feeling that the majority could be trusted.

But by then there were people around who had been sent just to dig up scandal, watching our every move, making something out of nothing." The hostess headlines proved to be the last straw. "That put the lid on it. We became wary and Des Walker refused to speak with the media under any circumstances. It's even worse now. The players know about me, know what I did in the game and in that sense I'm still one of them, but they aren't all that keen on giving an interview."

Antagonism between the media and the England camp intensified. While it is clear why the players rebelled against the media, it may not be quite so obvious why us in the media felt so aggrieved. You have to first understand the pressure on reporters. Covering a World Cup might seem like an ideal job; being paid to travel first class and stay in top notch five star hotels, and rub shoulders with the stars and be almost part of the entourage for seven long weeks on a 'football holiday' sounds like heaven but the reality is far from that, particularly when the tournament is being hosted somewhere like Mexico in 1986 where it was never easy to get to the training ground, there was always tension in the air with the local police, and it was dangerous at times with reports of kidnappings of journalists and security around the team hotel. In Italy the tension was of a different kind with the pressure on from editors to find something for the next day's edition.

The booing story, if I can return to that particular incident, also had a rather nasty side-effect; a monumental internal office row that nearly led to my early exit from the World Cup. After Robson's dressing room rant at the media, the England manager calmed down and after a day or two he was willing to find a conciliatory solution to the war between the England camp and the media. He knew it would be counter-productive in the long run to continue hostilities but the row within *The Mirror* offices lingered on, because I wasn't happy with the way I had been treated by the editorial back up team, especially the stand-in sports editor that night, Mike Bowen. On returning to the Forte Village after Robson's rant, I contacted the desk as usual to file my daily dispatch from the front, but this time I wanted to get something off my chest. Specifically that, having checked out the validity of a story and having reported back that it was false, I felt let down that the story should still appear in the paper and under my by-line.

I told Mike, someone with whom I had always got on well, that I suggested to the FA that the least we could do was to put it right, either to apologise, something that a national newspaper would never do willingly and it would take a writ and a long winded legal action before they would agree to or by way of a sensible compromise that was easily achievable and make a reference in my latest article to the fact that Robson had not been booed but had been welcomed by the locals at the match the other night. I relayed all the squabbling and recriminations that had gone on in the fall out and how *The Mirror* had been singled out for special rebuke by the FA, and I, on the paper's behalf, had pledged that we would do the honourable thing, take the balanced approach, and rectify the error by reporting the truth.

Again, in an unfortunate twist of fate, the sports editor Keith Fisher, was on a day off as was the editor Roy Greenslade, who has now reinvented himself as an expert columnist on media affairs while Fisher has reinvented himself on a local newspaper on the south coast where it is rumoured he also ran a fish and chip shop! Fisher always backed his men in the field, and I had never found Greenslade anything other than highly professional in the way he edited the paper. Mike promised to contact Fisher, who in turn, under the chain of command, would liaise with the Editor if need be.

Several hours later when I checked in after the day's work load, Mike had not been able to track down Fisher, and the news desk had not been in touch with the Editor, whether they tried or not, or how hard they had tried, or whether they had even been asked to try, I had no way of really knowing but I found it hard to believe that in the communications industry no one seemed capable of communicating to two important heads of staff.

My frustration was building, as the longer it went toward deadline, the less likely it was that I would be able to fulfill my obligation to the FA, although that was of little concern to Mike who pointed out, quite correctly, although I didn't really need it underlined, that my sole obligation was to *The Mirror*. In reality, it had been presumptuous of me to offer a form of an apology to the FA without running it past the office first and getting clearance from the editors; this was an error on my part, but I had assumed that *The Mirror* would back me up. It didn't.

It was at this point that my frustrations boiled over, and I made the single biggest error of my entire career, one that I have regretted ever since. With the ability to have direct access to Robert Maxwell I informed Mike that if he continued to prevaricate and to fail to contact his superiors and continue to refuse to make any editorial executive decision of his own, I would be forced, reluctantly, to take the issue straight to Maxwell. Even though everyone on the paper knew I had that power, it was something that I should never have exercised, never have even contemplated using and certainly not threatening anyone with, let alone actually doing it! But I did. It was unforgivable.

First of all, I waited another couple of hours in the hope of a resolution without resorting to Maxwell. Knowing this had to be the last option, I phoned Bowen again. Was there going to be a small item, however small, to redress the balance and point out our error? No there wasn't. After all my efforts, it was hard to believe that I wasn't just being fobbed off.

I placed a call to Maxwell's office. I got straight through to Captain Bob via his secretary, I explained the entire situation as succinctly as I could, knowing he was a busy man with a limited attention span to take in something that must have seemed pretty trivial to him.

Maxwell was not one to dither or think before he acts. He suggested that the man in charge of this debacle should be fired immediately for his incompetence! Blimey, I never thought that would be his reaction for one minute! I had never suggested firing Bowen, or even suspending him, or even flogging him with a cat of nine tails. I just wanted *The Mirror*'s proprietor to fulfill my obligations to the FA. I begged Maxwell not to take such an extreme view and that he should let me speak to him one last time, which I did.

I told Mike the proprietor's view, but he stood by his guns and reiterated that he was not in a position to take such action unilaterally and he still could not contact either the Sports Editor or the Editor, and that I should wait another 24 hours and sort it out when they were back. My gut feeling was that Mike had bottled it, had not even tried to contact his superiors, and wanted to leave it to them the next day. Or that the Sports Editor said he would sort it out when he was back the next day. Whatever was going on in London while I was in Sardinia, it didn't feel right.

Maxwell, though, was a law unto himself and in no mood to back down from his instant reaction and, indeed, Michael Bowen, deputy sports editor, was summarily sacked. I was appalled that I had been responsible for his sacking but once Maxwell is put into play, I should have known there might well have been an unpredictable outcome, and not the one I had hoped for. What I wanted never happened, there was no small item putting the record straight and the next day all hell broke loose in *The Mirror* offices.

Fisher, the Sports Editor, was angry with me, although, as he knew me so well, he could appreciate my frustration, and accepted my side of the story that I did not ask, nor seek, Bowen's sacking and would happily do all I could to facilitate his reinstatement. Despite all of that Fisher was highly critical of my actions, and rightly so. Now he had the unenviable task of trying to sort out the mess with the Editor.

I realised I had over-stepped the mark and instantly regretted my actions but I was still in shock about the repercussions and the sequence of events I had set in motion. My thoughts were with Michael Bowen and how I could possibly rectify the situation. I rang Maxwell again. I made every attempt to get him to change his mind. "Okay," agreed Maxwell, "I am only doing this because you feel so strongly about it" he said as he hung up. I could tell Maxwell was not happy with me in persuading him to back down in such a way. He thought I would have been pleased he had sacked Bowen but by now though the Editor was on the warpath!

Roy Greenslade was so angry and put out by my actions in going directly to Maxwell that he ordered me home from the World Cup immediately. The Editor was far more concerned that I had gone behind the back of the editors and had such powerful direct access to the proprietor that the central issue of my complaint was of no consequence and wasn't even discussed. I explained to him that I had spoken to Maxwell again and that he told me he would rescind his earlier decision to sack Bowen. "Not good enough," argued Greenslade.

Clearly he was not going to tolerate what happened, and it seemed to me it was more about me usurping his authority rather than the sacking of Bowen, which was bad enough. He insisted that I be on the next available flight back from Cagliari. I think he wanted me back from Italia '90 and would then take it even further and see if he had a case for dismissal - mine not Bowen's!

I played for time. I knew that as I was out in the field that the Sports Editor needed me there to cover England, playing for time might help my situation but if the Editor orders you home, then home you must go. However I made no effort to book a flight, and made a case that if the Editor wanted me home, then I would be expecting the Sports Desk to arrange my travel details, and send out my replacement. I thought I'd sit tight and maybe everything might be amicably resolved when tempers have calmed.

Keith Fisher did not want me to return, he wanted the best possible coverage for his sports pages and that was his argument to the Editor, stressing that it would severely diminish *The Mirror*'s ability to compete with their rivals if the paper's chief football reporter was taken off the assignment, and Greenslade took that argument on board, and when he had calmed down a tad, he was no longer insistent that I return to Holborn. By the way Bowen was indeed immediately reinstated, and in effect had been sacked for less than a day. I personally apologised to Bowen on the phone that day, and apologised to him again when I returned when the tournament was over. I feel as though I have been apologising to him ever since. I have the utmost respect for Michael Bowen, especially seeing that, although my actions caused great grievance to him and his family, albeit for less than 24 hours, he had the good grace to forgive me. This episode underlines some of the pressures journalists feel while on long haul assignments, even sporting ones, which the general public must think are endless fun and not exactly 'work'.

I wasn't exactly one of the elder statesman among the journalists at this time, but I had reached the top at a relatively young age and was therefore vastly experienced and only too willing to help the new boys on the block, providing they were polite and respectful, such as young Danny Fullbrook, who succeeded a young reporter on the *Daily Star* who had been assisting with the task of gathering the quotes after the matches at this World Cup, and doing the second tier player interviews in his capacity as No 2 football writer for the newspaper.

These were the days, prior to email, mobile phone and social media that we would file our stories the old fashioned way, on a landline phone from our rooms. Some of the journalists liked to find a spot on or close to the beach, with the tranquility of the location, to compile their articles, often by hand on a piece of paper. Some had Tandy's first generation laptop. The Press Association reporter, Martin Lipton, was always on his, so he earned the nickname Laptop. He's now on *The Sun*. I tried the Tandy but found it an awkward first generation piece of kit that was always losing connection just as an article was about to be sent. So I stuck to filing the copy the old fashioned way but I didn't spend hours agonising over every word and sentence. I worked for the *Daily Mirror* and the key was 'communication'. If you make it too complicated then the public will find it complicated to read. Simplicity was the art of tabloid journalism, so I would ad lib the story – I was invariably the first to finish. I would use my spare time constructively… sunbathing on the glorious spotless Forte Village Beaches with a bar never too far away. I found this tranquility and peace an antidote to the pressures of the job. It was a way of unwinding, relaxing, and it almost felt as if I was on holiday, it was form of meditation; with a nice tan to

The Sunday People's *Mike Langley (right) suffered the wrath of Bobby Robson when he took his wife into the England teams dressing room to escape the rain, when the manager planned a rollicking for the media.* Mirror *Sports Editor Keith Fisher is in the centre.*

show for it.

About 10 days into the preparation, before a ball had been kicked, I was first out of my room, having finished two or three stories for the next day's edition, and was already laid out relaxing on the beach. Suddenly out of the corner of my eye this figure approached me, marching down the beach, in his size 10 brogues, fully booted and suited, wearing a tie and carrying a small suitcase. The junior reporter told me he was checking out of the hotel but he wanted to thank me for all the help and encouragement I had given him during the tournament and how much he appreciated it, in contrast to the way others had treated him. He explained he was suffering from a minor breakdown and wanted to return home as he could no longer take the pressure.

I never saw him again.

TREVOR STEVEN

The Three Amigos - Gazza, Steve Hodge And Me!

I didn't think I would be going to Italia '90. We were staying at Burnham Beeches hotel after our final training session when the announcement was made for the final selection; Bobby Robson was knocking on doors and personally letting every player know, mostly good news, but for a handful it would be bad news. It was obviously a choice between myself and David Rocastle, it was brilliant news for me, but the opposite for Rocky, as he sadly missed out.

I had just started with Glasgow Rangers and enjoyed a good first season as we had won the league as it had gone really well and I was delighted to be going to Italy, which at that time was the focus of European football and I didn't want to miss out, so I considered myself very fortunate to have got one of the last places on offer.

And I was right to feel it would be something special, for that's how it turned out. It was a brilliant tournament; it was brilliant to be involved and experience all the excitement. I had been to the World Cup in Mexico but having been to one I knew how important it was and wanted to go again, but never thought I would get another chance,.

I went out there as a squad player, I knew I wasn't first choice, but knew that as in Mexico, the team that starts the tournament isn't necessarily going to be the team that finishes it, so opportunities would come along and it was about taking them when they arose. It was a frustrating start being on the sidelines, particularly as we didn't make a good start in the group stages, there wasn't a lot of quality football, and we all felt a lot of pressure in those early stages; there was a feeling that things weren't right behind the scenes, Bobby Robson was suffering media attention about his private as well as professional life, and there was a lot of criticism even before we even started. It was all set up for getting caught cold and being home before the postcards! The whole group were on the defensive around what we were doing, so with everything that was going on, we had not arrived with any great expectations from within the country itself.

But after the group stage we started to gain momentum, it was just an incredible transformation and over the five weeks of that tournament

I believe we changed the face of the game in our country. The population were elated by our achievements as we grew in confidence, and progressed. It became a very important tournament and from a personal perspective, I loved every minute of it.

There's no doubt for me that the catalyst was Paul Gascoigne, he had just come onto the scene but he did so like a rocket, both on and off the pitch. He grabbed the whole tournament from start to finish with his enthusiasm and passion for the game and off the field he was just the same, he was non-stop. His antics off the field were a welcome distraction and it was great to behold the way he wanted to control the game.

I got to see Gazza's antics up close because one week during the build-up Bobby Robson invited the wives and girlfriends out to our team hotel, but there were three of us without any female companions, my wife was pregnant so couldn't come along, and that left me with Gazza and Steve Hodge. I think Gazza was scared to death of women at that stage of his life, he was only interested in his football. So we ended up as The Three Amigos. However, Steve Hodge had no intention in participating and he would go missing mid-afternoon on a peddle boat with a book to relax on his own, or he would find somewhere else to hide away from Gazza, leaving me with him which made for a very bizarre few days!

In the evenings all the guys would smarten themselves up to have dinner with the wives and girlfriends, but The Three Amigos were spare. At times we sat with Mick Hucknall, another time with Nigel Kennedy, who were both invited to have dinner with the squad.

The evening with Nigel Kennedy was something special, with the world's greatest violinist trying to entertain us playing on his £200,000 violin with Gazza trying to nick it from him. It was bedlam trying to keep him from trying to play the master's violin.

Most nights Paul would be banging on my door begging me to play tennis with him, but I had usually put on the light by the time he came calling and I'd be reading before going off to sleep. He was constantly at my door, I seemed to be always doing my best to avoid him, he kept on nagging me until one night I played tennis with him at midnight!

I was having a cappuccino with Gazza at reception one afternoon and Bobby Robson walked past. "Keep it up with the coffee, Gazza" said the boss. Gazza smiled and nodded. What the England manager didn't know was that Paul had sneaked a couple of shots of Baileys into his coffee! Gazza kept us all amused, but he was also at the heartbeat of the team, I have no idea what would have happened without him in the squad. He played with great maturity in the tournament, always demanding the ball, using it well and creating, he played World Cup ties like was on the training pitch, no matter the opposition.

Equally he was the same off the pitch, non-stop, frantic; there was always something going on, and he played just like that, he would never stroll around during a game, he wanted to be in the thick of it, no matter where the action took him.

It was his birthday when we were out there, and a big cake was brought out for him. We all shouted "Speech, speech, speech!" but Paul said he was far too shy. Then he suddenly launched into a speech and we couldn't stop him. He didn't stop talking for about 15 minutes, telling all sort of stories about everyone and everything, taking the mickey out of so many of us. He was some character.

Paul kept everyone amused, but because we were away for so long some of the lads, especially the older ones, got bored very quickly and used to sneak out to the nearby town of Puli for what they called their Social Club. They would go off saying they were only going for one beer, but that went south very quickly and they would have a few and some arm wrestling, and then sneak back in. There wasn't a split in the camp, but some of the lads preferred an early night, while some had cabin fever and needed to break out, or they would come down for the team dinner wearing their jackets back to front or shorts, it was anything to break the monotony.

There was one trip to the Forte Village but much of it was spent sunbathing as well as a few beers at the beach bar - I wasn't involved too much but I did hear all the stories about Robbo's big toe the next morning!

I didn't play against Belgium but I felt I was getting more and more noticed behind the scenes, because I put a lot of effort into the training sessions, I was training well. I was not quite there for the Belgium match but David Platt's extra-time goal set up a difficult quarter-final with Cameroon, who were a very physical team. Again I was on the bench but this time I came on. It was a great moment; I felt like I was really in this now.

After my performance against Cameroon I trained really well and thought I'd start the semi-final. I knew it was between me and Chris Waddle but Bobby said he hadn't made up his mind. In the training session prior to the game there was has a session of crossing, shooting, and finishing and when it was the turn of the midfield players I scored from all four of my attempts on the trot, and all 'worldies', right into the top corner, left foot, right foot, with my head. Bobby shouted "Did you see that, four on the trot, four!" You would think I was close, and as we walked off the training pitch Bobby said to me that I had done well against Cameroon, and he said "You are in my thoughts, I've got you in mind, you're in my thoughts…" I thought I had got in.

By now my family had flown out to Italy. My brother and his wife were there. So when the team was named and I was on the bench I felt really down but it was a World Cup semi-final and I was on the bench. I would be ready if I was called upon, and I got on as Bobby switched it back to 4-4-2. I consider I got my chance because of my attitude and application on the training pitch. I came on and played on the right in front of Paul Parker and feel I made a contribution, about seven or eight minutes after I came on Gary Lineker scored.

As for the penalties… looking out at the frenzy of excitement in the crowd and then the recognition that we'd have to take a kick was like an out-of-body experience. Although I'd taken spot-kicks for Everton, I wasn't one of England's five takers. I was due to be sixth, though, so I had to believe I was going to take one and keep a calm head. I knew I could become a hero or a villain. Football is full of ifs, buts and maybes but this was on a different level. The emotions were so intense and it's difficult to relate to now. We started the shoot-out well but then suddenly it was over, after Stuart Pearce and Waddle missed the fourth and fifth kicks. All that opportunity had gone. We were completely deflated. It could have been so different. We were the better team in the semi and I don't think there was any doubt that we believed we'd have beaten a poor Argentina side in the final and I might have played in the final, had that chance came along. I'm sure Steve McMahon would have thought along the same lines, but I think Bobby would have considered me for that game. You have to believe it will be you, you have to live on the edge, be ready, be prepared, believe it will happen and that way you are geared up for the right level of performance.

Overall, on a human level, to have participated in a World Cup semi-final at that level for my country was massive and I feel, even to this day, that what we achieved has been under-estimated because Bobby Robson and the players should take even more credit considering the country had been out of top class European club football for so long. Factor in all the ingredients, and what we achieved in Italia '90 was phenomenal.

PETER BEARDSLEY

Gazza's special birthday surprise for son Drew

With so many Geordies in the squad; myself, Gazza, Pop Robson, the Waddler, and of course the manager, you would have thought that on occasions the five of us were all talking a different language! There were times when giving interviews that the press couldn't understand some of us!

The World Cup semi-final brings back some incredible memories, and there were some remarkable moments in that game, none more so than when Gazza got booked and the whole world knew he would miss the final. Yet the world class player Gazza was up against, Lothar Matthäus, couldn't have be nicer once it happened telling Gazza, "Get your mind back on the game." He was genuine, and I have total respect for the way he went about it, and so too was his manager Franz Beckenbauer who came into our dressing room after the game to seek out our manager Bobby Robson. He was all over Bobby, wishing him well. He was so humble, so nice, that I felt no malice towards them. In fact, after the way they behaved I wanted them to go on and win the final, which of course they did.

It was brilliant to be part of this squad, and even more so that Gazza was part of it. He was a superstar, a genius. He was a pleasure to be around, as a person and a player. He loved the game, and he was such a special talent. As for favourite Gazza stories, there are hundreds, but I suppose I do have a couple. He made us all laugh when he nicked the key to the kit van and stole half the kit, but my favourite has to be the day of his birthday which just happened to be the same day as my son who was born in 1989, and Bobby Robson had the families over for a week before the hard training started.

So May 27th was a special day for my son Drew, his first ever birthday, and for Gazza, and a great big birthday cake emerged when we were all around the hotel pool, and it came in the shape of a brush,

Gazza's first World Cup shirt signed to Peter Beardsley's son Drew

which was fitting. On it was written 'Happy Birthday Gazza'.

But as soon as Gazza saw it, he ordered it to be returned to the kitchen. Shortly, the cake returned. This time it had written on it: "Happy Birthday Gazza And Drew". He also gave Drew his first ever World Cup shirt, the one he wore against the Republic of Ireland and signed it to my son. Although Drew has the same birthday as Gazza, I am glad to say that's where the similarity ends! Only joking Gazza!

THE INDOMITABLE LIONS

One of the greatest giant-killings in the tournament's history, which perhaps provided the blueprint for Senegal's equally shocking 1-0 victory over France in Seoul 12 years later, was the opening game of the 1990 World Cup. Napoli, with Maradona their inspiration, had just won the Serie A title from Milan by two points, and later in the tournament the Neapolitans would delight in the victory of Cameroon against Costa Rica, so much so that the Argentinian, who had been suffering from an ingrowing toe nail and played with the aid of a protective carbon fibre "bionic toe", claimed he had "cured the Italians of racism". "The whole stadium was shouting for Cameroon," he observed, "wasn't that nice?" It was a prelude to Maradona ousting the hosts at the semi-final stage at the Sao Paolo, an event that still triggers fury in the rest of the country but quiet delight in Naples.

At the outset Cameroon were 500-1 outsiders to win the tournament; no one gave them a prayer of even winning a point, the opening game against the holders was viewed as a walk-over. "The Soviet Union is a tough opponent, but I'm generally pleased," Argentina manager Carlos Bilardo had said after the draw the previous December. "Our group is not the easiest but we should have no problems in qualifying for the second round." No one really took the opening game seriously as the World Cup holders faced the minnows from West Africa, a feeling supported by the number of English journalists who made the long trip to Milan from Cagliari.

Some of the broadsheet football writers travelled from the Forte Village to absorb the atmosphere of the opening ceremony but the majority, such as myself, stayed close to the England camp, believing there was more chance of a huge back page headline by staying close to Bobby Robson and his squad. It was convenient to 'report' the Italia '90 World Cup curtain raiser from the comfort of the sponsor's media room, armed with unlimited beer, convivial company, and a huge screen as well as the choice of a variety of six star restaurants at which to prepare for the 'big' game.

I contacted the *Daily Mirror* 'desk' thinking they'd want a page lead, roughly 20 to 25 paragraphs, perhaps less as the focus was now fully on England's opener in their group with the Republic of Ireland. The response was a lukewarm, "just give us four or five pars at the end".

Indeed, the outcome seemed to be such a foregone conclusion that the *Daily Mirror* sports executives had allocated a small little side item, as they concentrated on England's build up for which I had 'filed' acres of column inches that day.

What no one had anticipated was that Cameroon, comprising mainly journeymen players from the French lower divisions, would produce one of the World Cup's most unforgettable tournament openers. As you can imagine, as the drama unfolded so did a major re-think back at Holborn HQ as the sub-editors and page designers threw their original designs out of the 9th floor window.

Suddenly Roger Milla and his band of merry men were the new back page story, usurping England's traditional place at the top of the sporting agenda for the night. I had sat myself down in front of the big screen, along with quite a fee journalists, armed with only a small piece of paper to take note of the goals, and anything else that might be of interest, probably a Diego Maradona hat-trick and file the few pars on the whistle. Suddenly I was scrambling for more paper, searching for the team sheet to find out the names of all those new stars of the World Cup performing such heroics out there against the world champions, and was asked to file a thousand words on the whistle, then a thousand word re-write for the later editions, with the 'desk' sub-editors taking care of the quotes from their own TV monitors to speed up the process of getting the edition out to the printers.

The gulf in quality was staggering to comprehend and far from it being the world champion's superiority over the relative unknowns from Africa, it was the other way round. Argentina, four years after their triumph in Mexico, took on players who were, bar certain exceptions, amateurs, and were outclassed on the night. Despite the seemingly impossible task, Cameroon were fearless as their striker Emmanuel Maboang later explained, "This was an Argentina team who were champions of the world, who represented everything, who had Maradona, who was our idol. We knew that we were combatants. We'd left as amateurs, but we'd done five months of preparation, and we absolutely wanted to win this match. We had no doubt, because we knew each other so well. We said that, apart from Maradona, the rest of the team were beatable. We left without any complex, and everyone - even the substitutes - were confident because we'd played matches, we knew how each other played.

"We told ourselves that it was just football; it was 50-50, even though they were favourites. I'd already watched the World Cup in

1986, so I knew Caniggia, Maradona, all of Argentina's team, as did all of my teammates. We'd seen a lot on the television, watched their training sessions but even when he arrived at the stadium, we stopped our warm-ups and we all took photos with Diego."

Goalkeeper Joseph-Antoine Bell explained why his team were so full of confidence rather than having the inferiority complex they should have had. There had been pre-tournament rumours of an increasingly personal rivalry between him and the legendary Thomas N'Kono. "We weren't - let's not mistake it - stronger than our opponents, but the idea was that a team is not one good player next to another; a team is that one plus one can give you three. If we fought well together, if we were good within the group, we could produce something that could transcend the players on the pitch... and that's what happened."

Argentina started like world champions about to swat away their impertinent opponents, but struggled with the physicality of Cameroon. Yet this physicality cost the Africans as André Kana-Biyik was dismissed for a late challenge in the 61st minute. Yet the Cameroonians' still took the lead in the 67th minute, when Emmanuel Kunde crossed a free kick into the area, Cyrille Makanaky flicked the ball up, and Omam-Biyik leapt to an incredible height before planting a downwards header which squirmed under Argentinian keeper Nery Pumpido.

The World Champions had problems, not least controversial team selection; Jorge Burruchaga was surprisingly chosen ahead of Claudio Caniggia for the opening game and Pumpido's error highlighted their goalkeeping issues. "Everything was under control until Cameroon went down to 10 men and we got disorganised," said Carlos Bilardo after the game. Within six minutes of a red card for his brother, Omam-Biyik had headed Cameroon in front.

"[Omam-Biyik] was a great scorer with his head," Maboang explained, "When he scored, I was warming up with Milla, because we were going to come on, and the coach was watching how things went. [Kunde] shouldn't have even crossed, I know he never crosses with his left - he's right-footed - sometimes he'd do that [with his left] in training, but never in matches. He positioned himself, and I asked myself what he was going to do. We knew about his strong right-footed strike, but not with his left. I waited for an instant, and the ball rose. Francois jumped, and I knew - when I saw him leap - that he'd get on the end of it. I knew he'd get high, we knew he could do this, but we didn't know he'd get his head on it like that." Argentina's goalkeeper, a veteran of the 1986 success, fumbled the ball over the line. Maboang continued: "People can say that maybe 1000 times it wouldn't go in, but I'd seen Francois score so many goals in training, where it went in off the goalkeeper, where it bounced off the ground and went in."

Argentina struggled to recover against opponents who became increasingly frantic in defending their lead and Benjamin Massing joined André Kana-Biyik as he was shown a red card for an infamous x-rated lunge on Claudio Caniggia, losing a boot as he sent the Atalanta striker sprawling in agony. It was a cynical professional foul to end a long run from the blond-haired striker who had already hurdled two crude challenges and was struggling to regain his balance before being hacked to the ground by number three. "He won't get past that," shouted commentator Brian Moore, "an assault and a brutal assault it was."

That crude tackle become one of the defining images of Italia '90 but it gave the false impression that Cameroon were just a brutish side that relied solely on brawn. Physicality became their trade mark throughout their shock run all the way to the quarter-finals where the Indominable Lions met the Three Lions but as Bell makes clear, "The 1990 team was physical. For any team to perform, they need to know their strengths, and if you don't work on your strengths, you aren't very intelligent. Cameroon did well to use their strengths, and we were right to do so."

Maboang acknowledges the Lions overstepped the mark, "Maybe the image that remains, against Argentina, is Massing's kick on Caniggia, who had just gone past two players, but apart from that, we had cards which weren't justified. It was the opening match, and the officials could have been more tolerant. I spoke to the referee who oversaw this match, and I told him that Cameroon weren't particularly nasty during the World Cup. There was no karate, there were no anti-football gestures, Cameroonians don't like playing brutally. We're just well-built."

In the wake of Cameroon's win, African football became credible. The result was celebrated not only in Cameroon, where impromptu street parties erupted across the nation and a reporter from the *Telegraph* wrote, intriguingly, that "a lady in a floral dress and turban did a hand-stand", but across Africa and beyond. When they were finally knocked out a woman in Bangladesh committed suicide, leaving a note that read "the elimination of Cameroon means the end of my life".

"No one thought we could do anything here against Maradona, but we knew what we could," goalscorer François Omam-Biyik, said after the game. "We hate it when European reporters ask us if we eat monkeys and have a witch doctor. We are real football players and we proved this tonight."

Yet the opening match set the tone as there were precisely twice as many red cards in Italy as there had been in Mexico in 1986, which itself had seen more than any previous finals. "Cameroon neutralised Maradona mainly by kicking him," wrote Matthew Engel in *The Guardian*. "He spent much of the game horizontal despite wearing calf pads as well as shin pads. His 10 team-mates seemed too stunned to make any trouble but they were kicked as well, if they got in the way."

Yet the first red card, shown to the goalscorer's brother André Kana-Biyik for a foul on Caniggia, seemed harsh but French referee Michel Vautrot had little choice but to follow FIFA's new ultra-strict guidelines.

Brian Glanville, in his book *The Story of the World Cup*, insists that "a bruising game was made worse by [his] draconian refereeing" but in the following day's *Express*, James Lawton proclaimed the referee's victory over "a rising tide of wild and often cynical tackling" as "perhaps the greatest triumph" of the night.

Sepp Blatter, then FIFA's general secretary, boasted before the tournament began that, as a result of their fair play initiative, "players will behave in a decorous manner in all phases of the match". Shame the players were not listening! "I'm unhappy the referee was forced to intervene as he did, but I'm pleased that he did," Blatter said after the match, having criticised the behaviour of players who "want to destroy the game of soccer instead of letting creativity and genius flow".

Maradona declined to make excuses, "I don't think they had any intentions of beating us up to win the game. I cannot argue, and I cannot make excuses. If Cameroon won, it was because they were the best side."

"This was no fluke, the better team won," wrote David Lacey in *The Guardian*. "They won, moreover, after finishing with nine men on the field… Such was their superiority that the Africans still finished looking as if they had more men on the pitch than their hapless opponents."

The Cameroon story really took shape a couple of years earlier when Paul Biya, the country's president, had asked the Russian FA to send over a few coaches who wouldn't mind helping out for a while. The first to arrive was Valeri Nepomniachi, an unexceptional ex-player whose only experience of first-team management had been a single season at the helm of an obscure Turkmenistani club in the then Soviet Union's third division. Biya appointed him national team manager, even though he spoke no French and almost no English. At the World Cup his team-talks were translated by the man normally employed as a driver at the Cameroon embassy in Moscow. Nepomniachi only just made it to Italy, having come close to the sack after the country's hapless displays at that year's African Cup of Nations, where as reigning champions they lost to Zambia and Senegal and were eliminated in the group stage.

Just a few weeks before the World Cup President Biya called Roger Milla, a 38-year-old who had retired from international football three years previously and moved to Réunion, a tiny French-controlled island in the Indian Ocean, where he played for a team called Saint-Pierroise. Biya requested the striker's return and Milla replied that he was "always ready to be called to my country's colours". It was a conversation that would change that year's World Cup.

Nevertheless Cameroon's pre-tournament training camps in Bordeaux and Yugoslavia featured frequent defeats to obscure club sides in warm-up matches coupled with bickering about Milla's arrival and the delayed payments of bonuses due to the players. Goalkeeper Joseph-Antoine Bell became the voice of the players' demands for cash. On the eve of the tournament he criticised his team-mates in a newspaper interview saying they had "no chance of coping with Argentina or any other team" and that they "will go out in the first round without much glory". Even though his place had been guaranteed by Nepomniachi, Bell was dropped in the wake of his comments and N'Kono came in. "I used to believe that he selected the team," Bell said. "I don't any more."

Until just a few hours before kick-off in Milan N'Kono had considered himself unlikely to even be in the match day squad – Bell didn't like him, and wanted the relatively inexperienced Jacques Songo'o on the bench instead. Suddenly N;'Kono was first choice, a decision taken so late, and so unexpectedly, that his wife missed his moment of glory having decided to go shopping instead. "I thought it was a very bad team and we were going to lose," N'Kono told Jonathan Wilson in the latter's book on goalkeeping, *The Outsider*. "Suddenly the coach said I was going to play five hours before the game. I said no way. I had no confidence in the coach. The federation, the minister of sport, seven or eight people were telling me I had to play and I was saying I didn't feel ready. They said if I wasn't going to play they would play Songo'o, and if he didn't want to play they would put an outfielder in goal. I went to talk with the president of Cameroon, and eventually I agreed."

N'Kono's performances were so good that a promising 12-year-old midfielder from Tuscany decided that he'd prefer to be a goalkeeper, and bought his first pair of gloves. "It was N'Kono and his spectacular saves that made me fall in love with the position. He became my hero," the kid said. Many years later he named his son Thomas in the Cameroonian's honour. The young Italian's name was Gianluigi Buffon.

Milla hadn't been in the Indomitable Lions' Africa Cup of Nations squad earlier that year, when they'd fallen in the group stage. "Failure at the Afcon in 1990 permitted Milla's return," Maboang says, "because if we hadn't had that failure, we'd have gone [to the World Cup] with the same squad, without modifying anything. He was very sad to see Cameroon lose at the Afcon, because he saw our talent. He hadn't been there for the qualifiers, but thanks to the head of state, he joined us and came to the World Cup. We'd talked about it a lot, and we didn't want him there, but training session by training session, he earned his place legitimately. It wasn't easy for him. In the changing room he didn't talk much, but he's someone who's passionate about football, about his country, and he wanted to win."

Milla only played the final nine minutes of the opening game, but settled into his role as Cameroon's super sub and scored twice against Romania in their second game and twice again against Colombia in the second round, to become one of the players of the tournament. He returned in 1994, where he broke his own record as the World Cup's oldest goalscorer by grabbing his side's consolation in a 6-1 thrashing by Russia at the age of 42 years and 39 days.

Having played for Laval in the French second division, Omam-Biyik's performances earned him offers from some of the biggest clubs in Europe, but he refused to break an agreement to join Rennes. Shortly after the tournament he was asked in an interview with the *Guardian* whether his match-winning goal against Argentina had been the best moment of his career. "It was one of them," he replied. "The best 'moment', if I can stretch the definition of the word, was the whole of that wonderful time we spent in Italy – the experience we gained, the atmosphere, and the money."

Eleven minutes into their second match, Argentina's Pumpido broke his leg, and he would never play for his country again. Like N'Kono, his replacement Sergio Goycochea went on to have a fabulous tournament, excelling in the penalty shoot-outs that took Argentina all the way to the final even if he was beaten by the one penalty that really mattered, Andreas Brehme's in Rome.

★

The Guardian's David Lacy was one of the England press corp who actually went to the game on June 9, 1990. Here is his report:

The fanfare for Diego Maradona was drowned by the drums of Black Africa in Milan last night as Cameroon defeated Argentina, the World Cup holders, to open the 1990 tournament by destroying a whole package of preconceptions.

This was no fluke, the better team won. They won, moreover, after finishing with nine men on the field, the result of Michel Vautrot's determination to obey FIFA's guidelines in dealing with persistent and cynical fouls. The French referee sent off two Cameroon players but such was their superiority that the Africans still finished looking as if they had more men on the pitch than their hapless opponents.

This result, the biggest shock in a World Cup since Algeria's 2-1 defeat of West Germany in the opening phase in Spain in 1982, has immediately thrown the new tournament off its predicted course.

Argentina's chances of winning Group B already look slim On last night's evidence one would not give much for their hopes of defeating either the Soviet Union or Romania. Maradona began brightly but when he faded the whole team fell away, losing rhythm and confidence and looking just another poor side.

England, if they finish runners-up in Group F, will meet the second-placed team in Group B in Genoa in the second phase. Now Bobby Robson might prefer it not to be Cameroon. Better even than Maradona was the inspirational Francois Omam-Biyik, who scored the winning goal five minutes after Kana-Biyik had been sent off and departed blowing a farewell kiss to an adoring crowd.

The Third World has long since threatened to arrive on the wider footballing stage in style but nobody seriously expected Cameroon to make the entrance they did on a balmy Milanese evening after half an hour of noisy pomp and ceremony had made it a natural setting for Maradona.

Long after the finish, in a stadium empty except for reporters, the PA system suddenly burst forth into the theme music from Ben Hur. Certainly this was one race which had seen several collisions and the finish that the majority wanted. The Milan supporters, remembering the way Napoli had pipped their team for the Italian championship, made sure that Maradona did not feel at home by whistling and jeering every time he touched the ball.

Cameroon, and in particular the tall muscular figure of Benjamin Massing, one of four French League players in the side, fouled Argentina's new ambassador for sport at almost every opportunity. Maradona must have felt he was encountering a distant relative of Claudio Gentile.

Massing became the second Cameroon player to be dismissed when Vautrot showed him the red card two minutes from the end after he had taken out Caniggia, sent on by Argentina's manager Carlos Bilardo in the second half to give his struggling team an extra attacker, with a thigh-high tackle. Massing had been the first of three Cameroon players to be cautioned, so he had to go.

And so did Kana-Biyik, without the preliminary of a caution, for coolly tripping Caniggia just past the hour. To him fell the distinction of being the first player to receive a red card in the opening game of a World Cup since referees started carrying red cards.

FIFA had been specific in its instructions on how to deal with this sort of offence and Vautrot set the sort of disciplinary standards the World Cup needs to heed, otherwise there will be anarchy.

While there was a natural inclination to rejoice with Cameroon, ugly images of their tackling lingered in the mind's eye. But when all is said and done it was a joyous occasion which did not lack a sense of irony. Four years ago, when Maradona sent Burruchaga clear to score the winning goal in the last World Cup Final, their green-shirted opponents West Germany collapsed in the centre circle in despair. When the game ended last night the green shirts, what was left of them, dissolved into a celebrating heap, leaving Argentina to wonder if the new roof of the San Siro had not fallen in on them.

Cameroon never looked like a side which had been sent into the opening match to play stooge to Maradona. Their man-to-man marking system was tighter, they were first to the ball in all parts of the field, they created space with greater ease and opened up ever widening gaps near goal as the holders' defence became threadbare.

From the start Omam-Biyik's willingness to run at a retreating defence looked like causing Argentina problems. Not only that, Cameroon had more skill on the ball than their supposedly superior opponents.

There was little hint of a shock at the start, which was an anticlimax after all the hype. A couple of touches from Maradona might have given Argentina two goals had not N'Kono, keeping goal instead of the more experienced Bell, somehow blocked the danger.

A goal then might have settled the holders. As it was, they became unsettled by Cameroon's close marking and hard tackling and never got their act together thereafter.

Midway through the first half Burruchaga was just able to flick the ball away from an empty Argentina net after Omam-Biyik had caught them square with an early through ball. Seven minutes before half-time the same player produced a sudden shot from a narrow angle that nearly went in under

Pumpido's body.

When Cameroon scored Pumpido was badly at fault. Ironically the goal followed a gratuitous Argentinian foul by Lorenzo, who conceded a free-kick on the right.

As the ball came across, Lorenzo rose with Makanaky and it spun off the defender high to Omam-Biyik, whose header was well aimed but should not have carried the power to beat a goalkeeper of international class. However Pumpido appeared confused by its direction, reacted like a dosing slip fielder and allowed the ball to squeeze under his right hand and over the line.

Argentina could not believe it, the crowd could not believe it, the world television audience probably did not believe it and even now it seems like something out of a fantasy. It is one thing to beat Argentina with a full side but to finish on the attack with nine men is rather rubbing it in.

MIKE INGHAM

Former BBC Radio commentator

I was fortunate to attend eight World Cups and this was my favourite tournament, only let down by a dismal final. It was also my last tournament before becoming BBC Radio football correspondent and my role was as a commentator. All the daily briefings and press conferences were covered by my predecessor Bryon Butler.

I had been with Bryon in Sardinia two months earlier as part of an FA delegation looking to reassure the good people of Cagliari at a conference that their island would not be in any danger from marauders masquerading as England fans. This turned out to be an exercise in futility.

In those days at the big tournaments BBC radio was able to get into bed with television when booking the main hotels – so no expense was spared! Our base, as with most of the other journalists, was by a very long way the most luxurious that I was ever fortunate enough to experience. I would not have been able to afford to stay there on a family holiday. The Forte Village resort in Santa Margherita di Pula boasted white sandy beaches, numerous swimming pools, evening buffets under the stars and complimentary room service every evening of bottles of wine and canapés. One big difference in those days was that England were guaranteed to play all their of their group games in the same stadium just down the road unlike my last World Cup in Brazil where they faced three journeys and three overnight stays in three different cities. None of us wanted this group phase to end!

The team did not have the scenic advantage of being based on the coast itself and were more in isolation on higher ground at the IS Molas hotel, renowned for having one of the best golf courses in Italy. The players shared rooms and apart from the rest of the FA party the only other residents were broadcasting rights holders like my colleague Bryon who was given more accessibility to players for interviews.

Like Bryon I went on to experience being based in England hotels at five different tournaments and though this had its advantages, it could also lead to cabin fever! At Italia '90 any stir craziness among the players was nullified by Gazza, a professional court jester. There were some big senior players in this squad and some that didn't need any second invitation to break curfews and join escape parties to the local bar in Pula. Though they would be scolded and dressed down by the manager, ultimately the squad repaid Bobby Robson by reaching the semi-final and then turning in one of the best performances I ever saw by an England side. All this was in stark contrast to 20 years later when institutionalised under Fabio Capello in South Africa they were an embarrassment to the shirt.

Having been in the company of both Terry Butcher and Chris Waddle at other tournaments, I have been regaled with stories from Italia '90 and it was clearly a very happy camp with Gazza at the hub of it all. The Bryan Robson damaged toe story is now part of folklore. When Butcher had to face the manager the next morning and was the last to knock on his door he was greeted with "I knew it would be you Butcher". As he was receiving his bollocking Terry spotted Waddle and Gazza behind the England boss pulling silly faces and he started to snigger at which point the manager told him that this was no laughing matter!

On another occasion Bobby Robson, sitting with assistant Don Howe at one team dinner with the entire FA International committee also present, was impressed that his squad had attended wearing England blazers and white shirts and ties. At the end of the meal, when Butcher got up to leave after proposing a toast, the manager discovered that the bottom half of his attire was incomplete, he was wearing only a jock strap! To amuse themselves, some players took the waiters into their confidence and would have their food back to front – starting with coffee and dessert and ending with the soup.

Robson would eventually reap the benefit of this team spirit and camaraderie and on a number of occasions would be the unwitting victim of a prank himself. Peter Shilton in his autobiography recalls fondly watching his manager grapple to make the new technology of a mobile phone work and telling Stuart Pearce that he didn't think it was working. Pearce advised him that the best way to test it was to ring his own number, which he duly did only to find it engaged; lots of laughs and horseplay. Then there is the Gazza story in his own book about the flight to Bologna and being invited into the cockpit, only to flick a switch inadvertently and make the plane go into a dive!

Bobby Robson did most of his press conferences in Sardinia when we would break off from being serenaded under the trees by violinist Nigel Kennedy to ask the manager some 'searching' questions. The most intense of these was the day after the opening game against Ireland when the team had turned in a turgid performance and most of the tabloid headlines that morning were along the lines of "Bring them back home now Bobby!" Robson was even more animated than usual and went on the attack. Eventually, during the first lull in the proceedings, the void was filled by a question from the reporter from the *Daily Sport* asking Robson if he was concerned about the advertising hoardings being too close to the pitch. Just for once Robson was lost for words and later in the tournament the reporter was presented with a BBC badge for asking the question of the tournament.

I naively thought that every World Cup watching England was going to be like this. Italia '90 ended for the team *After Extra Time and Penalties* and the national team waited for me to retire before reaching their next semi-final 28 years later.

SEND THEM HOME!

Jack Charlton's Republic of Ireland squad pitched up just down the road from England's base in Sardinia. Ireland had finished runners-up to Spain in the qualifiers to make the finals for the first time. As with Euro '88, the Republic of Ireland were drawn to play England in the first group match aiming to emulate their shock 1-0 win in Stuttgart two years earlier. The date: 11th June 1990, the venue the Stadio Sant'Elia in Cagliari in Sardinia. After weeks of build-up we were all on edge as the big kick-off drew close.

Intrepid BBC radio commentator Alan Green was assigned a watching brief on the Irish camp, while his BBC radio team-mate Mike Ingham had a roving role but was often in the England team hotel. Greenie's brief was to be lead commentator on the England game and he went along to the team hotel to interview Big Jack prior to the opening game against England and detected an atmosphere vastly different to the England camp, and although the two hotels were in close proximity, they were a million miles apart in the way they were preparing for the opening World Cup tie.

Green's highly entertaining book in 2000 was billed as "the views from sport's most outspoken commentator", and that was a perfect description on the front cover of the tome entitled *The Green Line*. Greenie and I spent many a happy hour in each other's company to the point where we actually set up a join venture together called Voice of Sport, probably one of the first ever internet football content sites of its kind, a hard-hitting controversial platform that, at one time was talked about with a £60m price tag soon after launch that attracted some huge sponsors, and big name investors such as Adam Faith and Umbro, but then collapsed to virtually nothing at the height of the dot com bubble bursting!

Greenie had access to the England team hotel, something denied to the army of journalists both from the UK and abroad, but the broadcast media were treated differently. The media were permitted access to the England training camp, where all the interviews with Bobby Robson and the players were conducted. The team hotel was off limits.

Never one to mince his words either in his book or on the radio, his take on the Republic of Ireland camp might have reflected the reason why it turned out to be such a tough encounter for England in their opening World Cup tie. It should have been a routine win for England, but Big Jack's players were enjoying the *craic* and were in a wonderfully relaxed mood, as he points out: "There was a vivid contrast in the security deployed around the two camps. England maintained something of a fortress mentality. Only by pre-arrangement, or in exceptional circumstances, did you pass the guards. Ireland's hotel was open house. It was just as well for me as I'd interviewed Charlton and returned to my own hotel only to find that, for whatever reason, it had been recorded at an absurdly low level. We needed the interview badly. It was the day before Ireland were to play England in the opening match of the group. I had no choice but to return to the Irish hotel and beg forgiveness; hopefully Jack would oblige once more.

"The whole squad was out sunbathing on a small private beach. Jack stood alone on a rocky ledge staring across the Mediterranean. I'm afraid he looked like the typical Brit abroad; bare-chested, white shorts, brown shoes and socks, and a green peaked cap. He was smoking a huge cigar and probably wishing he was out at sea on some boat fishing. He caught sight of me out of the corner of his eye. 'And what do you want?'

"I explained my predicament. Most managers would have said 'that's tough' and brushed me aside. Jack asked only where I'd prefer to do this second interview. I think he liked to give the impression that he wasn't quite on top of everything that he should be. Those who saw Charlton, with the faltering memory and superficial grasp of detail, as something of a fool, misunderstood the man. He was fooling them. The great Johan Cruyff thought Charlton was one of the very best international managers."

TV producers brought together Bobby Robson and Jack Charlton, manager of England's first opponents Republic of Ireland, by video link from their respective team bases. "Did you get w'or telex, wishing you all the best?" Charlton asked fellow his Geordie. Robson, grinning, replied. "I'm still waiting for that one!"

After all the off-field headlines and interminable build up, we were all glad to be watching actual football! Gascoigne was picked in a side containing forty-year-old Peter Shilton, with Butcher and Walker in the centre of defence, Gary Stevens and Stuart Pearce were the full backs. Butcher's nagging doubts that his old Ipswich Town boss might overlook him had proved false. Gazza and captain Bryan Robson were now a firm first choice central midfield, with two natural wingers in John Barnes and Chris Waddle. The pairing of Lineker and Peter

Beardsley, which had proved fruitful at Mexico '86, were up front.

In the corresponding meeting two years earlier England had conceded an early goal and failed to find an equaliser. This time it was Robson's men who forged ahead in the opening minutes through Lineker; Chris Waddle floated a beautiful cross that landed in the 18 yard box, Gary Lineker read the flight, raced between Kevin Moran and Mick McCarthy and used his chest to steer the ball past the on-rushing Packie Bonner in the Irish goal. Lineker chased the ball but the single touch from his chest was enough to see the ball over the line.

This time Ireland chased the game. For the rest of the first half and most of the second the Irish players, employing the typical Jack Charlton style, pressed in search of an equaliser. With European champions The Netherlands also in Group F, it was imperative to Ireland's chances of qualifying for the knockout stages not to lose their opening match. Just when it looked like the English might be able to hold out for a victory Ireland received a big slice of luck. Combative midfielder Steve McMahon, on as a 69th minute substitute for Peter Beardsley, failed to control the ball on the edge of the English 18 yard box and Kevin Sheedy pounced and drove a left foot shot beyond Peter Shilton. It was unfortunate for McMahon who had just come on to the pitch but the goal had been coming as the English retreated deeper and deeper.

England should have had a penalty late on when Waddle went down in the area, but they had to settle for a draw amid a Sardinian storm. England were suckered into deploying the direct method that the Republic's charismatic manager, Jack Charlton, employed with considerable success, but England never got going. "No matter what people said about Jack's policy the Irish could make life difficult," Butcher explains. Paul Parker, on the bench that day, recalls: "The Irish side was full of players we met every week in the English First Division and the teams cancelled each other in a dull stalemate."

A turgid draw on a rain-lashed night darkened the mood, and instantly ended all the usual World Cup hype. The thunder and lightning was more spectacular than the game, however it was an improvement on the result in Germany two years earlier but the match lacked quality and the criticism was fierce.

'BRING THEM HOME' screamed one headline; no prizes for guessing which newspaper carried that one. Yep, spot on.

England had been bogged down by the Irish, none more so than England's ace marksman Gary Lineker, who has since come clean that he took one for the team by refusing to go off. He was desperate to leave the pitch but didn't want to let his team-mates down, and said he had been suffering with a troublesome tummy before the match and had a terrible sense that the worst was yet to come but, having refused to dash off the pitch and leave his nation a man down, he stretched for a ball and lost control of his bowels.

Lineker said: "I had a bit of a dickie stomach, I don't know where it came from. I'd been ill overnight and it was the opening day of the tournament and I'd woken up a few times with diahorrea. I didn't want to tell Bobby Robson because I thought he might leave me out the team, and I wanted to play, as always. Anyway, the game started and I was alright then about 20 minutes in I started cramping. I managed to get through the first half despite terrible stomach cramps. Somehow I made it through to half-time and I thought I'd be alright. We go out for the second half, we're 10 or 15 minutes in and I'm starting to cramp again and I think, 'oh, I'm in trouble here'. You know, it's a World Cup, you cannot say 'Excuse me, ref, is it alright if I pop off for five minutes?

"The ball went down the Irish left hand side and I ran across and tried to block something. Anyway, the ball went and I kind of go for it but I stumble a little bit. And as I stumbled, I... relaxed as I fell to the ground and it just went 'boom'! It was like, 'oh my god', but it was like everywhere. There's a bit, if you ever see the footage, where Gary Stevens comes over and asks what's wrong. He's looking over me saying 'are you alright?' And I just remember saying: 'I've s*** myself?' What do you do? Thank god I had dark blue shorts on that day. I'm shovelling it out and rubbing myself on the grass like a dog. It was amazing how much space I found after that though, I was stinking!

"In the end Bobby had to take me off, and I think Steve Bull replaced me and I went to the bench. Every ground pretty much has the dugouts right next to the tunnel, but on this ground, the two dugouts were on the opposite side to the tunnel so I had to go and sit on the bench with all of the subs. You could see everyone shuffling away from me whilst I sat on my own feeling sorry for myself."

Ironically England's opening performance smelt as bad as their star striker and Robson and his Boys of '90 woke up the next morning to a savaging in the media, not only from the notorious red tops battling a circulation war to be the most outspoken and critical but the international press too who decried the game as a war between savages, Roman newspaper *La Repubblica* asked "Is this all there is to England?" while the Milanese *Gazzetta dello Sport* disdainfully headlined its front page "No Football Please, We're English". Therefore it was not going to be a good atmosphere, to say the least, when the England manager, as had been pre-arranged, came to see the media at the Forte Village media room, as there was no formal training the day after the game.

BBC's Alan Green had followed the Irish teams for the majority of the time, and enjoyed the relaxed atmosphere within their camp, but on the odd occasion when he attended an England press conference he noticed a complete change in attitude and a frostiness toward the media. Having once asked Robson what he thought an innocuous question, only to receive a terse response with the England manager always suspicious of the motive of even the tamest of questions, Greenie attended this post match briefing wary of how it would go. Under the circumstances he suspected, quite rightly, it wouldn't go well.

He wrote in his memoirs: "The day after Ireland held England to a punishing 1-1 draw, Robson came to the media base at the Forte Village as he'd indicated that he would. I think he'd been expecting to come on the back of a win and now regretted being so amenable. It was a rather edgy press conference. Halfway through it, I put my hand up. Robson looked in my direction. "Given yesterday's scoreline, is there a result in tonight's match [Holland against Egypt in the same group] that would suit England best?'

"'I don't have to answer that question,' snapped the manager, 'and I won't.' I was dumbfounded. There was no edge to the question, nor any hidden agenda. This, I decided, was a man under considerable pressure.

"The conference broke up in farce. The representative from *The Sunday Sport* ("London Bus Found On The Moon") asked Robson what he thought of the advertisement hoardings. "What?" said Robson.

"'The hoardings. What do you think of the advertisement hoardings?"

"'What are you on about?"

"'Are they too close to the pitch?' This, of course, was the burning issue of the day! Robson, like all of us apart from the questioner, shook his head, made his excuses and left.

"On the day after the final, I bumped into the *Sport* reporter at Rome airport and gave him a prized BBC World Cup badge as a reward for asking the craziest question of the tournament. To his credit, he saw the funny side and immediately pinned the badge to his lapel."

Player power stories later emerged in the aftermath of the Irish disaster that had forced Robson to change to a back three system by his senior players, fuelling the sense he was a lame duck boss just seeing out his time.

In the event the other Group F match between the Netherlands and Egypt also finished 1-1, perhaps the ideal result for England with the group all square, the England manager could move on from the Irish debacle.

After the opening set of matches there was absolutely nothing to separate the four teams in the group, but that meant that there was no margin for any more error. The Dutch had not displayed the cutting edge shown when they won Euro '88, which offered some cause for English optimism. But another dark cloud was lurking on the horizon. As my colleague Michael Hart mentions, the fall-out from the hostess story continued. "There's people out there who don't want us to win the World Cup," said an infuriated Gascoigne in a TV interview, offering a greater depth and seriousness than his usual 'clown prince' image.

MICHAEL HART

How 'The Rotters' were behind the war between players and press

It was a great privilege for me to travel the world from 1970 to 2008 writing about sport for the readers of the *Evening Standard*. As the destination for most 15 year-old school leavers in Dagenham was the foundry at Fords, I was thrilled to be offered a £5-a-week job as a messenger boy at a small but busy sports reporting agency in Fleet Street.

I loved sport, particularly football, but knew I would never be good enough as a player to follow the likes of Jimmy Greaves, Terry Venables, and dozens of other Dagenham boys who made their name in the professional game. So the next best thing was watching it for a living.

I was lucky. During my time at the agency I must have impressed someone because one day they decided to promote me from messenger boy to trainee reporter. A couple of years later the *Standard* offered me a job as football reporter and suddenly I was no longer watching Millwall and Leyton Orient. Instead I was watching Arsenal, Tottenham, Chelsea and West Ham. And England! For Fleet Street's football writers the big England games provided the platform on which they could display fully their writing talents, demonstrate their depth of knowledge and offer their opinions. And in the context of big England matches, none were bigger or more important than the World Cup dates very four years.

World Cups were special. They presented the ultimate test of team and individual. They made heroes and villains, created legends and filed golden memories into the history of the game. There were disappointments, too, and in England's case lots of them. Winning the World Cup in 1966 remains unique, an achievement that has eluded some big coaching names like Don Revie, Ron Greenwood, Bobby Robson, Glenn Hoddle, Kevin Keegan, Sven-Göran Eriksson and Fabio Capello.

I watched Robson's team of 1990 gradually take shape as they prepared for the World Cup with an encouraging run of results – unbeaten in 17 matches until Uruguay's surprise 2-1 win at Wembley just before the tournament started. Despite this setback preparations were good. Robson knew he had a squad good enough to face any challenge from vastly experienced men like Peter Shilton, Terry Butcher, John Barnes and Gary Lineker to the unpredictable Paul Gascoigne and the new addition Paul Parker.

There was, though, a sense of unease in some quarters. To the regular England observer it was apparent that a sour atmosphere was developing between the players and the Press. The original source of this may have been the claims made in some newspapers about Robson's private life.

As I had learned from travelling with the squad over the years, many of these 'revelations' can be traced back to the tabloid Press and the news reporters they sent to write about the behaviour of England's fans, some of whom had a notorious reputation at that time.

These reporters had a job to do, just like me, but they often spoiled the relationships between the sports reporters and the players. This is what happened in 1990. England's opening three games were on the island of Sardinia partly because travel to the island presented problems that, it was hoped, would reduce the number of England fans travelling.

We had barely been on the island a few days when big headlines in the papers back home carried reports of an 'incident' involving England players at the squad's heavily guarded luxury hotel. An attractive Italia '90 hostess, Isabella Ciarovolo, was named in the reports.

The mood in the England camp changed dramatically. As far as the players were concerned it didn't matter whether you were a news reporter or a sports reporter. All bets were off!

Around 100 TV and newspapers reporters gathered in the little village of Pula to question Robson and his players about the allegations. The players were so angry at the suggestion of a *dolce vita* nightlife that they refused to talk to anyone.

Robson explained that the players would not be talking to the Press again. "For you to do this to them at this time is a disgrace," he said. "There is absolutely no truth in this report."

'The Rotters', as the news reporters were known by the sports reporters, were thrilled with their story. One tabloid apparently offered Isabella £20,000 for her exclusive story. She said nothing but there was no doubt that she was an Italia '90 hostess at the England hotel. The organisers moved her out of the England hotel, explaining that her English wasn't good enough. They found her a new position not far away at the Irish hotel – presumably because her Irish was better than her English!

This ill feeling between the players and press festered for days. I remember trying to get a quiet word with Paul Parker after training one day. He was sitting on the team bus. I signalled him to come out.

He sensed he was going to get a chance in the team. He was right. In the end he played six of England's seven games. I knew him quite well from his time with Fulham and QPR. When he got off the bus he stood by the stairs at the front. As we shook hands a cup of Coca Cola was thrown over us from inside the bus. Culprit: Paul Gascoigne.

Such incidents were rare during my 38 years covering England and what I learned from Italia '90 was the importance of the relationship between the players and the manager. That is all that matters. Robson's players loved working with him. They wanted to win for him – and they nearly did.

After all, in the end two missed penalties was all that separated them from a place in the World Cup Final.

DAVE BEASANT

lthough I was the fourth choice goalkeeper at the time, I'd had such a good season with Chelsea I felt I was in with a chance of making the cut and going to the World Cup. There was a 26-man squad named that trained at Bisham Abbey and we stayed at Burnham Beeches hotel, but we all knew the day was arriving when Bobby Robson had to reduce that squad to his final 22.

The goalkeepers were Shilts, Chris Woods, David Seaman and myself and as I had only had two caps at the time it looked like the manager would go with the more experienced keepers but I felt I was in the group on merit and still had a chance right up until the final day. The year before I had saved that penalty in the FA Cup final, now I had enjoyed a good season at the Bridge, and I didn't have a better opportunity of a World Cup.

I was rooming with Dave Seaman when the knock on the door came and I opened the door. Dave was stood up by the window, and I thought, 'should one of us walk out?' The England manager looked at me and said "Good news Dave…."

Out of the corner of my eye I could see David Seaman wince, he must have been thinking "Oh Christ, I'm not going to the World Cup!" He looked as though I was going instead of him, then Bobby Robson, still looking straight at me, finished his sentence, "Good news Dave… no more training for you!" There is no real way to break the news of this sort of thing to somebody, no one is going to take it well, and Bobby tried to make it in a light-hearted jokey sort of way. The other three to go home were all three Arsenal boys; Rocky, Tony Adams and Alan Smith.

"Right, I'm off then" I said to David Seaman, as I packed my bags and left the hotel, as the squad were packing up to leave for the airport ready for the journey to Sardinia the next day. Bobby Robson told me to keep myself ticking over as you never know what might happen, and so I went for some runs when I got back but there was no one around at that time of the year for proper goalkeeping practice or training.

A few weeks later I was on a Dave Bassett golf day, and in those days there were no mobiles, so when I finished my round and came into the club house a few people said "well done on your England call up!" I thought they were taking the piss. "Yeh, ok", I replied.

But they were insistent and told me I put Ceefax on and there was an item which said Bobby Robson was trying to contact Dave Beasant to call him up to the England squad as David Seaman has gone home injured. I went straight home, contacted the FA and was on my way to Sardinia. By the time I got out there the tournament had started, England had played their opening game against the Irish, and I thought it was going to take me weeks to get back into shape and regain my rhythm, and it took a little while, but nowhere near as long as I thought, and within a few days I was up to speed with the new Adidas balls that were flying all over the place.

It was great to be part of such a wonderful experience and I enjoyed all the larking around, it was such a good group of guys. Everyone wanted to sit next to Peter Beardsley at dinner, he was by far the most popular guy in the camp as Bobby Robson allowed us one beer with our evening meal and, as Peter didn't drink, there was a rush to get a seat near him so they would be first in the queue for Peter to slide their beer over to them.

I was unable to join Harry Redknapp for his first *'Arry's Heroes* TV programme, but was available for the second one, which was filmed out in Italy, with a couple of the England lads, John Barnes and David Seaman. Part of the filming was to talk about your memories of Italia '90 as we were out there it made sense. Wrightie told me that Bobby Robson often spoke to the senior players about a lot of things and they had been discussing what if a game went to penalties and they were telling the England manager "Get Bes on". They argued that my big presence in the goal as well as my knack for saving pens might work, while Shilts didn't have such a good record at penalties so there has been a lot of talk that I should have come on in the semi-final when it was going to penalties. More recently we have seen how Louis Van Gaal brought on Tim Krul for the Dutch in Brazil in 2014, but all this was a myth; I wasn't even on the bench, so I couldn't have come on! In those days you had to name the substitutes, whereas today the entire squad gets stripped and you can chose anyone you want. On that day Chris Woods was the substitute goalkeeper not me!

Yet, even the day after the semi-final, Robson was supposed to have said he had been thinking of bringing me on! He had convinced himself that he was thinking of bringing me on, even though I wasn't on the bench! It could never have happened.

Anyway I came away with a World Cup medal, albeit a bronze medal, as everyone who reached the semi-final was given a bronze medal, which made the play-off for third and fourth place even more ludicrous and irrelevant, and was just a filler before the final yet that play-off game was very important for myself and Chris Woods, and all the others who hadn't played, as it was an opportunity to earn a World Cup cap.

Bobby Robson told the squad that anyone who hadn't played so far would be in the team against Italy, provided they were fit of course. Neil Webb was the only one that wouldn't make it as he had been injured throughout the tournament and never got a kick. Chris Woods was overjoyed as this was his second World Cup and he hadn't got a game, and I was overjoyed as I was to come on in the second half and also earn a World Cup cap.

Then Shilts had a word with Robson. He wanted to go out on his 125th cap for England, announce his retirement and play in the whole game. I felt for Chris, as his chance had now gone, and I was none too pleased myself. We were both very much aggrieved.

If Shilts had realised the euphoria being generated back home, of course, he might have waited and it would have been a more fitting farewell if he had won his 125th and final cap at Wembley and made a perfect farewell in front of an appreciative crowd.

Instead his farewell was in a meaningless game, when he was caught trying to dribble with the ball and Italy scored, his England career fizzling out. For Chris Woods and myself we spent four days training for no reason, and it was a hugely disappointing way to end our particular World Cup.

FAN VIOLENCE AT WORLD CUP FINALS

Credit: The *New York Times* Archives

Two hours before the kick off of the World Cup match between England and the Netherlands on Saturday night, Italian police officers and about 1,000 English soccer fans exchanged rocks and tear gas during a clash.

According to Italian and British authorities, two officers and seven English youths were injured in the skirmish, which began when fans stormed a police barrier near Sant'Elia Stadium, on the outskirts of this southern Sardinian city.

The police, clearly responding in force to the first sign of provocation by English hooligans, responded with several volleys of tear gas after the youngsters hurled stones at them, witnesses said. After chasing hundreds of youths down backstreets and alleys, the police took more than 500 people into custody, but British officials said that over the next few hours all were let go.

After the game ended in a 0-0 tie, fans for both teams left the stadium quietly, many of the Dutch visitors planning to take planes directly to Palermo, Sicily, where they are staying during the first round of the finals. Nevertheless, the battle deepened worries that a night of trouble lay ahead for what was already the most dreaded match of the tournament.

Both England and the Netherlands are notorious for soccer hooliganism; their teams trailed by packs of rabid fans out to prove they are the nastiest around.

But police officers in riot helmets were out in full force in the heart of town into early this morning, hours after the match, and they easily outmanned young fans and local youths milling in the streets. For all the worries, there were no disturbances.

For months, people here had braced for the estimated 8,500 Dutch and 6,000 English fans who poured onto this island in the last few days from planes and ships. They were greeted with the tightest security net thus far in the month-long tournament.

About 3,200 extra police officers were assigned to duty in and around Cagliari, raising the total force here to 4,000; equivalent to one officer for every 60 residents. They closely patrolled every Sardinian airport and ferry landing, using dogs to sniff each arrival for drugs and pulling aside those suspected of being possible troublemakers.

At least 1,500 officers stood guard at the stadium, where no one could get in without undergoing a body search or a metal-detector inspection. The first of several checkpoints was set up nearly a mile from the stadium, and the police confiscated sticks, bottles and anything else that might be hurled at players on the field.

Large groups of English and Dutch fans were escorted by armed police into the stadium. One contingent of about 75 English youths was completely surrounded and ordered to maintain strict ranks by rifle-carrying officers.

Starting at midnight Friday, alcohol sales were banned throughout Cagliari and nearby towns, a restriction that has been in force on match days in Italy's 12 host cities, to the consternation of bar and restaurant owners and to all Italians who insist it is their inalienable right to drink wine with their meals. Restaurant owners in Rome and Milan were so outraged this week that many closed their kitchens for a day in protest.

Here, many soccer fans, including many young Englishmen, camped out for several days, drinking and behaving raucously on the streets.

Yet for most of today, along Via Roma, a porticoed boulevard of shops and cafes that is this port city's waterfront promenade, it was generally quiet until the clash just before the 9 P.M. kickoff. That street and its nearby train station were considered likely battlegrounds.

Dutch fans, wrapped in banners of orange, their team's colour, marched and chanted along the boulevard as they walked the two miles to the stadium. But they avoided contact with the English youths who also cruised the street. Some fans spent idle time at sidewalk cafes, where the strongest drink they could buy was a stiff cup of Italian espresso.

The British Embassy set up a special office in Sardinia, where the English team has been exiled for its three first-round matches to make it easier to monitor its fans.

One unexpected source of trouble turned out to be young Sardinians out to prove themselves against the northern Europeans with tough reputations. Late Friday night and early Saturday morning, several scuffles were reported near the train station and witnesses blamed the trouble for the most part on local youths.

That is not to say that the visitors have been angels.

Eight English hooligans were arrested Thursday after a barroom brawl, and another one was expelled from the country for pushing two Italians off a motorcycle. Last Monday, riot police charged bottle-throwing fans who had fought with local youths after a match between England and Ireland.

In all, 32 English fans were in jail pending trial and three were serving sentences of 20 days each.

Despite the focus on Sardinia, the worst World Cup violence before today had come from young West Germans who rioted in Milan last Sunday as their national team played Yugoslavia. The police fired tear gas after the youths smashed store windows, attacked a trolley car and vandalised subway stations in a rampage that lasted several hours.

Afterwards, at least 45 Germans were expelled from the country, and seven others, plus a Swiss, were given eight-month prison terms.

GARY STEVENS

Fun, football, and Robbo's toe mystery

Last November I flew back home from where I live here in Secret Harbour, Western Australia for an Everton reunion to watch the film *Howards' Way* about my former boss Howard Kendall and it was astonishing to get back together all in the same room after 30 years, it's just as astonishing to think it's 30 years since Italia '90

Ever since I returned early with injury I have taken a step back from 'soccer', I'm now working as a physio, but I have fond memories of Italia '90 even though I only played the first and the last game and watched everything in between and wasn't even on the bench. Everybody wanted to play in Italy, it was the hub of the game at that time, the tournament promised so much and I consider myself so lucky that this was my second World Cup.

From the time of the draw to actually getting there it all lived up to its promise, even though it was a slow start for England against Ireland when my Everton team-mate Kevin Sheedy scored a late equaliser. We had found it tough against the Irish in '88 in the Euros, and it was no different here in the World Cup. From that point, the Boss wanted to change a few things and although we had never even tried out a sweeper system, let alone played with one in a game, incredibly that's the system he switched to and it worked but I was a casualty as the boss opted to go with Paul Parker instead of me. It turned out that from that point I watched a lot of football and while that was frustrating at times, I got to play against the hosts in the last game. Of course it was hugely disappointing that we lost on penalties in the semi-finals, and we were a lick of paint away from being in the final where we would have been confident of beating Argentina but the last game holds special memories for me in front of a full crowd, it was the World Cup Finals, it was one of the highlights of my career.

Gazza wore his heart on his sleeve, and when he was booked in that semi-final the wheels came off, you would have thought it would have badly affected the way he played but it didn't. It couldn't. He is not someone who can hide, who can stop, he is always on the go. He was the best person to have around the camp to keep us all amused... for 10 minutes. After ten minutes you wanted him to go or you have to find a way to go. He was too energetic. The greatest players in the world had some kind of edge, some kind of flaw, whether it was Diego Maradona or Gazza in his own way. We saw those cracks.

We were also a group of young boys who needed, at times, to break out of 'prison' and it was Chris Waddle with his Geordie accent, who would invariably says "come on lads, who fancies going to Pula to the Social Men's Drinking club". He called it the Social Men's Drinking club, but it was just a bar we all liked in the nearest town, it was an escape route for a couple of hours, something that would be very much frowned upon these days, but back then the players did their best to keep it all under wraps and generally speaking we behaved ourselves, but we were young boys who needed a prison break.

It might have been Mexico or it might have been Cagliari, but in the hotel there was a stage in the night club, and one night Bobby Robson came in and there must have been 15 of us on stage playing imaginary brass instruments, thinking we were a Brass Band. He was not amused, as it was clear we probably had more than one or two drinks to be doing something like that - unless the England manager thought we had too much sugar!

One night our captain Bryan Robson was trying to sneak back through the room I was sharing with Trevor Steven. We heard a knock, and we snuck him in, then in the dark we heard a screech when he stubbed his toe and the next morning we saw a tail of 'claret' on the floor. I've no doubt that he probably couldn't remember half of what actually happened. But when we saw the blood on the floor next morning we knew what that scream had been for, Pop was one hell of a player and I'm not saying we would have progressed to the final or even won it had he been fit, but you never know. We certainly missed him when he had to go home early.

MARK WRIGHT

Bobby Robson told me his master plan, then told me to keep it secret

One of the biggest incidents in the entire World Cup campaign was the switch over from a traditional flat back four to the sweeper system which ignited England's performances, and there was the suggestion that it was player power that changed the mind of Bobby Robson. A lot of people have their own opinions why it was changed, and how it came about, and whether some of the senior players went to see Bobby Robson to lobby the change, but I actually know what happened.

Leading up to the selection of the final squad when we were all gathered at the Burnham Beeches Hotel there had been a slight worry about an injury I was carrying, but the manager selected me for the squad, and when he told me I was in, he pulled me to one side and said to me, "I want you fit, because I want you out there to play you as a sweeper - keep that to yourself." He elaborated and told me that he would not play me against the Irish as that would be more like a traditional English game, but in the second game against the Dutch, they had three at the back and had adopted a sweeper system, and he wanted to match them up. "Get it in your head you will be sweeper against the Dutch, and get ready for it," Robson said.

I had played that system so many times before, it was familiar to me, and it was clear to me that's why I was in the squad, and that Bobby Robson and Don Howe had planned it all in advance.

If you are competing for and playing for your country, you should be a confident footballer and assured about any system you play in, but I was very comfortable as a sweeper, so I wasn't shocked that we played it, as I was expecting it.

Everybody in that squad had the utmost respect for each other, so we all knew there was no guarantees of a place, you had to earn it. You knew there might be injuries so if you didn't start you might get your chance and, if so, a chance to keep that place. The competition for places was fantastic as we had so many outstanding players in that squad. If the manager stuck with Terry Butcher and Des Walker in the heart of the defence I could not have had any complaint, they are both great players. There was massive trust between the defenders and indeed the goalkeepers, we were all very confident going into the tournament. Some of the lads liked to break out from time to time but I didn't go. Having missed one World Cup, I had lost time to make up, and I wanted to be as sharp in my mind and body as I could be to get into the team and stay in the team, I didn't want to be even a little bid jaded from a night out, but there was no shortage of a glass of wine or a beer in the hotel.

Bobby Robson and Don Howe made it all work in Italia '90 because they made us all feel like one big, happy family; we were united, in it together, whatever system he played whoever he picked to play it. That's why we were united when the media targeted us, and that happened long before we got out there. We played a World Cup warm up match at Wembley against the Czechs but there was an abysmal turn out, a crowd of around 30,000, as the mood had turned against us, expectations were low, but it was up to us as players and management to galvanise the nation, to capture their imagination, to believe in us the way we believed in ourselves. We had to show them that we meant business and were not just going out there for the ride.

There had been much talk during the period leading up to the tournament about the benefits of utilising the sweeper system, as England repeatedly refused to follow the lead of continental sides and instead deployed more traditional defensive formations but for the Dutch game England manager Bobby Robson at last opted to make the sweeping change, recognising the benefits of selecting Mark Wright in the role. There would be suggestions that player power led to the switch, but Robson always maintained it was his choice.

Peter Beardsley and Gary Stevens, who had attracted criticism, lost their places as Paul Parker came in after being on the bench for the opening game but knew almost immediately that changes were going to be made, he just didn't expect to be picked as a wing back as he recalled: "Bobby took the bold initiative of dropping Gary Stevens and, in reverting to a 3-5-2 system, bringing in Mark Wright in defence and me at wing-back, a position completely foreign to me, not having even played there in club matches. But I was more than happy to try. Trevor Steven was the obvious choice to play in that position, but I think Robson wanted a more defensive player and one who could adapt during a match if an alteration was required.

"I have no doubt that in my selection and in making major changes, Bobby listened to the opinions of his senior players. Other managers might have seen this as a weakness, but Bobby had around him a group of players who had been playing internationals in some cases for six or seven years and they knew what it took to succeed at this level. Bryan Robson was close to Bobby, but I think it was Chris Waddle who advised Bobby to tighten the midfield, and he did. It might surprise some people to know that Sir Alex did the same; with Robbo, Roy Keane and Steve Bruce who were often consulted by him, out of strength, not because he had no idea what to do."

Robson would encounter some of the players he would later inherit at PSV who were in the Dutch squad, but a more pressing concern was that England delivered, and with a new system that the England manager probably didn't actually like very much!

By this stage, a 1-1 draw with the Republic of Ireland had prompted demands from the press to 'Bring 'em Home.' So why didn't Bobby announce these changes in advance, if only to distract the press from their negativity. "I don't think he wanted to confuse us. He gave us information as we needed to know it," says Terry Butcher, "There was laughter around the camp. There was light and shade, Bobby knew you had to have a blow-out at some stage."

"Bobby was [thinking] about changing because of the way the Dutch played," Gary Lineker observed, "he went to the experienced players – Bryan Robson, myself, Terry Butcher, Peter Shilton – and we all thought it would suit the type of players we had, particularly with Mark Wright, who was a natural player to come out with the ball."

The new system saw the swift Des Walker as cover for two central markers. When Mark Wright was originally selected he was seen as a back up to Butcher and Walker but by the second game he had become a pivotal figure in an unexpected change of tactics. The sweeper was still considered a very foreign concept by English football followers, part of a system many still saw as negative when in fact it allowed teams to keep the ball for longer periods, something that was desperately needed following the 'stone age football' we'd witnessed in the Ireland game.

Robson, who would later go on to be a key influence across European management, not least in the education of Jose Mourinho and in a roundabout way Pep Guardiola, introduced a tactical innovation which was rarely used in the English game and broke away from the 4-4-2 which had been the bedrock of the national team since Sir Alf's

1966 triumph with the 'Wingless Wonders'.

It is tempting to believe that the change was made in fear of the likes of Ruud Gullit, Marco Van Basten, Ronald Koeman and Frank Rijkaard who had humiliated Robson and England at the 1988 European Championships and perhaps it was, but the move had an unexpected by-product. The back five provided a defensive platform that released the midfield from their defensive duties, specifically this freed up Gascogine, while David Platt was free to join the attack. Against the Dutch it nearly worked; with England coming closest to breaking the deadlock in a tight game with a Holland team divided by their own in-fighting.

"The Dutch had some terrific players – Van Basten, Gullit, Rijkaard, Koeman - but they didn't seem half the team that won the European championship a couple of years earlier," Butcher observed.

Paul Parker revealed the instructions he received from his manager. "Holland were undoubtedly the best team I had ever faced up to then. They were effortlessly brilliant in all positions but my nerves disappeared once we kicked off. I did what I was instructed to do and that was to keep it simple. 'Do what you are good at,' Robson told me. I even got forward far enough to set up a Lineker 'goal', but it was ruled out for offside."

Where the side had been slammed for their display five days earlier, they were now praised for taking the game to the European champions and Gascoigne was able to more freely display his talents than he had against the Irish. His phenomenal turn to leave Ronald Koeman trailing was one of the best moments in the entire tournament.

The Dutch cause was not helped by Ruud Gullit having endured a lengthy injury lay-off, as he struggled to exert the same influence as that shown two years earlier and Marco van Basten never looked like replicating his Euro '88 hat-trick. England successfully dealt with the Dutch threat and almost won right at the end, Pearce's indirect free-kick going in without being touched.

Holland had arrived in Italy as one of the favourites to win the World Cup, but now faced the tricky prospect of needing a result against the Irish who were out for revenge following their unfortunate defeat in Germany just two years earlier.

For once Robson could look forward to some positive appraisals of the performance, he was right when he said, "It was a superb match, a complete contrast to the opening game. We created the better chances and, with any sort of luck, would have won." It was the first inkling that this could be a special summer for England.

Robson certainly had a better weekend than Jack Charlton, whose Irish side were widely criticised for their role in a dull goalless draw with Egypt. Ireland had squandered the opportunity to go top of the group after England and Holland played out a draw. Nevertheless it was not going to be an easy match as the Egyptians had already drawn 1-1 with the talented Dutch team in their opening group match in Stadio La Favorita in Palermo, Sicily. The two goalless draws meant that it looked quite feasible that all four sides could finish with identical records, leading to lots having to be drawn to decide who went home.

CHRIS WADDLE

I dreaded England's 4-4-2

I dreaded playing for England in a 4-4-2, I didn't play that way with Tottenham or with Marseille, but only when I joined up with England. Everyone raved about the football Tottenham and Marseilles played, that it was so good on the eye, everyone raved about the transformation of some of our players when they went to play abroad, Glenn Hoddle for example, he was fantastic at Tottenham but they didn't play 4-4-2, but he was world class when he went to Monaco into a more flexible formation; he was the same player, just trusted and given his freedom to express himself even more. Terry Venables was the same at Tottenham, he didn't want you to defend all the time, he wanted you to make things happen. It wasn't about playing attractive football it was about effective football, getting the best out of the individual, not forcing the individual to play within a system that might not suit them.

CHRIS WADDLE

During the World Cup we started with the traditional 4-4-2, but I was very pleased that Bobby Robson changed the system. Whether it was Don Howe, the England manager, or the players who persuaded him, the result was that we changed, and I don't know how it changed but I know it changed for the better.

Bryan Robson was a fantastic captain, unfortunately he was injured, so it had more to do with myself talking to Terry Butcher, we would sit and talk about the game and what needed changing, and Terry had a word with Bobby. In my eyes from what I had seen in France, we had to play three at the back to give us an extra man in central midfield, and play wing backs, and that is something that would suit us with the good footballers in our side. I made it perfectly clear I was sick of playing 4-4-2, that the entire world when asked about English football would respond instantly with "Ah, kick and rush." In France we heard it about the English way of playing. You would hear it from the Brazilians, Yugoslavians, as they were then, the England way is just kick and rush, they would say it straight away. We were renowned for how we played, kick and rush, up and down the field, win the ball, lose the ball, win it back and relying on set pieces but this England team could play differently, there were many technically gifted players and it was a big plus for me that by changing the system we changed the mentality of the English game for a while, it had a profound effect on English football, certainly in the eyes of the rest of the world.

We proved we had technically adept players as good, possibly even better, than anyone in the world. Over our history you can trace back those technically gifted players who weren't trusted in an England shirt, it goes back to Rodney Marsh, Alan Hudson, Frank Worthington, Stan Bowles, Matt Le Tissier, and Glenn Hoddle, who should have won 150 caps not 52. The guys who play it off the cuff but supposedly don't have the 'legs' to run up and down the park so the managers are always 'not sure' of their worth. We had players like John Barnes, who was fantastic, but sometimes I felt like I was playing full back as you would hardly ever manage to get into the final third. If anything good came of this tournament it was that we could bridge that gap on technical ability and we could see how it has developed over the years.

I was in the campaign to change things at the World Cup, having experienced a variety of systems at Marseilles where players would be afforded a lot of freedom, I had learned how you would get the best out of players, rather than how they had to fit into the system. I was fed up whenever we played someone and the press would be raving about their star man, a Hagi, or Stojkovic, or somebody else, but they were allowed to go and play and hurt the opposition, the shape was built around them, not the other way round. All of a sudden I go to Marseilles and I'm regarded as world class, but I'm the same player, except that they want me to fill a certain area, conserve my energy for when it matters the most, and then look for the space as they will give it to me as soon as they gain possession and go to hurt the opposition.

When it was decided to switch I had a spring in my step, there was a chance to change the way people thought of English football being played at a 100 miles an hour, playing the percentage game, bullying teams. But no one was playing 4-4-2 apart from us, the Irish and the Scots. Other nations had caught up on our physical side of things and had the technique to go with it. But now we had exactly the same tools as them, we no longer had to play kick and rush.

It was a warm day when we played Belgium, we needed to look after the ball, so it made sense in my eyes, and a lot of the players were all for it. Whether the manager listened to the players, or listened to Don Howe, or already had a Plan B, the outcome was the right one, it was the right system to go forward with the players we had, and once we changed we had the match for the better teams. I knew Enzo Scifo from playing against Bordeaux when I was in France, I knew how good he was, but we had great players. I enjoyed the Belgium game – they could easily have beaten us, but we could easily have beaten them in normal time, it was end to end, a proper cup tie. Platt's goal was fantastic, what a goal, it deserved to win that game.

For the fans, players and coaches, they could see how England can play, it was a step in the right direction, and how football could change in our country for the better.

THE WRIGHT MAN AT THE RIGHT TIME

op spot in the group was in England's sights should they beat Egypt but equally the unfancied supposed whipping boys of the group also had a chance to qualify and join Cameroon in representing Africa in the knockouts.

The night before the match Paul Gascoigne was restless, roaming around trying to persuade someone to play table-tennis, begging them for a game when everyone was looking for an early night before such an important game but Gazza was as hyperactive as usual and, not needing an excuse to expend his excess energy, he was 'high' on winning money from bookmaker Gary Lineker on the filmed races that entertained the players most nights.

The win just about put him ahead on the trip, or the "holiday" as he was now starting to call it. Whether he was kidding himself or not, he didn't think he was feeling the sort of pressure everyone else must have been under. As Mel Stein wrote in his biography of Gazza: "He'd even bribed the waiters to serve him bottles of fizzy water topped off with a generous amount of wine. He was with footballers, making people laugh, ignoring journalists when he wasn't taunting them, taking part in all sorts of sports, and best of all playing football. Whether it was in the world arena, or on the grass of the hotel with the local kids, it was all he really wanted to do."

As for taunting the media, he was the last of the entire group to maintain his interview black-out, and behind anyone he spotted giving TV interviews he would hold up a centre fold of Playboy, pointing to the naughty bits!

Bobby Robson even accepted an invitation to have lunch with a collection of football writers before the game and received a gift from them ahead of his departure as England manager. "It was time to be gracious, and it all went very well," he said later, "I must admit I gave it some thought before I attended. But I have never been one to bear grudges – say your piece and get on with life."

Another unexpected change saw Robson drop Terry Butcher to the bench. After serving him so well for Ipswich Town and England and becoming such an iconic figure in the England team it was Butcher, rather than Wright, who was sacrificed as the sweeper system was put on hold, with Wright picked ahead of him. It was another massive

<u>*Bobby Breaks Bread With His 'Enemies'*</u>

The senior football writers invited Bobby Robson to lunch before the final group game against Egypt. Despite the growing animosity he held toward the media, he decided to attend which just goes to show that he was very forgiving!

On the right (closest to Robson): Bob 'Bomber' Harris (ghost writer of Robson's books), Colin Gibson (the then Telegraph chief football writer and member of the Morris Men), me, Keith Pinner (representing one of the main sponsors).

On the near side (obscured): Steve Curry (The Express/Morris Men), Jeff Powell (Daily Mail), Michael Hart (Evening Standard), Bob Driscoll (Daily Star) and Paddy Barclay (bald head), David Lacey (Guardian) and Stuart Jones (The Times/Morris Men) also attended but isn't in shot.

I introduced Keith Pinner to the Football Writers Association which began his long and influential involvement in the game. Keith died in June 2019 at the age of 74. He was an honorary president of his beloved Manchester City. He was so popular and respected in the game that FIVE former City managers attended his memorial service at the Etihad; Tony Book, Peter Reid, Brian Horton, Frank Clark and Joe Royle. Also present as a speaker was former Manchester United manager Sir Alex Ferguson and ex-Everton and United boss David Moyes, in charge of Real Sociedad at the time, who travelled from Shanghai to Manchester, via Munich, to pay his respects.

decision by the England manager that needed to pay off. It was not a decision some of the players approved of but the manager told them it was for just the one game, as he wanted to revert to the traditional flat back four for the Egypt game.

Steve McMahon, who had been dropped following his calamity against the Irish, replaced the injured Bryan Robson who would soon be flying home early for a second successive World Cup, while Steve Bull came into the attack.

Paul Parker recalls, "Egypt were seen as make-weights in the group, but our manager made sure we never believed that. I remember how tense we were before the start and during the match because there was no free-flowing football or chance to show why we were supposed to be a superior footballing nation. The Egyptians made life difficult for us and we had to work hard to see them off. They had a couple of brothers playing for them and, for all Robson's words of caution, I was surprised how capable they were as a team."

It wasn't looking good at half time with the score goalless while Holland were beating Ireland 1-0 and if both scores remained the same, the Dutch would win the group, Ireland would be bottom, leaving England and Egypt to draw lots for second and third places.

The performance was less impressive than against the Dutch but it produced the desired outcome as Wright headed in Gascoigne's free-kick for the only goal. Niall Quinn equalised for the Irish, so England actually finished top by a clear two points!

Bobby Robson knew he had at least one more match left as manager which would be against Belgium in Bologna, as England at last entered the Italian mainland and joined the real World Cup party.

Wright's header proved to be his only goal in an England shirt yet it was Paul Parker who excelled in a right wing-back role and the transformation of the team seemed complete, "the whole atmosphere changed from how it had been after 90 minutes against Ireland, where it was doom and gloom and papers demanding we come back."

In the bath the team sang *World in Motion* which had reached No 1 in the charts back in the UK and even those who didn't play joined in the singing and landed in the bath "some reluctantly and fully dressed with the help and encouragement of Gazza" reveals Mel Stein.

For now it was now farewell to Cagliari and onto Bologna. For the media, it was farewell Forte Village, it was a wrench to leave.

TERRY BUTCHER

Seeing the media conflict from both sides

ENGLAND
TERRY BUTCHER

Time has flown by, I can't believe it all happened 30 years ago. We've had a few get-togethers since, a few programmes to mark the occasion, a documentary, and whenever we do get together it's like time travel, we are straight back to that time when it all happened. To go through the tournament, so far into the competition, and what we achieved, just one step from the final, we were so close, we formed an unbreakable bond, a bond for life. We will never forget it, we made some great friends, and irrespective of how long we are separated, or lose touch, whenever we get back together that bond is so special.

I am sure the players who reached the World Cup semi-final again in 2018 will know how we felt, they would have experienced that bond, they will always remember being part of it.

At Italia '90 we had a lot of really good players, manager and a team, there was so much energy, it was fabulous, the best experience of my life in football, the football and the camaraderie. There were such great characters in that team, great people as well as great players. People talk all the time about 'spirit' but if ever there was a case of spirit within the dressing room, then we had it. It says a lot that an international team had a better spirit within the dressing room than happens at your club, that takes some doing, but that's what we had, it was unique, it was special. It was also my last tournament and the semi-final was my last England game as I didn't play in the third and fourth place play-off, in fact I didn't play much football at all after that, so that tournament came just in time for me.

Talking about unbelievable characters, Gazza would be top of that list, they don't come more unbelievable than him. He was funny, he loved laughing at himself, and he wanted people to laugh at him. He loved to be loved. Chris Waddle roomed with him, and I was in the room next door with Trevor Steven and there were times when Chris would come knocking on our door to get away from him but Gazza would be banging on our door to try to find him or to get in with us. If you let him he would be everywhere, nothing was sacred, but he was funny. He was also a bit afraid of the older players like Robbo, Shilts and myself, because we were not worried about giving him a clip round the ear and tell him to behave himself. If he did something wrong, over-stepped the mark, we'd give him a whack on the head, or I would chase him around the grounds and into the building to try to catch him.

While he loved having a laugh, and there were many laughs when Gazza was around, and at times he could be a pest, he was deadly serious when it came to his football. A court jester off the pitch, he was a phenomenal talent on it. I don't think people realise just how good he was. He showed it against the Czechs to cement his place in the squad, when he went past people from midfield, that was something unique; a midfielder able to dribble past players in those areas and then find yourself straight into their back four, caused mayhem. He would also do his defensive work, he was all over the place, had a relentless amount of energy, and although he gave a penalty away in the quarters, he was back there showing he was prepared to do the hard work as well. Sometimes, though, you need to relax, whether on the field or preparing for a game. Gazza would do neither, it never got into his head that there was a time to relax, he was on the go all the time, whether in a game or whether it was back in the team hotel.

In the semi, I don't think we did a lot wrong. To be fair we actually didn't lose to Germany, we lost a penalty shoot-out which is recognised as a lottery; a one to one situation which as a team you have no control over. I'd rather lose a semi-final the way England did in 2018 than lose on penalties. It was really harsh to lose on penalties, hard to take, as the semi-final is the hardest one to take when you lose, so if I have any regrets about Italia '90 is that we didn't make the final where we would have had every chance of winning it but, even so, it was a sensational time.

Having been so deeply involved in the media since, working for so long with experienced journalists at BBC Radio 5 live, it has definitely given me a different perspective about how the media interact with football, especially the England team. I have crossed over to the other side, so to speak, so I no longer see it as "them and us". Having been in the England camp during Italia '90 when it was all kicking off with the media and now seeing the relationship from the media's point of view, it helps a lot in the way I approach the job of analysing players, the team and the manager when I am working for the media, and I was lucky enough to be part of the 5Live team for some major tournaments. It was strange being in the England team hotel when things had come full circle; I was no longer one of the England squad, but tasked with criticising the England team, if need be. But times had changed between players and the media with the advent of the Premier League, and the relationship becoming even more remote.

In Italia '90 the fall out with the press got so bad that we ended up not talking to them. However that brought about its own peculiar problem, as some players had been contracted to do columns for national newspapers. So on one hand we were refusing to talk to the press, but on the other some players were continuing to chat to journalists for their ghost written columns. But within the camp, it was accepted that the players had no choice as they were under contract to write their columns. But the attitude toward how certain things were being reported created a siege mentality against the press, and that was a consequence of a lot of the news guys out there who, in the absence of genuine news, went in search of stories.

My approach to being 'on the other side' is to tell it honestly and I believe players appreciate that. If they think they are getting honesty they will accept what you have to say about them, even if, at times, they might not like what is being said. When I was a player I hated it the most when I didn't agree with things said about me, if I didn't think they were right or views were given in a dishonest way, it was unacceptable, for instance, if attacks on you were personal.

The right approach is a balanced one, which I am sure players appreciate. If they have made a mistake, they know it, and won't argue with you if you say they had made a mistake, even though they won't be happy that their mistake has been highlighted.

But, of course, then having to mix with the players in their team hotel if I had called out any mistakes or made any critical comments, was a strange experience. But I love being part of the media team with 5Live in World Cup tournaments, it is special.

FAREWELL CAPTAIN MARVEL

Bryan Robson had been England's best player throughout his namesake's reign as England manager but having already flown home after the second game in the Mexico World Cup, the same happened again four years later in Italy. The official line was that he had suffered a torn hamstring and this remained the accepted truth long after the event when it was later revealed that it was a broken toe caused by an incident when one of the players (Gazza who else!) dropped a bedstead on his foot! The reality is that a series of events had unforeseen consequences that led to the toe incident in the hotel room.

Normally the loss of England's prolific goalscoring midfield captain to an avoidable injury would have seen huge negative headlines back home but this time around the incident was hushed up. I should know as I did some of the hushing!

After such a fraught build up and the recriminations following the dour draw with the Irish, the mood in the camp was far more relaxed after an impressive performance against the Dutch and squeezing past Egypt to qualify from the group, which hadn't look at all likely after that opening game. Only three games in and it had already been a roller coaster of emotions within the camp.

It might have seemed a touch premature to be giving the players a day off just three games into the tournament, but Bobby Robson could see that his players had become bored and listless because of all the intense build up to the tournament on the training ground and hidden away at their team hotel, and the England manager wanted to reward them for qualifying from the group and after all the pressure felt they needed to unwind. Unwind they certainly did and, in the true traditions of players of that era, they 'refuelled' as Graham Taylor later describe it.

The modern thinking is that players need to be close to the city centre and be more like tourists and see the sights and be part of the location rather than hermits. Managers tended to be extreme, for every Fabio Capello, who imposed strict isolation on his squad, others are far too lenient. After so many weeks away from home and by now fed up with the gizmos, gadgets and games the FA had laid on for them, the players opted to spend some time at the Forte Village on one of their rare days off as Gary Lineker's wife was staying there with some friends close to the England party, so it was the natural place to which to gravitate. They just wanted a change of scenery but were no doubt aware that this was where the dreaded enemy 'The Press' were staying!

The media group would split into cliques, something that might not have been encouraged with the team groups, but it was inevitable that journalists would mix with their mates. My group were nicknamed The Morris Men; we enjoyed each other's company but I can only assume it was dreamed up by those outside of this group, and not in any complimentary way! One suggestion I heard was that we were all dancing in step together, there were one or two other suggestions I won't bother to repeat!

The Morris Men comprised Colin Gibson, the *Daily Telegraph* chief football writer, Stuart Jones, chief football writer for *The Times*, Steve Curry, chief football writer of the *Daily Express*, and myself. We travelled everywhere together; same flights, same hotels, same dinner venues, same after dinner clubs or drinking holes. There was a great camaraderie, but also implicit trust that, despite being on rival newspapers, we would often share inside tips, stories, and quotes. Or if there was an exclusive we would make each other aware of what we were doing so it didn't come as a surprise and we could prepare a story for our own paper with an inside track.

Colin Gibson was the first to leave our group when he opted to move up to Sports Editor of the *Daily Mail*. When he heard that I was leaving *The Mirror* for the *Express*, he took me to lunch and offered me a post on the *Mail*, but he was unable to pull it off, as I was committed to the *Express* with a lucrative offer from owner Richard Desmond himself. Colin then moved into football administration, first with the Football Association as Head of Communications and straight into one of their biggest controversies with Sven-Göran Eriksson. He enjoyed his new position during the World Cup tournament in 2002, but quickly became a high profile victim of the Eriksson-Faria Alam affair. Once it became public knowledge that the FA chief executive at that time, Mark Palios, had also been sleeping with Miss Alam he lost his prestigious post and Colin quickly followed him out of the door. Colin's mistake was to try to make a pact with the devil, a Sunday newspaper, to protect his FA employers by spinning a particular version of the story which was not precisely the truth, but it backfired badly. It underlines the pitfalls even for a vastly experienced journalist such as Colin, to deal with newspapers when the stakes are high can have dire consequences.

When I first started out editors often called the sports desk, and its personnel, the "Toy Department', because of the softer life style and easy going approach that accompanies sports coverage as opposed to hard-nosed news gathering. The two extremes often merge and more often it is hard for those on the receiving end to distinguish between the two, that's why it was an error of judgement on Colin's part to try to deal with the sector of the industry that takes no prisoners. He could have continued for many years in his role as FA's head of communications had he not been caught out being so naïve as to attempt to pull off such a clandestine deal behind the scenes. The tables were turned on an ex-journalist by a current one. It was dog eat dog, at its best, or worst, depending on which way you look at it.

Colin moved on to become head of communications for the Cricket Board of England and Wales, and as cricket was his first passion, being a none too shabby performer in his own right in his youth, more recently he has moved overseas.

The other two Morris men have both passed away. Stuart Jones, a heavy smoker, departed to his beloved Caribbean to see out his final few days with incurable lung cancer, while Steve Curry had a triple heart bypass but survived for a further 20 plus years before departing more recently.

Yet memories of the Morris Men will linger on in Fleet Street legend for sure, none more so than the exploits of the Morris Men at Italia '90. It would be a surprise if the drinking session with the England World Cup stars is not part of that legend.

The morning of the 'Battle of Broken Toe' we spent in our rooms filing copy to our respective newspaper having stored some material knowing it was to be a day off, so no media briefings at the training camp. We then planned lunch together at the beach-side restaurant, followed by a spot of sun bathing before watching one of the late afternoon World Cup ties in my hotel room which was the nearest to the beach and by far the biggest so it could accommodate us all very comfortably. My balcony alone contained two large sun loungers, a hammock and a table and four chairs, overlooking the sea.

Stuart and I enjoyed hours of sun bathing, the larger sized gentlemen in our four-man team, Colin and Steve, were not that keen, propping up a bar, having a sing-song and reciting Shakespeare was much more Steve's scene and Colin was the head of the social committee, so enjoyed a group gathering and a chat.

The four of us gathered at our usual spot on the beach, but it wasn't long before Steve and Colin were restless and opted for a stroll along the water's edge to cool down before deciding which one of the numerous beach bars to have a beer in the shade.

Stuart and I waited for quite some time, in fact just seconds before the next World Cup tie was due to kick off before hastily trying to locate the other two. After a short look around we assumed the pair were lost or drunk or probably both, so we made our way back to my room having missed the first half. We had only strolled about 150 yards when we caught sight of half a dozen England stars with Steve and Colin propping up the bar nearest to our spot on the beach. They actually hadn't gone far, but had stayed quite some time. Wisely we did a quick U-turn, beating a hasty retreat to find another path to the hotel determined to watch what remained of the game. Knocking back the beers were the likes of Bryan Robson, the captain leading by example, Chris Waddle, Trevor Steven, Terry Butcher and Paul Gascoigne.

After the match Stuart made his way back to his room to change and prepare for the evening meal and the late night entertainment. It was dusk by the time I received a loud knock on my door. There stood Colin and Steve. Well, I say stood. More like swayed. Neither of them were able to utter a word, at least not a decipherable word. Still in their shorts and covered in sand, they looked like synchronised divers as they simultaneously belly-flopped face down onto one of my two double beds, snoring before they even hit the mattress.

I got ready and left them spark out. And they were still snoring away as I left the room for dinner and when I returned. It seemed like a sensible solution for us all to enjoy a relatively early night. Steve and Colin needed to sleep it off but I remember wondering what state the players would be in.

The next day was the last at the Forte Village before moving onto a new venue to prepare for the knock out stages. It was rather a downer of an evening as we had all got used to the sheer luxury of the Forte Village, having spent six weeks there using it as a base, with a media centre stocked up with the sponsor's booze and food and all the amenities to help you put up with such a lengthy time away from home concentrating totally on work, although fitting in some down time as well; although there might have been a few who liked the time away from home.

At around midnight, as we were making our way outside of the Village in search of a local bar, Steve received a message to call Bryan

Robson, Steve was close to Bobby, but also had a firm friendship with Bryan. He was a big Manchester United fan, and had known Bryan for some considerable time. Although the England/FA party and its entourage were decamping from their hotel base at around 9.30 am the following morning, and the media group were all packed up and ready to make their own journey to the venue for the last 16, Bryan would be heading off to Cagliari airport to catch a 6.30 am flight to Rome, where he would then make the connection to London and then the shuttle home to Manchester.

He would be making the journey alone.

I decided that I would go straight back to my room for a good night's sleep, although the other three continued with plans to continue to a local bar for a final drink.

The media had heard the captain was carrying an injury, indeed he'd come off after an hour of the goalless draw with Holland, but no one had said just how serious it had been nor did anyone have a clue that he was on his way home and would be on the first available flight to Rome. Bryan had told Steve that the information he was giving him was strictly confidential for the time being, although an announcement was being planned for the next morning, but too late for anyone to be able to catch up with him on his way home but he didn't have any objection if the four of us just happened to turn up early at the airport and he wouldn't object to us having a brief word with him before his departure.

I was back in my room for around 1.30am that night to finish off the packing and to prepare for an early morning alarm call. We all decided we needed a 5am alarm call and that we would be straight out the door, into the car hire and straight to the airport knowing the car had to be returned before we caught the flight to Rome and to change our tickets to ensure we were switched to the same flight as Robbo for what would be a major story with only the four of us having the inside track. It was a cracking story, a great coup for the four of us representing different sectors of the media, so not really direct rivals.

Robbo was rewarding us for keeping quiet about what had occurred during the drinking session at the Forte Village, of which Steve and Colin had first-hand knowledge, and had confided only in Stuart and myself. It was old school journalism, we still believed what happened on tour, stayed on tour. But that was much harder to control with the sporting media mushrooming with so many hardened hacks around discovering the gossip, and just one wrong word out of place and the cat would have been out of the bag.

Robbo had confessed to Steve that when he and the other England players had returned back to their team hotel from that boozy all day session in the Forte Village, Bobby Robson was none too pleased to hear about some of the antics. Gazza was still riding the bike he had taken from the Village and the manager rightly suspected that Gazza wasn't alone in the high jinks.

Robbo told Steve he had gone back to his room for a shower to sober up, but cracked his toe getting into the shower. I have also subsequently heard that he was actually in his room with Gazza larking around as usual and lifting up the bed which then fell on Robbo's toe. Whichever version is correct, Robbo confessed that it was a self-inflicted injury and not an authentic one he picked up in the game as had been stated by the FA.

The four of us, of course, respected the confidentiality of this episode. Not for a second was it tempting to write an exclusive article by naming informed sources and the like. We knew the accuracy of the story, but there were always more stories down the line, and we still believed in the integrity of the job, and the sanctity of confidentiality, so if someone tells you something in the strictest confidence you respect it, irrespective of how big a story it would have been on the day.

Although still very much blurry-eyed, the Morris Men were quickly on our early morning mission to travel to Rome with Robbo the next morning. We had paid up our bills, and were on our way long before our colleagues were awake.

Colin, who was the tour leader of the Morris Men, had organised the trip down to the last detail, so he was in charge of returning the hire car. I was put in charge of the tickets and passports. I put my own in my top pocket, and the three others on the car dashboard. When we arrived at the airport, with all our luggage to contend with, I made the dash to the check in counter to book us all on the same flight as Robbo. When I got there, I could only find my own passport and tickets.

Oh no! I'd left the others on the dashboard, and there was no time to dash back to retrieve them! The other guys all rushed back to the parking lot, while I was the only one able to switch tickets and get on board the flight. Needless to say the other three were livid. If they'd known better they might have thought I had done it intentionally! I'm sure it must have crossed their minds. We were all highly competitive journalists, well, perhaps not Stuart Jones on *The Times*, he was far too high brow for scrabbling around chasing stories. But they had known me long enough to know that is something I wouldn't do to them. There had developed a unique bond between us which included an uncompromising trust. They knew that had I pulled a fast one like that the Morris Men would be no more. So, they knew it was not a deliberate act to sabotage their opportunity for a one to one with the departing Robbo, leaving me with the 'exclusive'. Well, it wasn't an exclusive as I promised to call them immediately we landed in Rome, where I would pass on all the quotes to them. My paper wouldn't be the least bit concerned if *The Times*, or *The Telegraph* had the quotes, nor indeed *The Express*, as they saw The Soaraway Sun as the only real rival of importance to them and possibly the increasingly popular *Daily Star*.

My fellow Morris Men had an insight into my character, they knew how disorganised I could be, they knew I was a non driver, with no sense of direction, who could fall asleep the moment I got into the car, and this particular morning was no different. This was a typical act of incompetence on my part of which there had been many previous examples. I was good at my job, maybe, but a disaster when it came to things like this. How they must have regretted putting me in charge of their passports and tickets!

I felt for them, and felt so awful. I knew they were angry, it was so frustrating to get up early, rush to the airport, to be part of the day's big story, one of the biggest of the World Cup, only to miss out. While the tabloids would only be interested in the big headline and the semi exclusive quotes, the other guys would have been keen to have written about the 'colour' feature-type material that would have gone with actually being on the flight home with Robbo. Instead they were left waving us goodbye from the tarmac like lemons. Whoops!

On board Robbo was worried that the real reason for the injury would emerge, but I reassured him that none of us would break a confidence, which would undoubtedly have seen him ridiculed across the nation's front pages if the truth had got out back then. That made him feel just a touch better, as I know he would have trusted us. But he knew that it was a self inflicted injury and that made the pain of his World Cup exit even harder to bear. But, of course, it was a huge embarrassment and as well as the four Morris Men keeping quiet about it, the England captain would expect the players to have kept the secrets of the dressing room but Gazza broke ranks when he discussed it in his autobiography.

In his own autobiography, *Robbo*, he contradicted Gazza's version of events when he turned to the contentious issues around this injury, when he wrote: "The gaffer was less impressed with his players - and this one in particular - after a bit of messing around left me with a bloody big toe. This was an incident that Gazza claimed in his book ended my World Cup, which he now accepts was a load of rubbish. We were at our training camp in Sardinia, and our first match was still several days away. A few of us fancied a last drink before the tournament started, so we went to a local bar. Gazza says Bobby found out we were missing and sent the police after us. Well, we did hear police sirens as we walked back to the hotel, but that was nothing to do with us. There must have been some trouble in the town. When we got back we went to Gazza's room and started larking about. I tried to tip Gazza off his bed and caught my big toenail on the corner. I had no shoes on and it ripped the top off my toenail. It was bleeding badly, so I went into the bathroom to try to staunch the flow. I had to have an injection in it to kill the pain to play in the first game. Bobby went mad at me and rightly so. He comes over as a nice Uncle Bobby, but he could be tough if he felt he had to be and he had a right go at me for pratting about that night.

"Gazza says in his book that we were absolutely legless, which isn't right. He also says I broke my toe, which I didn't. Worst of all, he says, that it was after the second match and was the real reason why I went home from the World Cup. It happened, so I've said, before our first match and I had to pull out of the tournament because of an Achilles injury, which I got in our second match. I have told Gazza he got it totally wrong about that night and he was distraught. he said, 'I just didn't know what was going on then, Bryan. If I got the story wrong, I'm sorry.' As we all know, Gazza has had his problems. He has been in such a mess at certain stages of his life that there was a lot he couldn't remember clearly. We've not fallen out. We've managed to stay pals even though he's given me a few headaches over the years."

Well, that's not how the Morris Men remember it, and only Colin and myself are still alive to tell the tale. Strangely, there was no mention of the Morris Men turning up at the airport, or that I was on his flight to Rome when he penned his autobiography! But the truth was still raw way back then.

On the day of the World Cup draw in Leipzig for the 2006 tournament in Germany, a good friend and associate of mine Andy Sutherden of Public Relations company Hill & Knowlton hired me to join David Platt and Martin Peters to provide expert media comment to TV, radio and internet for one of his sponsors, ostensibly to discuss England's opponents and World Cup prospects, but also to promote Gillette's newly sponsored official 'FIFA inaugural Young Player of the World Cup' award. At one stage David and I were sharing a radio booth doing back-to-back local radio shows. One of the main discussion points was about retrospective best young players of the tournament as a way of promoting the sponsors new initiative and, talking about Maradona, Bryan Robson's name cropped up and I kind of cheekily asked David if he knew the real reason why Robbo was forced to fly home disconsolately from Italia '90, and how his broken toe had come about? I knew David had known because he, like me, was there, of course, but he wasn't saying. Live on air Platt challenged me to divulge all, but I brushed that aside. A few minutes earlier, while off the air during a break in broadcasting, we had both been talking about Robbo's injury - and we both knew the truth.

Paul Parker's version, as he discovered inside the camp, was that Robson damaged his left toe while having a test of strength "in a lifting competition" with one of the team hotel's cast-iron beds! "The actual bed dropped on Bryan's toe." Parker added, "Just as well it never became public knowledge at the time."

That Gascoigne was involved in such a serious mishap was hardly a surprise. He was a central figure on and off the pitch, as Lineker recollects: "He was bright in those days, witty, and his practical jokes were unsurpassed. He'd drive you crazy occasionally, especially playing with him – he never passed unless he was either exhausted or you had no alternative but to give it him straight back."

BRYAN ROBSON

I will now nail the truth!

I look back on Italia '90 in one way with a great sense of achievement as it was my third World Cup Finals, but also in another way, that again it was a great disappointment having suffered the shoulder injury in Mexico and now having to comeback early from Italy and then be out of action for some time after that.

What I remember most about Italia '90 is being captain of such a fantastic group of lads who fought back from such adversity, there were so many problems for the manager Bobby Robson, and the lads getting so much stick before the tournament and then doing so well that they might even have won it. For all those reasons the lads had a terrific World Cup. Everyone moaned about our performance against the Irish but it was a much tougher game than anyone realised at the time, but we knew it would be tough as they beat us in the Euros. They were determined and had some very decent players, the media didn't understand how difficult it can be, especially in opening games. Holland had won the European championship two years earlier and had outstanding players but we did well against them, and even Egypt had some good players, two brothers who were outstanding. The Irish and the Dutch struggled in their other games, so it wasn't that easy to navigate out of the qualifying group.

Sorry if it's a bit of a pun, but I want to 'nail' the reasons why I came back, and they were not because of the incident with Gazza and my toe nail! I got back to see a specialist about my Achilles which I felt snap during the Holland game. I had an operation immediately I returned to Manchester with the club surgeon and then had to have a second operation in London with Mr King who has performed this type of surgery on Olympic athletes.

I managed to do a bit of TV, first in the studio with Terry Venables and Jimmy Hill, and it was disappointing not to be out there with the lads.

I asked the surgeon what the problem was and he said it was wear and tear over the past seven years and it could have happened in three months or three years but it was always going to happen. People keep telling me I returned from the World Cup because of what happened with my toe and Gazza but that is bollocks. It all came about when Gazza mentioned it in his book.

What happened was that we were larking about in my room when I tipped Gazza off the bed and as the bed slid along, the bedstead dropped on my toe, but it didn't break the toe as some people have said, it flicked part of the nail off and bruised it.

I came back because I felt my Achilles 'ping' against Holland and I snapped the Achilles, it had gone, and I couldn't walk as a result of it. I always got on really well with Bobby Robson and when I was injured in Mexico he asked me to stay on to help with the morale of the group, and he asked me if I would do the same in Italy but Sir Alex wanted me back to have an operation straight away so as not to miss too much of the new season, and in Mexico it was my shoulder so I was at least mobile, this time I could hardly walk and my mood wasn't good and I didn't feel it was right to be in a bad mood around the camp, so I flew home.

I broke my legs when I was 19 and 21 but other than that I don't think I had that many injuries, certainly not as many as people seem to think; they say that I was injured all the time, that's not the case. The problem is that I was injured in two World Cups and they are massive so that has been highlighted.

Gazza got up to all sorts of tricks but I suppose the one that stands out for me is the one that involved my missus and the other players wives and girlfriends. They were at our hotel until we got down to more intensive training and we spent a day on the beach where all the girls took out pedalos. Gazza thought it was a brilliant idea to go out to each pedalo and tip the girls out of them. They were not happy about that, and my missus was one of them. But he was up to all sorts of things, some made us laugh, but some of them were not quite so funny. At times he would upset Bobby Robson. The manager told us not to over do things but Gazza was always on the tennis court or playing table tennis, and would be out on the golf course when the manager told him not to. He was competitive in everything he did, but generally he was a load of laughs.

We had great fun as a group with our race nights with Gary Lineker and Peter Shilton as the bookies but one night we got our physio Fred

Street to break the seal on the racing video so we knew who won a particular race. We all bet on every horse apart from the one we knew would actually win. Then we persuaded Gazza to bet a couple of hundred quid on this horse, which at that time was a fair amount of money. The horse was at long odds and started at the back and worked his way to the front, just winning on the line. Gazza won an awful lot of money but the bookies were not happy, especially when they later found out what had been going on and they kicked up a huge fuss and said they shouldn't have to pay up!

PETER SHILTON

Bobby's Mogadon pre-match speech went on and on... until I had to ask him to stop!

Bobby Robson liked a team meeting, and before the Belgium game he gave one of his longest team meetings before we left for the ground. The players loved Bobby, and we all respected him, but his team meetings could go on a bit, and the lads used to call him 'Mogadon' and we would say we don't need sleeping pills after one of the boss's team meetings.

So we arrived at the stadium after one of Bobby's classic lengthy team meetings. At the stadium each player has their own routine, some like to leave it late before they change, some like to change to give themselves plenty of time before they go out to warm up. Those changed first went out for a warm up, but when we came back in, and with some players still not changed yet, Bobby sat us all down and started the team meeting all over again, making virtually all the same points all over again. I'm thinking "Christ, this is going to turn into another of Bobby's 'Mogadon' meetings". It was already going on far longer than any of would have liked. The 'curtains' came down for a few; Gazza never listened to Bobby's team talks at the best of times, and I could see him going into this little world of his own, and the rest of the players were also looking perplexed, and started looking at each other, then they started looking at me as the senior player. They wanted Bobby to wrap it up, as they were beginning to lose concentration anyway on what he was saying. Some had not even got changed yet!

"Excuse me Boss...," I started. Then Bobby looked at his watch and said, "Ok lads, I'll finish off now then, I think I lost all track of time."

Bobby always got everyone's name wrong, and the one I remember the most is when he called Mark Wright over, then went into a deep thinking mode, and told Mark he didn't need him, so Mark left, then Bobby called him over again, and started to talking to him thinking he was Mike Kelly the goalkeeping coach!

Gazza was the real joker of the pack, but I tended to steer clear of his antics if possible. I can remember in Albania for a World Cup qualifier, we were allowed into the stadium the day before and Bobby Robson insisted that our session was strictly private as he wanted to practise set plays and didn't want the opposition finding out what he had planned. As we ran onto the pitch we saw thousands of fans streaming into the stadium, there must have been 3,000, and Bobby told us "we will leave the set plays for today". At the end of the training session two stay on for some shooting practise. Chris Woods went in goal and about three or four of the lads, including Links and Gazza, started shooting practise which lasted about 10 minutes and I was watching the finishing session. Gazza went over to the crowd as he went over to take his shot, and waved his arms at them as the crowd started to shout "whoosh" as he ran up and then shot, and after his shot Gazza put his fingers to his lips and the entire crowd feel silent - you could hear a pin drop. He did this a few times and every time they build up toward his shot until it reached a crescendo when he struck the ball, and then they fell totally silent. Only Gazza could do something like that.

My best moment of Italia '90 was reaching the semi-final, it was a great achievement, and beating Cameroon I thought I had a pretty good game in terms of what I had to do. My worst moment was that fluke of a Germany goal. It was a free kick so I was on my line ready for whichever direction the free kick might come at the goal over the wall or straight at me but they knocked it square, so I came out a few yards to narrow the angle but it took a wicked deflection and went more or less over my head into the net. I was caught square on facing the shot, whereas the technique would be to be sideways on to get back using your feet and then jump into it, but being square on it went over my head, something goalkeepers can't legislate for, it was a fluke deflection. I was pretty pleased when Gary Lineker equalised as I felt I had a really good game and made two or three good saves, particularly one from Klinsmann, only to be beaten by a fluke.

I'd saved a penalty from Andreas Brehme before when he shot to my right, so I figured he would remember that and shot to my left. I guessed right, as I guessed right in all of the four penalties I faced, but they all went into the corner just inside the post like rockets giving me no chance to make a save.

Some of the lads didn't want to take the pens, but Chrissie stepped up, he had been really great in the game but unfortunately his pen went over the bar and we were out. We were so close, it's the worst feeling going out on penalties when we were the better team.

ON TO BOLOGNA AND BELGIUM

England were now based at the Novotel in Castenaso where Gazza was given a belated birthday present by his advisors Mel Stein and Len Lazarus of Union Jack swimming shorts, bright socks and underwear. A birthday cake from the hotel was delivered to the side of the pool and with the TV cameras there Chris Waddle said, "how many birthdays are you going to have?" His Geordie room-mate didn't wait for a reply as he slammed the cake into Gazza's face!

Gazza's response? "Lovely, chocolate"

The build-up contained the usual Gazza antics that both amused and infuriated the England camp in equal measure, depending on your sense of humour and how much of Gazza's whirlwind behaviour you could take!

Paul Parker recalled: "On the day of the game Gazza was playing tennis against an American couple at the team hotel. That kept him occupied. I think he'd had a swim and a sauna as well – things that you were not supposed to be doing, but that was Paul. He was a total one-off. He never slept. His whole purpose in life was to communicate with people, that's all he wanted to do."

Of course his team-mates have always been supportive, and to the majority it was a way of eating up the tense hours before kick-off. Gazza was better than calling in any comedy act. For the management, though, it was a constant nightmare and an endless source of worry keeping track of Gazza's erratic and unpredictable movements and wondering what might go wrong.

This was a tie that would determine England's stature as a potential World Cup challenger, with a quarter-final against Cameroon the prize for victory. The game had the potential to change the mood of the campaign overnight.

Paul Parker sets the scene: "Bologna was a beautiful ground with its own church and a long passage underneath to get from the pitch to the dressing room and I remember noticing how I was no longer nervous. I sat in the dressing room listening to 'Soul to Soul" on my head set, oblivious to the outside world. It was a sort of ritual I had developed during the competition and I was not about to drop it now with a possible final no longer a pipe dream.

"As soon as we came out onto the pitch in front of a huge and vociferous crowd I got racist abuse from the Belgium fans and, I fear, from some of our own as well. I found it bemusing that the Belgians should stoop to this, but luckily it made little difference to my performance."

Racism and hooliganism, the twin towers of England fans abroad, were never far from the scene, they were a headline waiting to happen, and the English always seemed to be a major incident away from expulsion. Trouble was never far away regarding the army of travelling fans as they became as much a target, sometimes the victims, as well as the perpetrators of their evil intent. As if to underline this, an England fan from Coventry was in intensive car after being struck by a car. Sadly, he later died. English vandals decimated nearby Rimini. Tanks lined the streets to the ground as armed police conducted searches.

The players, though, were oblivious to the growing fears of the tournament organisers and within the FA, of the mounting issues with the fans that might derail Bobby Robson's team, more so than the threat on the field posed by Belgium.

The management kept the players away from these issues as much as they could, and instead players like Paul Parker were overjoyed to be involved, which made them hugely motivated as he explained: "The side of the draw that we were in suited us. But Belgium were very experienced and had a great player in Enzo Scifo. He was a fantastic footballer – and he knew he was good too. There was an arrogance about him... I was nervous because the only tournament football I'd had for England was as a youth player. I had so many No. 12 shirts leading up to that World Cup because I'd been on the bench so many times. I thought I'd go to the World Cup and only be doing warm-ups. Lo and behold I ended up playing six games. And that tournament was the first time I'd ever played at wing-back."

England players suddenly realised they were three victories away from the final, and expectation was growing back home, but once they arrived at the stadium, they had that familiar feeling of a job about to be done, they were vastly experienced internationals. Peter Shilton: "There was quite an atmosphere in Bologna. I remember walking out before the game, looking at the stadium and thinking how beautiful and unique it was. There was that brickwork around the tower inside the ground. It felt different to anywhere I'd ever played."

With the stakes rising Bobby Robson again switched Mark Wright to the sweeper role and reintroduced Terry Butcher. Again Gascoigne thrived in the new formation with ever-growing confidence freeing him to use his prodigious talent to pull the Belgians from one side of the pitch to another.

England's World Cup changed on that balmy night in Bologna when, following a tense 119 minutes which could have gone either way, David Platt swiveled and hit an unforgettable last-gasp volley in extra-time to secure a last 16 victory over an Enzo Scifo-inspired Belgium. In truth the Belgians had been the better team for much of the 120 minutes and had struck the woodwork three times so England were extremely fortunate to go through. "They deserved to beat us," Terry Butcher later confessed, "but that's football and David Platt made his name with the volley that won it."

For a player like Chris Waddle, who had adapted to the nuances of the new system by plying his arts in France, it was a case of adjusting to a new style of play, "In the first 20 minutes we were still getting used to our system, because Bobby Robson altered to a 3-5-2 at that World Cup. We had a lot of technical players and to get the best out of them a 4-4-2 probably wouldn't have taken us past Belgium. So Bobby was brave enough to change it. I went into midfield with Gazza and Steve McMahon, so for me it was a little more like how I played at Marseille, where I had that license to go inside and find space. For years for England I wanted to be given a bit more freedom and I think John Barnes was in the same boat as me. It was really frustrating. I used to watch teams and think about the rave reviews their flair players received while the system we played was all about running up and down.

"In 1990 it was different. We had a good balance to that team with John playing off Gary Lineker, and David Platt, after he came into the side, timing his runs well to get into the box. The defence was quick with Des Walker and Paul Parker, and Mark Wright was ideal for bringing the ball out from the back. Football-wise we were as good as anyone else."

But, again, as the game ticked gently through the 90 minutes and then deep into extra-time, the tension grew. Not only was a place in the quarter-finals at stake, both teams knew that Cameroon, the rank outsiders, were waiting. It was reasonable to assume that if England could snatch a winner, they would be odds-on favourites for a place in the semi-final and then, who knows?

Yet Belgium were a high quality continental team and it showed in their technique to take immediate control of the tie. It was a worrying start for England as Shilton observed: "I made a save early on – for us to go 1-0 down then would have been a bit of a disaster. There was also a bit of a let-off when Jan Ceulemans turned and hit the angle of crossbar and post, so we rode our luck there."

But England had gained in confidence as the tournament progressed, and even in this match there were signs of that progression as Waddle makes clear, "We managed to get on the ball a bit more later in the first half and had a good spell when I thought we were going to score. John Barnes actually did score, with a volley, but it was wrongly ruled out for offside. If VAR was around back then it would have counted."

However, Enzo Scifo, one of the tournament's shining lights took command and in reality deserved to have given Belgium the lead as Parker confessed: "Early in the second half Scifo hit the post with a tremendous 30-yard shot, and how that didn't go in I don't know."

It was one of the defining moments of England's World Cup, but for Shilton he was far more relaxed than anyone watching in the stadium or in their millions back home, "people laugh when I say this, but I never thought when I dived that Scifo's shot was going to beat me. It did bend a bit more at the last minute and ended up hitting the middle of the post. But I was sure it wasn't going in." Really? Everyone else watching on thought that was curling in, even his team-mates but Shilts was one of the world's greatest keepers, no longer in his prime perhaps but experienced enough to know. So let's bow to his expertise.

For Waddle it was hardly a surprise that the man most likely to undo England was Scifo, as he explained: "I had played against him in France, so I knew he was a real talent, and I told the lads that if he gets within 30 yards of goal he'll shoot. I'd seen him do it a lot. A minute or so after that Scifo effort I got the ball and released Gary [Lineker], who spun in behind the Belgium defence – we always had a good understanding like that."

For Parker it was Waddle who was England's shining light in this game, "Scifo was an arrogant opponent, but a brilliant one, twice almost scoring, but I felt he was upstaged that day by Waddle. Chris was a top class player at the height of his career. He was a calming influence in front of me and he made my World Cup a whole lot easier by his encouragement, his positioning and his great skill."

Bobby Robson made the decision to bring on Aston Villa's David Platt in the second half and it lifted the team. "With about 20 minutes to go Bobby took off a more defensive player in McMahon and brought on Platt," Paul Parker recalls, "his game was all about ghosting into the box. Bobby was looking to win the match. David wasn't going to win you big tackles; he was a player who would make forward runs and try to nick a goal."

David Platt: "I started as a substitute. I can remember little snatches of the game. John Barnes having a volleyed goal harshly disallowed, Belgium hitting the woodwork twice, I can still see Enzo Scifo hitting the post with a tremendous strike from 25 yards. I was at the other end of the bench from Bobby Robson and didn't have much contact with him. Having since been a manager I now know that the emotions he must have been going through were far more intense than mine. I came on for Steve McMahon [in the 71st minute]."

Robson made another brave move. Steve Bull: "I had started the game before against Egypt, when Mark Wright scored, but Bobby changed it for the Belgium match and I was sitting on the bench – it was still amazing to be there. I came on for John Barnes in the 74th minute, and Bobby just asked me to do exactly the same for England as I do for my club."

Gazza's booking against West Germany in the semi-final is the one that is shown over and over again, the one that spawned the tears and one of the World Cup's most iconic moments, but who remembers when Gazza got booked for the first time? The second yellow might have been his undoing but the first was just as unnecessary. Shilton: "Just before the end of normal time, Gazza got booked for a bad tackle from behind on Scifo. It was a little bit of petulance and he shouldn't have whacked him. Obviously that rebounded on him later on in the tournament."

At 90 minutes there were mixed emotions within the Belgium camp with most feeling huge disappointment because they believed overall they had out outplayed England and should have gone through without the need for extra time or potential penalties, while others were uplifted by being the better team and so felt that they would eventually prevail in extra time. Parker could understand their optimism, but added, "Their chances were highlighted because they hit the post. But we created opportunities too." Steve Bull recalls a 20-yarder from the left-hand side of the area with his right foot that the keeper just pushed around the post, the Wolves man recalls: "I thought: 'Oh my word, if that had gone in I'd have been massive back in England.'"

Waddle felt the game was drifting towards the dreaded penalty shoot-out, and perhaps both sides were satisfied with that: "As the game went on you could see both teams thinking that they didn't want to give anything away, so you become a bit more cautious, playing no-risk football. I couldn't see anyone scoring." Shilton agreed: "As the minutes ticked away, it started to cross my mind that this could be our first penalty shootout with England."

It might have been fatigue, both psychological as well as physical, that appeared to allow both sides to settle for penalties, but the England players would rather have avoided it as Parker recalls, "I was thinking whatever happens, Peter Shilton is going to take one before me." It was a long and tense night. John Barnes, whose performances had been concerning Robson, had controversially had a goal disallowed, while Walker and Wright were carrying injuries from the start, as England faced extra-time for the first time since 1970.

But there was no need to worry, Gazza sorted it out. Setting off on a long lung-bursting 40 yard run from within his own half with just 2 minutes left in extra time, he beat a couple of men before a desperate Belgian hauled him to the ground – free kick, central about 40 yards from goal and Gazza decided to do something different as Waddle reveals: "Just before the end of extra time Gazza took off on a run from inside his own half and was brought down. To be fair they probably had to foul him because there was a good chance we would have scored or at least created something. I remember standing over the free-kick with Gazza and saying: 'What are you thinking here?' When he told me what he had in mind I thought it was quite an awkward ball that he was trying to play. Normally you'd try and clip it right to left for people to go and head. So when Gazza went to play it I was thinking: 'I can't see this happening, it's too straight.'"

Into the 119th minute and Gascoigne stood over the ball waiting to take a free-kick which would also probably be the final kick of the game. It was central and too far out for a shot and too central to fizz in a cross so he floated a 40 yard pass towards the back-post where David Platt was standing. Platt watched the ball drop over his shoulder and, with his eyes bulging through concentration, he hooked it across the face of 'keeper Michel Preud'Homme's goal and into the net. At that moment England were alive. The country was swamped with an optimism summed up by Gary Lineker's face in the ensuing celebratory scrum caught by the TV cameras. In pubs up and down the land there was an emotional release after 119 minutes of unremitting tension.

It later transpired that some of the Belgium players heard yells from the England bench as they thought Gazza might take a short free kick, but in the traditional English style when the pressure is on, it is best to loft it into the 'mixer', get it in the box and hope for the best.

John Motson recalled: "Bobby Robson and the England bench were signalling frantically as to what they thought they should do with this free-kick but I don't think Paul Gascoigne was paying any attention at all. Gazza floated his free-kick into the penalty area and David Platt, who was quite new then to international football, swivelled and volleyed it into the net."

Paul Parker could see what Gazza had in mind: "Gazza had a big run-up but slowed down as he got to the ball and sort of stunned it, almost putting backspin on it. It was like the ball hit a soft-padded wall and dropped down."

Steve Bull thought it was aimed at him, "Platty was stood in front of me. I was shouting: 'Leave it, leave it.'" There was no chance of that happening. The ball went over the head of midfielder Franky Van der Elst, who knew instinctively as he missed it that Platt was behind him and would score. But no one expected execution of such perfection, and it seemed that it even surprised the goalscorer who dropped to his knees in thanks.

Waddle was a genius with the ball, one of the great technicians of that England era and even he was in awe, "Platty's technique was second to none. If you were trying to demonstrate how to volley a ball over your shoulder, I don't think you could get anything better than that. His timing was perfect. If Messi or Ronaldo scored a goal like that today, we'd rave about it."

John Motson, commentating on BBC1 in extra-time after 119 goalless minutes: "Gerets challenges Gascoigne. Free-kick given to England …"

Platt: "It was the last minute. There was a free-kick in the centre."

Motson: "… Gascoigne shaping to take it …"

Platt: "Gazza was on it. I was in the box trying to get a yard or half of space."

Motson: "… and chipped in …"

Platt: "I was spinning, the ball dropped over my shoulder and I just tried to get something on it."

Motson: "… and volleyed in …"

Platt: "There wasn't a great deal of power. It was all technique."

Motson: "… and it's there! …"

Platt: "I saw it going in and fell to my knees."

Motson: "… by David Platt! …"

Platt: "Everything was intuitive, the way I met and hit the ball and then dropping to my knees. Instinct just took over. I'd never ever dropped to my knees after scoring before, I don't know why I did.'

Motson: "… England have done it! In the last minute of extra-time!"

Platt: "But when you score a goal like that you just go outside yourself for a bit, everything is surreal. The adrenaline surge is so great it's as if I really was in a different place, a different world."

Motson: "… That's the biggest smile in world football tonight – David Platt of Aston Villa."

Platt: "Don't get me wrong, the goal wasn't a fluke. I had an eye for getting on the end of that sort of ball and the technical ability to finish those chances off. I worked hard on practising overhead kicks and volleys in training at Aston Villa but, even so, if I had re-enacted that chance against Belgium 10 times in training the next day there's a very good chance I wouldn't have scored once from it. It was just one of life's rare, perfect moments."

Motson: "He turned, volleyed and what a good finish."

Platt: "The one place where things didn't go right was almost as soon as I left the pitch. One minute I was euphoric and the next I was being hauled off for a random drug test. It was hot and you're so dehydrated after playing that it took 40 minutes – which passed very, very slowly – for me to produce a sample. I was in a room with a couple of Belgians who were seriously unhappy because they'd just been knocked out. I didn't know what to say. By the time I came out the other players all had their suits on and the euphoria had passed."

Motson: "One of the most dramatic goals in the World Cup – and probably one of the best. England through to the quarter-finals of the World Cup."

Bobby Robson showed how much it meant as he danced a jig of delight on the touchline. It hadn't been easy but England's victory was one in the eye for those who had forecast an early departure. At the very least they had matched their quarter-final placing from 1986, and gone further in Italy than such nations as Brazil, the Netherlands, Spain and USSR who had already departed.

Platt: "After finally getting back to the hotel and having something to eat I decided it was too late to phone my then girlfriend, now my wife, Rachel. For some reason I thought she'd be in bed and annoyed if I woke her up. In reality everyone was having a party and expecting a call from me. Nowadays my mobile phone would have been going mad with texts and voice messages but in 1990 the England squad were isolated from everything.

"If I hadn't scored that goal, I might still have ended up playing in Italy [Platt went on to play for Bari, Juventus and Sampdoria] but, realistically, I'm sure it was the catalyst. Italian clubs were looking for international names and, before that goal, I was only really known as a club player with Aston Villa. We've got a home in Sardinia now. The goal was a big catalyst."

Paul Parker: "Seconds later the match was over and I had never known such an outburst of emotion. There was a night of immense celebration, starting in the dressing room where the normally parsimonious Robson allowed us a couple of beers, and continuing back at the hotel where we sneaked many more into our rooms. The adrenalin was flowing and there was laughter and banter into the early hours as we re-lived Platt's moment-of-a-lifetime and our own contributions to the downfall of a very good team."

Gazza paid tribute to his room-mate. "I was dead pleased for Chris. I knew there were knives out for him, but I also knew he was a great player. He can do things I can only dream of. Somehow he was never fully appreciated when he played for England."

The mood was more positive after the Belgium win with the players even talking to the media again. Parker observed: "That Belgium game, emotionally, was something else. I think all of a sudden the players started thinking: 'Hang on a minute, we could really go and do something here.' You could see what it meant when Chris Waddle and Terry Butcher were doing that silly dance. Those two had been through a lot together for England.

Parker added: "Our revelry was tempered in some measure by the fear of the press. There was a worry that they might knife us in our finest hour, as they had done to Bobby Robson and to Steve McMahon who had been accused, I believe, of getting involved in some corporate activity during the championships. Michael Hart, a respected reporter with the *Evening Standard* had always been good to me and after the Belgium match back at our hotel he started talking to me as we sat on the stairs.

"The next thing I knew Gazza had drenched us with a bucket of water. He screamed: 'Headlines… Parker has water thrown at him'. Hart did not take offence and nor did I because it was Gazza being Gazza. One-to-one he was a great lad, but any more than two people became an audience for him.

"There was a sense, at times, of mutual suspicion between the players and the press because we had stuttered rather than swaggering through the competition so far and it is true we had not played at all fluently. I knew a fair number of the reporters already and I got on well with Pat Sheehan of *The Sun*, Ben Bacon, Rob Shepherd, Barry Flatman, Hart and Stammers and the photographer Bob Thomas. I saw no reason not to speak to them because there had been no individual criticism of me, I would have been informed from home if there had been, and I have always believed it is the duty of players to speak to the press, and through them the public, win, lose of draw. Players are happy to talk when they are winning, but not when things are going badly and the press remember that. You are a small cog in a big machine and I realise after I had returned that you have to give sometimes."

The Belgians still believe that this was a glorious opportunity wasted, as Franky Van der Elst later confessed: "The worst thing was that [after the goal] we couldn't do anything – we did not get the chance to put it right. I was heartbroken. You come into the hotel and the first thing you do is empty your cupboard and fill your suitcase. It was very hard. And it dragged on enormously. When you get home you get another kick. On the way home you are still together with the group and you digest the loss with the team. But at home, the first days I went to the bakery, and that was it. I stayed at home a lot, trying to avoid people. If I look back at it, I was involved [as Platt's marker]. You still feel guilty. It was my fault. But Platt also did a great job."

"I remember going over to the fans and clapping them," Chris Waddle says of the immediate aftermath, "their arms were going up and down, so me and Terry were so happy that we just started to do the same. That image was shown everywhere and it's funny because it's almost part of that Belgium game now. People talk about Platty's goal and some of the incidents, but they'll always say: 'Remember at the end, Butcher and Waddle doing that dance?' I think we were on such a high because two years previous, in 1988, we lost all three games in the group stage at the European Championship finals and got hammered. And even before the World Cup, it was like: 'Get yourselves home, you're not good enough to compete.' Suddenly, though, it felt different. After what seemed like hours in the dressing room, we went back to the team hotel and Terry got a big tray of beers in for us. And then another."

Waddle swapped shirts with Nico Claesen, his old Tottenham team-mate, as the fans were signing "Let's all have a disco", as they danced around excitedly. Gazza, who had hugged his manager following that late goal, with Robson pushing him back onto the pitch, almost thought about joining the fans' disco. He even forgot his self imposed media ban and gave an interview to Jim Rosenthal.

As he admits himself, that goal changed David Platt's life; an unlikely hero, at 24 he was winning just his eighth England cap. "The day after the goal, I had to attend a press conference where there was a table with one chair behind it for me," he recalls. "In front of me were around 500 journalists from around the world. Before then all I was used to was a handful of local pressmen, who I knew, in a small room. I had to learn fast how to handle the media and so did my friends and family back home. They were inundated with requests for interviews and they were following my girlfriend Rachel trying to get a picture of her. One newspaper ran a column titled: '20 things you didn't know about David Platt'. I didn't know most of them myself!"

Later Platt revealed that his moment of history was worked on at Villa's training ground. "Often, after training, Sid (Gordon) Cowans, the Villa reserve keeper Lee Butler and I would take some balls on to the pitch and try a few different things," revealed Platt in an interview with retro football magazine *Backpass*. "I would try some spectacular volleys and overhead kicks. Sometimes they came off and other times they were hopelessly off target. But looking back I suppose, subconsciously, they were habit-forming and in that game against Belgium it was quite a natural thing for me to attempt that spectacular volley. My goal meant we were through to face Cameroon in the quarter-finals and it turned everything on its head."

Platt became a successful export to Bari, Juventus and Sampdoria before finishing his club career at Arsenal and Nottingham Forest.

JON HOLMES
Football agent

World Cup takes place back home, not at the venue

I was at the Holland-Germany game and had no idea why Rudi Völler got sent off but knew it was some bust up with Rijkaard, and from there I travelled by train to Bologna. At that time I was agent to Gary Lineker, Peter Shilton and John Barnes and before the game I met up with a few of the journos including Harry and Paddy Barclay. Paddy said to me he was shacking up with a girl back at his hotel but as we all know, it didn't last long with Paddy as she turned out to be the eventual wife of Chelsea chairman Ken Bates.

A lot of the journos thought it was a dismal, uninspiring tournament and moaned that the football wasn't very good but they failed to appreciate the excitement generated back home, the people were going potty about the World Cup. I think it's true to say that the real World Cup doesn't actually take place in the host country where tickets are limited, but back home - especially if your team is doing well. England were doing well and that was reflected in the mood. The journos had already been out there for some time, and they were out of touch.

Back at the team hotel the players were naturally elated after beating Belgium. I saw David Platt fleetingly and told him, "If you are not happy now, you never will be". I only saw the players for a few minutes, but it was clear John Barnes was aggrieved as he had scored a perfectly good goal that was disallowed, but these days with VAR it would have stood. I spotted Nigel Kennedy in the hotel and he was delighted as a Villa fan that David Platt was the hero.

I saw Gary and told him I had lined up tickets to come back for the final, and hoped England would be there. I told him it was a timely win against Belgium with such a late goal and at that point Gary had only the one goal, but he got the two penalties to win the game against Cameroon and of course the equaliser in the semi.

I was back for the final and saw the three Tenors live before it but it would have been such a wonderful occasion had England been there and had they got there, as they deserved to do, they would have won it.

ENOUGH TO MAKE YOU SPIT

The last 16 tie in Milan provided one of the World Cup's most unsavoury incidents as the Netherlands' exit at the hands of West Germany was marred by the appalling sight of Frank Rijkaard spitting more than once at Rudi Völler both before and after both players were dismissed. They continued their "discussions" as they marched off the pitch, but they would later kiss and make up - or more accurately star in an advert for a Dutch butter company together and make up.

The San Siro was a home from home for Rijkaard as he starred for Arrigo Sacchi's formidable Milan side of the late Eighties and Holland and Germany's rivalry was hardly a secret. The teams entered the knockout stages of Italia '90 in starkly contrasting form. The Germans had stormed the group stage, smashing in ten goals in three games, while Holland were mediocre, only scraping through to the knockout phase after three draws, including a desperate performance against Egypt. Their famous threesome of Gullit, Rijkaard and Van Basten were off form.

It all started when a crude tackle on Völler earned him a deserved booking. With the referee's back turned Rijkaard spat in the German's curly mullet as he ran past. By the time he had complained to the official it was too late. He too was booked. Tempers frayed again moments later. A melee in the Dutch goalmouth, in which Völler was clearly the injured party, saw both men sent off. The Marseille man was incredulous as Rijkaard spat at him again as they departed. This time it was captured in glorious slow-motion as it landed on Völler's ear. There was disgust in the TV studios. Big Jack Charlton later said "I'd have chinned him."

By the time Völler returned to the dugout from the shower, Germany had won 2-1 but no one was talking about the game itself. The incident remained a mainstay of Italia '90 reflective. Despite Völler accepting his apology with good grace, Rijkaard was christened "the llama" by the unforgiving German press corps.

"That day I was wrong," Rijkaard admitted years later. "I always had respect for Rudi, but I went berserk when I saw that red card. I talked to him after the match and apologised. I'm very happy that he accepted. I have no bad feelings about him now."

If anything could heal the divide between Völler and Rijkaard, it

Best mates Frank Rijkaard and Rudi Voller advertise Dutch butter

would be an advertising deal. In 1996, when the marketing men at Echte Butter brainstormed their next campaign, the two adversaries were pictured in matching cream robes, sharing slices of toast on a resplendent spring morning. The image was captioned "Everything in butter again", a reference to an old German proverb. The protagonists donated their fees to charity and the hatchet was buried.

Scotland's World Cup had started and all but ended with a shock 1-0 defeat by tiny Costa Rica. Dave McPherson still has nightmares over that Group C opener on a warm afternoon in Genoa. Alex McLeish anchored the Scotland defence in a rearguard that also included McPherson, Richard Gough and Maurice Malpas. McPherson, known as Big Slim in his Scotland days, said: "We were expected to win the opening game comfortably, maybe even by two or three goals. Certainly, Andy [Roxburgh] told us their keeper was a has-been who wouldn't come for cross balls and, sadly, nothing could have been further from the truth. We were lulled into a false sense of security as we settled for knocking the ball into the box for target man Alan McInally in the hope the keeper would spill something at the feet of our strikers. Who were we kidding? The guy was like a flying salmon. He came and picked everything out of the air. Andy had stressed the need to test the keeper early on and he came and caught a couple of balls easily. We should have taken that as a warning, but instead we thought he'd just got lucky. It wasn't all on the coaching staff, by the way. As players we were experienced enough and should have slowed the play down, shown greater patience and settled for getting the ball wide and delivering greater quality into the box. We put in plenty of endeavour and sweat that day, but lacked quality in our final delivery and the element of luck and good fortune any side needs to win a game of football. Our tactics never worked out and they were well organised and hit us on the break just after half-time for the only goal of the game. Mo Johnston had a couple of chances and I also went close with a header which, had it gone in, would have made it a completely different game. We weren't arrogant in the build up and we didn't suffer from nerves on the day. We didn't under-estimate Costa Rica either, but we knew that first game was our best chance of securing a win, especially with games against Sweden and Brazil to come."

The keeper Scotland manager Andy Roxburgh thought was a dud was 30-year-old Luis Gabelo Conejo, who conceded just twice - a goal each against Sweden and Brazil - as the Costa Ricans finished behind the South Americans and qualified for the last 16. He was injured for the second round game, a 4-1 defeat to Czechoslovakia, but still did enough to be named in the team of the tournament alongside Argentine number one Sergio Goycochea.

Scotland wore a yellow, white and blue shirt in the first game of the tournament but after the defeat the kit was reportedly criticised by then manager Andy Roxburgh. For the final two matches the traditional dark navy kit was worn. The Scots recovered to beat Sweden 2–1 in their second game but agonisingly lost to Brazil in their third match thanks to a late fumble from goalkeeper Jim Leighton that allowed Brazil to score the only goal on a rain-soaked night in the Stadio Delle Alpi in Turin.

Roxburgh should have known it was going to be usual the Scottish tournament of blunders when he named his team before Costa Rica and called out 'Nally', his nickname for Rambo, and Ally McCoist misheard and made for the number nine peg, not knowing he was a sub. McPherson added: "I was sharing a room with Craig Levein, right next door to Ally and Alan, who were also room-mates. We weren't slow in reminding Ally of his gaffe. We may not have qualified but that tournament remains the pinnacle of my career. A World Cup finals in Italy? A game against Brazil? It was an unbelievable experience, I enjoyed every second. We exited narrowly in the end to the Brazilians and there was an additional bonus for me when I was asked to address the media afterwards with Andy. We made our way through the stadium – we must have walked three miles – and just before we reached the press conference we bumped into Pelé. I shook his hand and we exchanged a few pleasant words. I was made up."

The Republic of Ireland were making their first appearance in the final stages of a World Cup. After emerging from England's group unscathed, Jack Charlton's men beat Romania on penalties. The Republic's first finals was an unqualified success even though they didn't win a single game! Three draws had earned them a last 16 crack at the Romanians and after a turgid 0-0 draw, keeper Packie Bonner and centre half David O'Leary were the penalty shoot-out heroes.

The Irish bowed out gracefully in Rome, a solitary goal from the prolific Toto Schillaci saw Italy triumph before 70,000 screaming Italians. Unknown outside his country, Toto became one of the most famous sportsmen on earth. "I'd had a great season for Juventus, scoring 23 goals, but I was one of the last to be called up," he recalls. "The press helped me a lot and I was just so happy to be in the squad because I didn't expect it. It seems so recent still. Whenever there's a World Cup, I always think back to 1990. It was a beautiful experience, truly unforgettable and it brought me worldwide fame."

Hosts Italy had begun nervously, only edging past Austria in their opening game thanks to their very own super sub. "I didn't expect to get on, I'd been dreaming away," added Schillaci, who now runs a football school in Palermo. "I remember that cross from Gianluca Vialli and I was standing in-between two huge defenders, like bulls they were. It seemed like the ball was being controlled by something else, it arrived exactly where I was standing and I managed to head in. That's how it all started."

Schillaci continued to score goals, netting against Czechoslovakia and Uruguay, before his fourth goal put the Irish out - he was on fire. With golden boy Roberto Baggio mostly subdued, Schillachi and his iconic eye-popping celebration was the talk of the tournament. "I knew it was a great moment and I tried to do my best while not thinking about what it all might mean," said Schillaci. "I didn't have the kind of pressure that some of the other players had because they already had big reputations. Anything I did would have been better than expected, so I felt quite calm." He was calm enough to score an opener in their semi-final against Argentina, but it wasn't enough as Caniggia levelled and the hosts went out on penalties. Against all odds, the holders made it back to the final.

Italia '90 was the lowest scoring World Cup tournament. Ireland got to the quarter-finals without winning a single match and scored only two goals in total. The Soviets had been among the pre-tournament favourites but never showed signs of being capable of winning and finished last in their group. Even Brazil failed to impress as coach Lazaroni used five out-and-out defenders in his starting line-up. Most teams seemed to play to avoid losing rather than to win, which was especially evident in the knock-out stage when half the matches went to extra-time and/or penalties.

STEVE STAMMERS
English journalist in the Scottish and Irish camps

T he Scottish preparations for the 1990 World Cup were in many
ways a sign of what was to come. I would like to make one
point clear from the outset, I was working with the London-
based *Evening Standard* at the time and was one of the few English voices
in the press corps but not once did I ever experience any hostility or
feel marginalised.

Of course there were divisions and agendas within the press and
the daily papers, evening papers, regional papers and both radio and
television but it was never uncomfortable for me – and the players
and manager Andy Roxburgh were approachable and affable. But
affable was not the word you could use for the weather in Malta where
Scotland prepared for a week ahead of Italia '90 . Acclimatisation was
the objective. Great idea; a week of hot weather but there seemed to be
a flaw in the plan. Because the players were then given a week off to go
back to Scotland which for all its beauty as a country is not known for
its tropical temperatures. It was a tad chilly and fairly wet which meant
that the advantage of going to Malta was negated. The heat for which
Scotland had prepared was evident when Roxburgh and his players set
up base camp in Santa Margherita Ligure some 25 miles from Genoa.

But the relaxed atmosphere of Malta gave way to intense security
at the Scotland hotel. There was a ring of (armed) Carabinieri around
the entrance. No parking within a mile radius of the hotel. It was
park up and then a get a taxi. Thorough does not come close. But
once through, the co-operation was excellent. Distant maybe but no
problem. And all seemed set fair for a three-point start against Costa
Rica. Who? Well it was time for me and my colleague Peter Gardner
from the *Manchester Evening News* to find out about these unknowns
from Central America.

First we had to find where they are staying. It was near a town
called Savona some 50 miles away and off the beaten track and while
Scotland basked in five-star luxury, the Costa Ricans were based in a
humble albergo in a sleepy town. So sleepy that their security guy was
dozing outside, rifle balanced between his legs and in front of him an
empty plate that had clearly once held pasta. Now I knew my Italian
O-Level would come in handy one day and I asked the sentry if the

Costa Rica squad were in the albergo (an inn rather than a hotel). They were absent – trying for the *third* time to get accredited in Torino. Yeah like Brazil (also in the group) had to go three times! So myself and Peter now had to formulate a plan for when the players came back. Who do we speak to?

Fortunately there was a squad picture in reception. We studied the faces and when the players returned we gave them the once over. A glance at the photo, a glance at the players and we were agreed, "That is Mauricio Montero." We approached, it was our man and he agreed to have a chat. "Dos periodistas ingles" we said and we managed to find out he was going to face Maurice Johnston – a somewhat controversial member of the Scotland squad who had turned down a return to Celtic and signed for Rangers. On decent money as well. Our man Mauricio? He played for Deportiva Alajuelense where he earned $20 a week and doubled his wages by working part-time as a petrol pump attendant. Talk about manna from heaven. His last words were "don't underestimate our team."

On June 11 at the Stadio Luigi Ferraris, Costa Rica won 1-0. Jubilation for Mauricio. For Maurice, not so much. But it was the post match conference that provided another highlight. Roxburgh faced up to the media flanked by Roy Aitken and Alex McLeish. A few "any injuries? Must be disappointed" type questions reflected the unease. Then came the voice. A loud and booming voice that in reality did not need the assistance of the microphone that had been passed to him. The accent was distinctly North American. "Mr Roxburgh, before this tournament Rod Stewart said that if Scotland were to have any chance they must beat teams like Costa Rica by four clear goals. What is your answer to this most famous supporter?" McLeish looked bemused and I swear he took off his headphones. Roxburgh looked a combination of fury and frustration while Aitken stared the inquisitor straight in the face. Roxburgh – nonplussed – said: "Are you Scottish?" To which the inquisitor replied : "No sir, I am Canadian." Aitken interjected, "We are only answerable to the Scottish fans." It was at once brilliant and bizarre.

Now comes the credit where credit is due moment. The following morning, rather than hide away in a sulk, the Scotland squad went round the port of Santa Margherita Ligure and faced up to their fans. It must be stressed that there was not one hint of trouble from any Scotland fan. None. While England fans were less than impressive in Sardinia, the Scottish supporters were exemplary. And while England players on such a sortie after such a result would have been the target for fearful abuse, there was passionate but never verbally violent debate between players and fans. It was a remarkable sight. Scotland's history is littered with a proud production line of magnificent players who never achieved the results to match. Think of that list – Law, Bremner, Dalglish, Souness, Baxter, Johnstone – world class. And that history is also littered with heroic failure – Scotland beat a powerful Sweden outfit in their next match only to lose – unluckily – to Brazil in the final group. Once again, they were home before the postcards.

Following them into Santa Margherita came the Republic of Ireland. Talk about a contrast. They had shown in the European Championships of 1988 that they were a capable outfit under Jack Charlton and Ray Houghton has never had to pay for a drink a Dublin after he scored the winner against England. Now they breezed into northern Italy. Gone was the massive security. It was possible to sit by the hotel pool with the likes of David O'Leary, Chris Hughton, Mick McCarthy, Tony Cascarino, Kevin Moran, Andy Townsend, Houghton and Frank Stapleton and discuss tactics, bonuses, transfers… anything you wanted. They were to face Romania in the last 16 in Genoa with the winners to play in Rome in the quarter-finals. So were they nervous? "No – it is home or Rome," O'Leary told me. A dour game against the Romanians in searing heat ended goalless after two tedious hours and so to penalties and the winning strike came from O'Leary. Andy Townsend scored one and when I asked him afterwards what words of encouragement were said to him as he went up to take his kick he revealed, "All I heard was the lads saying not to worry that I was wearing number 13!"

That was the Irish in Italy; a squad with proven winners but with an atmosphere that was relaxed. Of course there was a meeting with Italy to come in the quarter-finals and a defeat to a single goal from Salvatore Schillaci but for many of the squad, a more significant event came a few days earlier. No-one was more moved by meeting Pope John Paul II than goalkeeper Packie Bonner – a devout Catholic who was singled out for a one-to-one talk with His Holiness who had himself once been a goalkeeper at semi-professional level. A lifetime memory for Bonner but something of a bitter aftertaste following the defeat to Italy. "It was difficult and we knew it would be," said McCarthy after the defeat. "They were given a lot while we sometimes got free-kicks we didn't want because we were still in possession."

But the last word went to Charlton. Ireland had given Italy one tough match. Not, however, in a physical sense. Italy manager Azeglio

Vicini disagreed. He claimed the Irish were too aggressive. When the accusation was put to Charlton afterwards he just said with a face reflecting genuine disbelief: "Did he say that ? Did he actually say that?" End of press conference. End of my World Cup 1990.

THE REAL STAR OF ITALIA '90

"I'll tell you something," Roger Milla told *France Football* after Cameroon were finally knocked out, "if we had beaten England, Africa would have exploded. EX-PLO-DED. There would have been deaths. The Good Lord knows what he does. Me, I thank him for stopping us in the quarter-finals."

Cameroon's preparations had been shambolic, their squad was divided, their players felt unappreciated, but for all that it took two Gary Lineker penalties to beat them in the quarter-finals when England came from behind to win 3-2 just as it was starting to look like Cameroon would be swept irresistibly to a showpiece reunion with Argentina in the final.

Having shocked Argentina in the opening game most experts thought it was a fluke. Then Costa Rica put Sweden and Scotland behind them in the group and advanced through to the second round. With Mexico banned for illegal use of overage players in a FIFA youth tournament and the US only in Italy to learn before hosting the next tournament, most people predicted a poor showing by Concacaf in this tournament. Costa Rica, complete unknowns before the tournament, gave their confederation some fine moments when they were needed the most.

Of the other lesser known nations United Arab Emirates had been the whipping boys in West Germany's group, conceding 11 goals in 3 games and South Korea had fared little better in a tight Group E where Uruguay, Spain and Belgium all qualified for the knockout stage while the other African team in the tournament, Egypt, could consider themselves slightly unfortunate not to progress from the 'Group of Death' containing England, Holland and Ireland when conceding only 2 goals.

Yet if doubts persisted about the value of Cameroon's place in the second stage they were banished when Roger Milla scored two goals in two minutes of extra time to knock out an exuberant Colombia prompting his famous hip-swinging corner-flag dance to set up a quarter-final meeting with Bobby Robson's revived England. Gazza was fascinated by Milla's antics and loved his goal celebrations, so naturally he practised them in training until he had perfected them and he was determined to copy him should he score against the Africans!

The performances of Roger Milla altered the worldwide perception of African football

Had the tournament panned out as expected, England would have faced a repeat of their infamous Mexico '86 quarter-final clash with Argentina but the holders had begun the tournament with that shock defeat to Cameroon so instead the 1986 champions faced a clash of the titans with neighbours Brazil in the last 16. The 1990 vintage were the poorest to have represented Brazil since 1974 and Diego Maradona conjured a 1-0 win, drawing several men before playing in Caniggia for a late winner.

Despite the fact Cameroon had claimed three notable scalps in Argentina, Romania and Colombia, Milla says they relied on the element of surprise. "No team could ever again do what we did in 1990. The element of surprise is not there. Everybody knows everything about all the teams now."

After squeaking past the Belgians, England thought they knew everything about Cameroon. They thought it would be a bye but it was anything but; it was nearly bye-bye England! Bobby Robson and his team committed the cardinal sin of taking victory for granted and by the time they were walking out to face the first African nation ever to reach the quarter-finals they were not prepared for what hit them.

The source of England's complacency was a scouting report. Paul Parker takes up the story, "Howard Wilkinson was our scout and his verdict was 'you have got yourself a bye into the semi finals' but it was never going to be that simple, especially as Cameroon had beaten the holders Argentina, sensationally, in the opening match of the tournament." Parker was sure that Wilkinson's verdict was viewed with "justifiable scepticism" by the players. However that was not the feedback that came through, instead the majority of the players thought it would be an easy win.

Wilkinson had been unimpressed as he watched them suffer a 4-0 defeat by USSR in a dead rubber and reported back to Robson that England could relax. Robson trusted Wilkinson's judgement and relayed the information to his players, but the match in Naples would prove anything but easy. "Some f★★★ing bye," joked Waddle afterwards.

Parker added: "We got to the stadium in Naples and 45 minutes before kick-off Bobby Robson simply disappeared. He had been shattered and drained by the whole World Cup experience, and all that had gone before, and we discovered later that he found a doctor's room with a couch and curled up and went to sleep. Don Howe, unable to find him, took charge, gave us our last minute instructions and then prepared to send us out onto the pitch to do battle.

"There was an air of false security developing, not helped when the star-struck Cameroonians wanted to swap shirts *before* the match had even taken place. They were clearly in awe of us as we lined up in the tunnel along side us, staring at us not in menace, but like fans. Just as the referee prepared to lead us out there was a loud shout emanating from one of the side-doors and from it emerged Robson. Bleary-eyed but refreshed, our manager gave his instructions along the lines of 'England Expects' and off we went.

"Not that his words made much difference because we gave a distinctly lethargic performance and we were surprised how good they were."

According to John Barnes, Cameroon made an impact even before the match by breaking into song in the tunnel. "We responded with a few 'Come on lads' and head butting the walls and stuff – we were vociferous but they were much more cohesive than us and rhythmical."

England ended up with a fortuitous win in Naples, riding their luck as much as they had against Belgium in the previous round but that only served to raise optimism and expectation still further as the other teams left were hardly setting the tournament alight, it even sparked optimism it could be England's year.

David Platt concedes that if he hadn't scored the Belgium goal, England might not have gone through and it would have been a very short tournament for him. The Aston Villa midfielder was preferred to the more defensive Steve McMahon for this match and he justified the selection by heading England into a half-time lead from a stunning Stuart Pearce cross. In truth the goal came against the run of play as England struggled to cope with Cameroon's runs from midfield, the Africans created two big chances in the closing moments of the first half but their control let them down.

The game turned when Roger Milla came on early in the second half, now Cameroon's domination had a degree of composure and, after appeals for an England penalty were turned down at one end, Mexican referee Edgardo Codesal gave the first of three spot-kicks on the night as Paul Gascoigne made a desperate lunge on his hero - Kunde made no mistake from the spot. Moments later Roger the Dodger was at it again, strolling on to a through ball to set up Ekeke for a simple finish to put the Africans in dream land.

Gazza was distraught. "I wanted the ground to swallow me up. I could feel my face burning. To come all this way and then give away a stupid penalty. I just felt I'd let everyone down. I prayed, I really did, that he'd miss it, but no luck. Two minutes later that bloke Milla again, unbelievable he was, chipping the ball through and one of the other substitutes, he'd only been on the field five minutes, runs onto it and we're 2-1 down. We've drawn with Holland, beaten Belgium and we're losing to bloody Cameroon. Right I said to myself, don't get angry, get even."

At that point it seemed as if Cameroon could score at will, England were all over the place defensively and Robson swiftly changed systems to a more attacking 4-4-2 with Trevor Steven replacing Terry Butcher.

As time ticked down it was clear the Neopolitans were willing the Cameroonians to victory. England looked finished as they mounted several desperate attacks. Up in the press box the 'See Naples and Die' headlines were being dusted off for the morning editions and England were grateful to Peter Shilton for keeping them in with a shout by making a vital block from a cheeky backheel.

Then came the moment that would change the course of the night and ensure Robson bowed out a hero. Cameroon had won many admirers for their cavalier approach during the tournament, but their defensive discipline had always been suspect after the side ended with nine players when they beat Argentina. Those frailties were evident again as a flick from Wright found its way to Lineker who took a superb first touch before being hauled to the ground by two players. The Mexican referee again pointed to the spot, earning England their first penalty since February 1986. "Never a more vital penalty for England," whispered BBC commentator Barry Davies and it really was all or nothing. Robson's legacy as England boss effectively hung on this kick but Lineker coolly converted and the nation collectively breathed a huge sigh of relief.

Cameroon had been just seven minutes away from making history with a place in the last 4 but they still continued to create chances forcing Shilton into several saves. In the final miinute of the first period of extra time a fine run and through ball from the effervescent Gascoigne set Lineker through again before N'Kono brought him down, the striker made no mistake from the spot, blasting the ball down the middle. Cameroon looked visibly deflated and somehow England and their talismanic striker had snatched victory from the jaws of defeat.

"I have to admit it," Terry Butcher confessed, "Cameroon tore us to pieces. We knew they had some extremely talented players but we weren't prepared for their teamwork and effort. We were down 2-1 with about 15 minutes to go when the manager replaced me with Trevor Steven. Sitting on the touchline I couldn't see us scoring until Gary [Lineker] panicked them into giving away a penalty. Another in extra-time put us through but my goodness it was close."

Paul Parker felt England pulled through with a combination of Cameroon's naïve defending and England's "extra mental toughness". "They gave away two penalties needlessly and with more experience of the big occasion I feel they could have held on and beaten us. One of their players was clean through at 2-1 and only his desire, I recall, to finish with a flourish stopped him nailing us. At 3-1 there would have been no way back.

"My header into the penalty area led to Lineker being fouled for the first of his two penalties and we got back to 2-2, I think we were always going on to win from there. Had we lost, it would have been the biggest upset in the tournament and I remember thinking how fans at home must have been feeling as we floundered our way through the match. The whole episode was embarrassing from start to extra time finish and the talk afterwards was of relief and escape. How would we have gone home if we had lost? As for Belgium-style celebrations, they were long forgotten."

As for the hero of the hour, Gary Lineker admitted that he wasn't quite as cool stepping up to take the first penalty as he appeared to those watching the game. "When I stepped up to take the first, all sorts of negative thoughts were running through my head."

By this point, as Maboang notes, the Cameroonians' race had been run. "Apart from Milla, Bell, N'Kono, and a few older players who were aware that we were going far, [many players] were already tired mentally before the England game. I wanted to go home and have a party. The semi-final or final didn't mean much to me. We'd said that we were fed up and we wanted to go home, and to be honest, the sports minister said that we'd already done our maximum and that we'd done enough to go home. [He said] they didn't even have the money to pay for more matches, the hotel can't be paid for the semi or the final, there wasn't money to pay the match bonuses. There was no pressure, our work was already done, and we wanted to go home.

"Several players had already packed their bags [before the England match], and we didn't care. I didn't even watch the semi or the final, I wanted to go back to Yaounde, to Douala, to eat, drink and see my family. I was sick of it."

Their achievement has never been eclipsed, although has twice been matched by Senegal in 2002 and Ghana eight years later.

Cameroon's performances in 1990 - defeating the reigning champions, rattling England and coming within minutes of the semi-finals - remains arguably Africa's finest, and most vivid, performance on the biggest football stage. For the first time a team from sub-Saharan Africa had advanced past the group stage, and for the first time an African side had reached the last eight. "Honestly, we didn't really think that we were writing history," Bell says. "We thought about the present moment, that we had a match to win and we wanted to win it. It's only afterwards we said: 'That has never been done before', because don't forget, if you think too much about history, that can put the brakes on you, it can block you, because it can seem enormous."

THE GUARDIAN'S REPORT

David Lacey in Naples

Bobby Robson's eight-year career as England manager nearly ended in tragifarce here last night but the team are in the semi-finals of a World Cup abroad for the first time after a victory over Cameroon notable more for its courage and resilience than any overall quality of performance. England now move 600 miles north to Turin to meet West Germany in Wednesday's semi-final. After this latest example of the English ability to muddle through, Franz Beckenbauer may be relieved that the match is not being played just up the road at Monte Cassino.

The Germans will be expected to win, especially after the way England's defence nearly threw the game away last night. Nevertheless they will have noted the way England, 2-1 down with eight minutes to play, saved themselves, courtesy of two penalties from Gary Lineker, one in extra-time, and hung on after the team had undergone drastic re-organisation following an injury to Mark Wright.

From that point of view England's win had heroic undertones not dissimilar to the victory over Belgium in Bologna in the second round. And whereas then David Platt had brought England success with a volley in the last minute of extra-time, this time he gave them the lead with a header midway through the first half.

The fact that Platt, starting the match last night with McMahon kept on the bench, had so quickly confirmed his position as Bryan Robson's successor in the matter of scoring important goals gave England a buoyancy which was wholly misleading. The ship of optimism was holed below the water line and had Cameroon taken just a fraction more of their chances England's hopes would have been torpedoed long before the finish.

As it was the Africans scored twice in the 61st and 65th minutes to bring the opposition to the point of collapse. Lineker's coolness from the penalty spot saved England, ended Cameroon's historic World Cup and kept Robson's job alive for at least another 90 minutes.

In a way the game was a microcosm of his eight years in charge of the national squad. England's performance was both creative and chaotic, pragmatic and indecisive, bad in places, just unlucky in others.

There were several good things in attack. Again Gascoigne's readiness to take the ball deep into enemy territory gave England's attack a fresh dimension.

Pearce, moving up from full-back, was a consistent threat on the left and played an important part in the opening goal. Platt already looks an established international footballer and Lineker's forbearance remains a source of wonder. Massing almost beat a tattoo on his shins last night and inevitably collected another yellow card.

But the picture at the back remained confused throughout. Wright was not used as a sweeper but rather as a spare man in a flat back four. With McMahon absent from midfield Cameroon often had space and men to spare with the result that Pagal and Libiih were able to get men in behind defenders at unexpected angles and embarrassing moments.

When Platt met Pearce's cross with a firm header past Nkono after 25 minutes it seemed that England only needed to produce more of the same to earn themselves a comfortable victory. Cameroon were always likely to prove suspect in the air given the right quality of centre.

However, once Makanaky and Omam Biyik had begun to turn England's defenders the whole scene changed. Libiih missed two chances in three minutes shortly before half-time and the appearance of Roger Milla for the second half was full of dark omens for England's wobbly defenders.

With his ability to stand off opponents, maintain close control of the ball and create angles for others as well as moving into scoring positions himself, the 38-year-old Milla would be a danger to any defence. In England's case he took on the role of executioner.

First he moved on to a through pass from Pagal and went down as Gascoigne, who probably did not know much about what was going on, tackled him. Shilton made a valiant effort to reach Kunde's penalty but was still beaten by it. Two minutes later Ekeke replaced Mfede and two minutes after that Milla sent in Ekeke to put Cameroon in front.

The world had begun to tumble around England's ears. At last Butcher, the white man's burden, was taken off but when Wright suffered a badly gashed head he needed six stitches but says he will be fit for the semi-final in a collision with Milla in the 85th minute, England had to reorganise.

Wright eventually returned, head bandaged, but could not head the ball with any safety and played on the right wing. Steven filled in on the right of the defence with Parker joining Walker at centre-back.

Shilton made one of the most important saves of Bobby Robson's England career when he dived to stop a shot from Omam Biyik in the 87th minute that he could only have seen at the last instant. Early in extra-time Omam Biyik shot wastefully over the bar.

Lineker's first penalty and only the third in Robson's eight years as manager in the 82nd minute was awarded after Kunde's flailing foot had brought him down. His second, at the end of the first half of extra-time, came when he hared past the last defender on to Gascoigne's pass. This time Nkono was the offender.

'At one time I thought we were on the plane home,' Robson admitted afterwards. 'We never underestimated Cameroon but they still surprised us through their speed, strength and running off the ball. We pulled it out of the fire and I don't really know how.

'I thought we showed a lot of spirit and a willingness to fight to the end. They were the better team when they went ahead but it was a see-sawing saga of a match and now we're in the world's top four in 1990 and I'm proud of our football for having achieved that.'

Brave words, but last night, when all is said and done, England were lucky to get another chance. Still, they are worthier semi-finalists than Argentina.

Cameroon: *Nkono Massing, Ebwelle, Kunde, Tataw, Mfede (Ekeke, 63min), Pagal, Libiih, Makanaky, Omam Biyik, Maboang (Milla, h-t).*

England: *Shilton, Parker, Walker, Wright, Butcher (Steven, 75), Pearce, Waddle, Gascoigne, Platt, Lineker, Barnes (Beardsley, h-t).*

Referee: E Codesal (Mexico).

STEVE HODGE

My fondest memories were many, starting with the week in Sardinia with the families was a great start to the tournament, Mick Hucknall and Nigel Kennedy came to our hotel. Also in the build up going on the pitch with a few England players and waving to the crowd at a Cagliari game that we went to watch pre-tournament and getting a huge roar from the crowd.

Having a chat with my former team mate at Nottingham Forest Hans Van Breukelen on the pitch before the Holland game, then watching Gazza destroy Gullit, Van Basten, Rijkaard and Koeman against Holland. The wild celebrations at David Platt's winner as all the subs ran on the pitch. The Cameroon players singing a song in the tunnel as both teams prepared to walk on the pitch in Naples.

For me just being on the bench in a World Cup semi-final and seeing the legendary Franz Beckenbauer standing at the German bench just 30 feet away, the penalty shoot-out, the incredible tension, walking off the pitch with my arm around Stuart Pearce, Lothar Matthäus about to get on the German bus after the game and turning and clapping our bus in appreciation of how well we had played.

Receiving our medals on the pitch together with the Italian team after the game in Bari: Carlo Ancellotti, Baggio, Donadoni, Vialli, Schillaci, Baresi, Maldini and the Mexican wave. The camaraderie of all the squad and staff, the incredible scenes at Luton airport on our return.

I was available for the first two games, having played against Tunisia, I thought I may be involved against the Irish but sadly from my point of view Sir Bobby didn't select me which was disappointing. I then tweaked a groin before the Egypt game which was going to take two weeks to settle so I knew my tournament was probably over. Then Paul Gascoigne and David Platt burst in to the tournament and there was no way in even if I'd been fit. I stayed bright and breezy, Bobby would not have taken anybody in the squad who he thought might sulk if things went wrong for them, we all got swept away with the possibilities and the draw had been kinder to us than it seemed before the tournament - we faced Belgium and Cameroon!

I'm not sure if I would have started games, we had some quality wide players, I think that was one of England's strongest squads ever. It was a tough few weeks mentally for me but I wouldn't have missed it for the world. It was a privilege to be part of my second World Cup even though personally it didn't go well for me. My World Cup was four years before in Mexico when I went there thinking that I wouldn't play but ended up playing in every game. Four years later and I was a better player and believed I might have some involvement but it wasn't to be.

To experience all those highlights, travelling round a fantastic football mad country, experiencing every emotion good and bad with a fantastic group of players and legendary manager and ending up with a World Cup medal is a memory to cherish.

I never thought as a kid watching football in the 1970s that I would be a footballer, never mind an England footballer and go to two World Cups! I'm very proud of that. I remember watching Ossie Ardiles on TV at 1am in my bedroom as a kid in 1978 winning the World Cup, eight years later I'm playing with him at Tottenham, I've always loved the World Cup. As Brian Clough used to say "the hard bit is getting yourself in the squad and on that plane", and "once you're on the plane anything can happen".

My two World Cups both turned out differently to how I'd expected but both squads were very good and it was a privilege to have been selected for both by Sir Bobby Robson, a truly great man.

AND NOW FOR THE GERMANS

In his autobiography *40 years in the Commentary Box*, John Motson made it clear on numerous occasions he wasn't a fan of Italia '90 and thought England were fortunate to progress to the semi-finals. He commented, "Towards the end of the match against Belgium in Bologna, most of us had settled for penalties before Gascoigne floated a free kick forward and David Platt scored with an acrobatic volley. It is worth recalling, too, that they were 2-1 down to Cameroon in the quarter-finals with eight minutes to play. 'Had it stayed like that', Bobby Charlton said to me in the hotel the following day, 'it would have been England's biggest humiliation since we lost to the United States in the 1950 World Cup.' The unthinkable was avoided largely because the Africans, who had beaten holders Argentina in the opening game, had not learned how to tackle properly. They conceded two penalties, both nervously dispatched by Lineker, and England were through to the semi-finals."

"Determination and the riding of luck has taken England through," proclaimed Barry Davies on air at the end of the match, which was a fair summary. There was no question England had enjoyed some good fortune, but they had also shown character to claw their way back into the contest when all looked lost.

An overjoyed but at the same time clearly relieved Bobby Robson said in one TV interview: "I've had 17 heart attacks, I feel 92..." Bob Wilson in the London studio for the BBC signed off by saying "we've all aged 10 years" before handing over to Des Lynam in the stadium. "You think you've aged 10 years?" asked Lynam, possibly deep down conveying how painful the night was for most of the country. "What a traumatic night it's been," he said, which didn't quite seem the right words to use to describe England reaching their first World Cup semi-final since 1966.

As with the previous round against Belgium, ITV went up against the BBC and went on air half an hour earlier and had 1966 World Cup winning captain Bobby Moore in the studio with Elton Welsby as they sought to lure viewers - a lost cause as the Beeb also came out on top at the World Cup and Euros.

Sadly the ITV broadcast would be mostly remembered for the contribution of Big Ron Atkinson, who unwisely declared on air that hard-tackling Cameroon defender Massing did not have a brain. Although Brian Moore – who made reference to the incident in his autobiography – attempted to defuse the comment by making clear he meant a "football brain", Atkinson brought the issue back up at half-time and made a comment which could be interpreted as racist. They thought they were off-air as they chatted, but other nations taking ITV's live feed heard the words and complaints started to mount from overseas. It would be an unfortunate pre-cursor to the circumstances in which Atkinson would leave ITV in 2004.

ITV editor Rick Waumsley said after the Cameroon match: "We absolutely deplore any kind of racist remarks and our commentators are given very strong reprimands when they say these things." But Atkinson kept his co-commentary seat for the remainder of the competition and for the next 14 years was a mainstay of ITV's coverage. Yet the incident emphasised that issues of racism, and indeed hooliganism, were not going to be cured by events at Italia '90. Far from it.

Motty and other broadcasters such as Radio 5 Live's Mike Ingham and Alan Green, were not considered to be 'reporters' or even 'journalists' as such. Of course they were, but they were the acceptable face of the media, they were 'broadcasters' so didn't quite have the nasty edge to the Fleet Street pack. Hence they had greater access, knew far more, as they were not interested in reporting the tittle-tattle. Although I seldom dined with Motty and his TV chums, whenever the other Morris Men were on assignment elsewhere, then Ingham, Green and their usual expert analyst Terry Butcher, plus Michael Hart and his fellow *Evening Standard* reporter Bill Pearce would be the ones I'd chose to spend an evening with; they were trustworthy, totally professional and genial characters.

It wasn't my intention to pick up the inside gossip, I enjoyed their company and that was the sole motive, but after a few bottles of red around the table, the inside track was fascinating, but, of course, all in confidence.

Motty could roam the team hotel freely and as he said in his book in the aftermath of the Cameroon tie, "England's hotel was on the outskirts of Turin, and the mood was like that at the end of a school term. Everyone seemed to be of the opinion that we had already met or exceeded expectations, and that anything we did now would be a bonus.

"Out on the lawn Bobby Robson's hairdresser, who had flown over from Ipswich, was giving the England manager a haircut, much to the amusement of all concerned. In a corner of the bar Steve McMahon was sitting alone, having lost his place in the side after playing against Egypt and Belgium."

Motty would never have dreamed of saying it at the time as he prepared to commentate on England in his first, and as it turned out, only, England World cup semi-final, he had spied a few of the players all packed and ready to leave - clearly some didn't think they would beat the Germans. Quite an alarming thought.

Again in his memoirs Motty wrote, "When I got to the stadium, the first person I met in the media centre (we used to call it the press room) was Gordon Taylor, the chief executive of the PFA. 'All the boys are turned out, John', he said, pointing to the assembled journalist places, 'they just want to go home.' I didn't tell Gordon, that I had seen a few packed suitcases discreetly placed around the foyer of the England hotel earlier that day."

Cameroon returned to a rapturous welcome, with the government announcing a national holiday to enable everyone to celebrate. "When we arrived at Douala airport, the aeroplane had to pull up and come around again," said Omam-Biyik, "because the runway was totally flooded with people." The players' victory parade lasted two full days, and ended with President Biya conveying honours not only upon the players, but their coaches, the support staff, and even journalists.

Cameroon's successful run, along with Egypt's respectable showing, led FIFA to increase Africa's quota of spots from two to three for USA '94.

And now the Germans stood in England's way; by far the best team in the tournament, they had eased through their group without breaking sweat and seen off the Dutch and the Czechs with their usual efficiency. In Matthäus they had the player of the tournament so far and many home feared for an England team that had just been run ragged by Cameroon.

PAUL PARKER

It seems like yesterday

ENGLAND
PAUL PARKER

It doesn't feel like it all happened 30 years ago, it feels as its always been there, whether it was 10, 15, or 25 years ago, it still reflects something special in the history of the game, and the way football has developed in this country.

Many people are like me these days and fed up with football in its new age where it has a five year memory scan and it's all forgotten. It's the quest for immediacy, everything is the 'greatest' of all time; the greatest team, the greatest goal, greatest Player, greatest this and that without any real knowledge of actually what came before the Premier League in 1992. I'm sure no one can remember who won the first Premier League or even care.

But what happened 30 years ago is going to gain more and more significance as there will be a wealth of media attention as there is now a lot of nostalgia for the tournament in all its glory, for a time when, certainly for international football, there were tougher games and better teams.

Too often I hear, 'well you only got to the semi-final, what is there to celebrate?' But that fails to appreciate the significance of what was achieved in Italia '90 when an England team went into a tournament with such low expectations off the back of such a poor Euros, the manager under extreme pressure and even the players not really believing they were going to go very far under all the negative circumstances. That was definitely how I felt, I was even carrying an injury that needed warming up all the time and injections either side of the groin area.

Okay, we had good fortune but great sides always also need some luck, as club sides do when winning the Champions League, and sometimes you build up momentum whichever competition you are in, and that was true of this England team as Scifo hit the post, and a back heel by a Cameroon forward looking as though it was going to be a simple goal let Shilton make a save.

You don't see the full picture when you are immersed in the moment, and it was actually the first time I saw back our semi-final against West Germany the other Sunday when it was shown on BBC recently. I'd forgotten how good we were in that match. Suddenly it had more meaning and now I believe even more that we were the better team and deserved to be in the final.

We should have beaten Germany but I felt the country should have done more for us after what I think we did for the country, what we achieved was out of the blue and lifted the nation. You see MBEs handed out for someone moving a chess piece from left to right, but what we did was to achieve radical change for the way the game was perceived in England coming off the back of a European ban for what happened at Heysel and with a Sports Minster who was against the game because of the hooligan element. Collectively we did much for the country, but when it came to honours the country did nothing for us.

Re-watching the semi again it was hard to watch how I tried to block Brehme's shot that I deflected over Shilts. I asked myself whether I could have attacked it more as a defender. But you really do need to be brave to run straight at it without trying to protect yourself. Jimmy Hill was critical saying I shouldn't have turned my back on it but as defenders you tend to turn sideways to protect yourself rather than taking one in the face for the team. But the truth is I couldn't believe it when I have now seen it back how it ended up a goal.

Of course there wasn't social media back then, but I spotted a lot of tweets about Shilts. Many made the point that he was one of the world's greatest goalkeepers in his prime, but he was now 40 and this was his final tournament for England. Shilts stepped forward to narrow the angle for the shot, which left him out of position when the ball looped up. A younger, more athletic keeper might have got backwards quicker and retrieved it. Shilts at 20, 30 would have got it I'm sure, but at 40, it was asking a lot to have the same sort of movement in your feet. If you ask me why Bobby Robson had a 40 year old keeper at his first choice keeper than I would have to say it was probably out of sentiment for the guy being the best for so long, and this was his final goodbye.

Also when it came to penalties, why didn't Dave Beasant at 6ft 6ins come on with a record of saving penalties. I know I put Dave Seaman out of the competition in training, but Chris Woods was capable, so too was Beasant and much, much younger.

I was the first player booked in the semi-final and 15 minutes later

*Paul Parker, far right, was one of the guests during a live
2002 World Cup streaming show hosted by me,
other guests were Harry Redknapp and the late Peter Bonetti.*

might have got a second yellow for a challenge that even my wife, watching the re-run on the BBC with me, thought should have been red! But I explained back in those days you had to commit murder to get a second yellow, it was a different game.

Which brings us to Gazza. Ah Gazza! One of the stories of the World Cup was how he poured water over myself and a journalist when he thought I was giving an interview when he was so dead against the media at that time.

I was on the England team coach after the Cameroon game when I spotted Michael Hart of the *Evening Standard* whom I knew very well and had given my first interview to when I was an 18 year old at Fulham. I went to the side door, down the steps where the loos usually are, and was having a chat with him, not actually giving him an interview, just chatting as friends, as he was saying how pleased and proud he was of my performances in the tournament. Gazza saw us, assumed it was an interview and threw water over both of us. It was nothing aggressive, just Gazza being Gazza.

Chris Waddle was Gazza's room-mate until the wives and partners arrived at our Cagliari team base, then as Gazza and Trevor Steven were on their own, they paired up. After a while Trevor was going crazy, he couldn't sleep as Gazza couldn't sleep, and wanted to play table tennis at night or do something. Trevor is one of the nicest guys you are ever likely to meet, always immaculate, but he was haunted by Gazza. He ended up hiding from him in other player's rooms with Gazza knocking on doors trying to find him. "Where's Trevor?" he kept saying. Chris, though, seemed to have an immune switch with Gazza, he was more comfortable in dealing with him, but even Chris needed a break from him and he was delighted when his wife arrived and poor old Trevor became his room-mate.

The players enjoyed the one room that everything had been placed in; the TV, video games, table tennis, these were good times shared by the squad, and there was space to come in and just sit around chatting. Trevor was fine when Gazza wasn't in there, but when Gazza walked in the atmosphere changed, we were all like mice when the cat came in, wondering who his next victim would be. If he set his sights on you, you were buggered.

There's the famous incident when Gazza was playing an America couple at doubles but he was by himself, and it was on the eve of the semi-final and Bobby Robson caught him. 'What are young doing?' the England manager shouted at him. 'Hang on gaffer, it's match point!' he replied. And Bobby let him carry on until his match was finished!

CHRIS WADDLE

What Gazza Got Up To The Night Before The World Cup Semi-final

After the World Cup in Mexico in '86 there were a few changes for the Euros, but '88 was a disaster and we were slated in the press, but no one appreciated that the teams that beat us, Russia and Holland, ended up in the final, they were outstanding teams, and we were in a period of change. But we were poor, and we expected to take some stick. Fair play to Bobby, he stuck by his squad although he added to it, and I was very confident going into Italia '90 on the back of a good season with Marseilles in

an excellent team. I joined up about a week and a half late as the season finished later in France. When I arrived at the hotel, I was back rooming with Gazza, and knew what I was in for, I had roomed with him long enough to know what to expect. No sleep! But at least Trevor Steven was relieved he didn't have to room with him any longer.

The issues with the media began with our last warm up game when we left Sardinia to play Tunisia, which was a 1-1 draw and the headlines were far from flattering, along the lines of 'Keep going to England, don't stop in Italy'. It was clear we were getting plenty of stick and no one thought we had a prayer of getting anywhere near a final, how could we not beat Tunisia and stand any sort of chance?

The group games were predictable, they are always very tactical, you don't want to lose, there are a lot of nerves, and you are always in with a chance if you play it tight. We should have beaten Ireland, Holland is always difficult so a draw against them wasn't bad. Meanwhile, the Germans had started very well, but for us it was a terrible group to get through and we eventually did it with a set piece against Egypt reverting to 4-4-2. But we were not fluent enough and no one gave us much of a chance in this competition, so we had to change against Belgium.

One of the main problems was the boredom, no matter what games were laid on, and distractions within the camp, boredom was getting to us, it was doing our heads in, so seven of us decided to break out it was like *The Great Escape*. There was so much security around our hotel, even a tank out the front! But the seven of us sneaked out somehow, jumped into a couple of cabs and headed to the nearby town about ten minutes away to find ourselves a bar. We also sneaked back in and thought we had got away with it. Somehow, though, we had been spotted.

Bobby Robson was none too pleased to say the least, and the message got around that he wanted all of those who were out without permission to come to see him and sort it out. The message was also pretty clear that if any of the culprits didn't own up and he found out about they risked being sent home! I had a chat with Gazza and told him I'm going to see Bobby and do what he suggests and hold up your hands, "let's tell him and take the consequences". The next day we went to see him and apologised. We all got a strong talking to. He wasn't going to accept any more stupidity. He told us there are fans and the media who might see us and it could cause so much trouble. We would need security with us, we shouldn't be risking going out to public places. Bobby doesn't hold a grudge, I will say that about him, and he said that was the end of it, but if it happened again you would be risking being sent home. I thought to myself "I'm not doing that again".

One of the seven didn't own up, and Bobby didn't find out otherwise he might have been on the next plane home - I'm not telling who though! The day out at the Forte Village was different. Bobby knew about that as it was more of an organised day out, he gave us all a day off, time to sunbathe on the lovely Forte Village beaches, to chill out for the day. He wasn't daft so he knew the lads would have a few beers and he didn't mind that too much.

I'm sure, though, he did mind, and mind very much, when Robbo tried his party trick of lifting up the bed when someone was lying on it and the slid down the bed and fell off the other end as there was no headboard. This time he lifted the bed, but it fell on his toe, and the nail flew off, and the next day against Holland he also injured his Achilles. I was in the room when Gazza was on the bed and Robbo tried to tip him off it and the doc had to be called in to patch him up.

Bobby knew how to handle his players, he knew when he needed to bollock someone or when he needed to laugh it off, and that applied more so to Gazza more than anyone else. Often Bobby would laugh at Gazza's antics like the rest of us. Bobby knew when he needed to go mad with Gazza, and when he needed to give him some leeway.

Bobby's main concern was keeping Gazza's feet on the ground. Bobby handled Gazza well, let him express himself at times and knew how to take him, and he got the best out of him where it mattered - on the pitch. He liked his players to be sensible and disciplined but he also knew when to let them off the leash on occasions. He knew you were dealing with characters, not robots, and there were some like Gazza who could be as daft as a brush or act the clown.

Equally it can go too far, and Bobby knew when to act if he needed to. He also knew he couldn't change Gazza. It would be like asking John McEnroe not to argue with the Umpire, and if he didn't argue he wouldn't be the same player. You have to give Bobby a lot of credit in the way he knew when to press the right buttons with someone like Gazza; when to tick him off and when to laugh and walk away.

The night before the World Cup semi-final was a classic, and my favourite Gazza story of the tournament. We had our usual team meeting, talking tactics the usual stuff, and you could see Gazza doing his usual thing, taking absolutely no notice. He would never look at the tactical board, he never listened to any of the team talks, he just went out and did his own thing.

Later that night Bobby was walking around the grounds of the hotel and in the distance he could see this kid with no shirt, no socks, with his shorts twisted up almost to his waist.

"Gazza, Gazza," yelled Bobby at him "What do you think you are doing?"

"I'm playing tennis, gaffer", he replied.

"What!" said the England manager, "It's late, we've got a World Cup semi-final tomorrow, what are you doing?"

"I'm bored, gaffer" Gazza replied.

"And who are you playing?" said Robson

"I'm playing the waiter of the hotel," Gazza told him.

"By the way" asked Robson, "what's the score?"

"It's 5-5 in the fifth set!"

Bobby couldn't believe one of his star men was playing five sets late into the night before the World Cup semi-final.

How do I know all of this? Well, Gazza came racing back to the room to tell me everything that he did and what the manager had said. It hardly surprised me as he couldn't keep still, he had to be doing something whether that was fishing, running, tennis table, tennis or whatever.

MARK WRIGHT

My semi-final fitness test: Bobby Robson threw a ball at my cut head!

We all saw that re-run of the World Cup semi-final on TV recently, it brought back so many memories, but people also noticed that I was walking out to face West Germany with a strip of tape over my eye.

I got a cut against Cameroon when I 'went after' Roger Milla. I was covering the left back position when the ball was up in the air and I could see Milla going for it but I was out to get him, so I went smacking in, but he got me, I think it was his head, but it might have been his elbow, whatever it was, I came off worse.

The wound needed five or six stitches, they glued it up and put tape over it. A few days later Bobby Robson looked concerned in training when he came over to me bouncing a ball as he walked along. "You've got a cut eye," he said, "I'm a bit worried with the semi-final tomorrow. Are you fit?"

"Of course, I'm fit, it's only a cut" I replied suddenly fearing for my place.

Bobby threw the ball at my head. I never flinched and headed it back he said "Yeah, you've passed, you're fit".

He was making sure I wasn't frightened to head the ball, which would be a problem for a centre half but I'd played with cuts before, and even a broken nose, it's the sort of thing you did back then, get on with it.

"Don't you worry, Boss", I told him, "I've played with a broken nose and a cut eye before, no problem." Well, that was my fitness test, the manager throwing the ball at my head!

I imagine the England manager was more worried about Gazza the day and night before the semi-final, than he was about my cut head, as he was up to his usual tricks. Gazza could never keep still, never settle, was always on the go, it was great entertainment for everyone, he was the life and soul of everything that was happening. But he didn't pick on certain players for his pranks or he knew he would get his bottom kicked. Terry Butcher would give him a smack if he got out of hand. Gazza knew not to mess with the big centre-halves so I never had any cause to give him a smack. He would give Chris Waddle and Steve Bull the run around, and of course the day before the semi-final he was playing tennis in the boiling hot sun, and got himself sun burned.

Memories of Italia '90 are always with me every day. I have pictures of it on my walls at home, and whenever I walk past them I have flash backs, and then there was a recent re-run of the World cup semi-final on TV. I came to it late, so had recorded it, then got distracted again, but when I started to watch it, after Gary Lineker equalised, all the memories came flooding back, Terry Butcher going off as we chased the game, reverting to a back four with myself and Des Walker marking Jurgen Klinsmann and Rudi Völler, and then Karl-Heinz Riedle coming off the bench late on.

Years later Riedle turned up at Anfield and we became team-mates, so he says to me "I've got something to show you". He whipped out his World Cup winners medal. "You git!" I said but he then said, "You were the better side on the day" which made me think, wow that's how close we came to winning it. It was a very good solid performance by that England team, and maybe we deserved to have got more out of it. Seeing it on TV brought it back but it's always remained fresh in my mind and all of the team's minds; the excitement to be playing the best countries in the world.

The highlight for me was the whole thing. Just being there was an honour, playing for England was an honour. The stand out moment for me, well you might think I would say scoring against Egypt with the goal that took us through the group stages, but that's not it. It was actually being there, at a World Cup, playing for my country, and being part of such a great group, where we were in it together as a team and came out of it together as a team, it was all amazing, especially as I had missed out on the World Cup in Mexico because I broke my leg playing for Southampton against Liverpool.

I was naturally devastated at missing out as you'd expect and it killed me watching it all from home, with my leg in plaster, but Bobby Robson would call me from his hotel room out there in Mexico and say, "Wrightie, how are you? We are missing you, and we will try to win it for you." What a special man he was!

TORMENT IN TURIN

Terry Butcher was one of the most prominent personalities in the England squad and, having played under Bobby Robson at Ipswich Town, he knew the England manager better than most, and also how far he could push him. The Big Man had a wicked sense of humour and his antics were only bettered by 'daft as a brush' Gazza. But he knew how to lighten the mood.

On many a convivial evening with the BBC Radio 5 broadcast team of Mike Ingham and Alan Green, Terry would be among our dining companions, and he never tired of telling us his favourite Italia '90 World Cup stunt he pulled on the England manager conspiring with the entire squad to pull it off ahead of England's biggest game since 1966.

To alleviate the boredom and to lessen the tension, he led the entire squad one evening in eating their meal back to front, which completely flummoxed a bewildered Bobby Robson. They all ordered their meal with coffee as their starter, followed by dessert, and worked their way to the soup. Beside each player Terry placed two bottles of wine! In fact they were wine bottles filled with water. The England manager went spare when he spotted all the wine bottles! Another time Terry came down to the meal early, looking like the best dressed England player, resplendent in his England blazer, collar and tie - but he had nothing but underpants on below the waist!

Terry revealed that one of Robson's motivational tools was a flip-chart. During Italia '90 Bobby would put up the scheduled flights home and challenged his players to make sure they would not be making that early trip to the airport. Togetherness was forged within the group and the ability to get stronger through the tournament was the key to success. He said: "We weren't great in 1990 in the early stages, but got better all the way to the semi-final. It's not about peaking too soon, it's about getting to know each other, forming a bond and some of the players have suffered disappointments and that would drive me, as a player, to say, 'That's not going to happen again.'

"They need to be saying, 'We're not coming home early.' Bobby (Robson) used to love a flip-chart and he'd tick the flights off as an incentive."

Butcher reflects on how respect for the manager was key. "Bobby came through it so well. You are cocooned away in your hotel, we were two to a room... no iPads, no internet and five phones. We had Monopoly and Peter Beardsley, that's all we had! The squad was really tight, we got on really well, Gazza kept us on our toes, he was electric on and off the pitch. We had a glimpse of it against Czech Republic [in a pre-tournament friendly] when he made goals and scored. But Bobby didn't put him in for the first game, only when we changed it to play the Dutch did he put him in, then he changed the system and Gazza got his chance, David Platt got in. Even Paul Parker didn't start the tournament. Players wanted to do it for him, they fought for him. They knew what to do, it was part of the system and everybody had no worries. Anybody could sit with anybody at the dinner table, anybody could play with anyone.

"We became a bit of a machine, you know. We knew what we had to do, who was doing what and gradually it all just clicked. I think there's a pattern there, if you look at the teams that have won the World Cup, they all have that spirit and togetherness. They're able to laugh."

Gary Lineker tells how, as the players awaited their manager's arrival for his team-talk head of the West Germany semi-final he had scribbled 'even money he mentions the war' on Bobby's flip chart which he subsequently hid from the manager's view. Robson duly arrived with his opening gambit: "Well lads, we beat them in the war" and the room dissolved into laughter and the boss hadn't the remotest idea why.

John Barnes' highly educated background meant he had an intellectual take on many aspects of the psychology of the game. He believes such basic nationalistic traits manifested themselves into conflict that invariably influenced the team-talk of his patriotic manager and also the atmosphere in the dressing room, perpetuated by senior players in the England ranks. "We were all well aware because Bobby, and we all loved Bobby, Bobby's team talk always revolved around 'remember the war' – now of course when you're playing against Germany that's very obvious but you've had the war of independence against America, you've had the Crimean War against the Russians – how many wars have we had against France? People think it must just be against Germany, but you know England have fought against everybody !

"When you played for England, I've never actually said it, but a lot of the talk also from people like Terry Butcher, Bryan Robson, Ray Wilkins... Terry used to headbutt the wall and say 'they shall not pass', he was a real warrior and he also bought into this thing about the British Empire and what have you.

"But I always felt, well why should it mean more for us to play for England or for the French or the Germans or for the Tunisians or the Algerians to play for their country? And of course, in that respect, particularly having lost a war for example, and feel hard done by because of the nature of things. It maybe should mean more to the Argentinians to actually beat us but I went along with it because I'm a young lad who doesn't want Terry Butcher to headbutt him!"

Interest was growing and press conferences became packed out, as the nation started to dream that 1990 could become comparable with 1966. Previously England enjoyed five-day gaps between matches but now it was down to just three and with hosts Italy losing on penalties to Argentina the night before, England were now one of just three sides left who could win the World Cup. Robson was convinced Argentina were there for the taking, with the bigger challenge lying immediately ahead of them. The West Germans were favourites, boasting the strong Inter Milan trio of Andreas Brehme, Lothar Matthäus and Jurgen Klinsmann.

Barnes had gone off injured against Cameroon and was ruled out as Beardsley finally returned, but the side was otherwise unchanged. The semi-final with the Germans in Turin's Stadio Della Alpi on July 4th 1990 was watched by 30 million back home, the biggest TV audience in the country's history for any single sporting event, not far short of twice the previous record held by the Tyson–Bruno fight!

Jimmy Hill and Terry Venables were in the TV studios and alongside them injured captain Bryan Robson. Hill opens the coverage by admitting that he is "frightened out of my life". Des Lynam's opening words summed up the enormity of the occasion, "This is the most momentous day for English football since 30th July 1966."

The BBC began their coverage with a montage contrasting the classes of 1966 and 1990. The highlight is Bobby Robson shaking his head back and forth as he considered the possibility of winning the World Cup: "Well, I've been in the game now 40 years it would be lovely to... to win the... the biggest prize the game had to offer, the world championship." Of England's biggest match for 24 years the England manager said "If we can win tonight, we're in the final, with a great chance of beating Argentina. Great chance. This is the big one.

Germany's the big one."

Robson admitted that "4–4–2 saved us" against Cameroon, but while that was his preferred formation, he was always likely to return to the extra defensive cover of a sweeper system for the Germans and made just one change from the side that started against Cameroon: Beardsley for the injured Barnes. Des Walker and Mark Wright were passed fit, although Wright had six stitches above his left eye. England's five substitutes included Trevor Steven, so impressive when he came on against Cameroon, and Steve Bull of Second Division Wolves.

After a comfortable passage through their group, West Germany had seen off Holland in a fractious second round game that saw Franck Rijkaard spit at Rudi Völler with both men being sent off before they edged out Czechoslovakia in the last eight thanks to a Matthäus penalty. Manager Franz Beckenbauer brought in two impish schemers, Thomas Hässler and Olaf Thon, for Pierre Littbarski and Uwe Bein. Völler also returned, having served his one-match suspension for the Frank Rijkaard spitting incident, Karl-Heinz Riedle dropped to the bench.

England (5-3-2): Peter Shilton; Paul Parker, Terry Butcher, Mark Wright, Des Walker, Stuart Pearce; Chris Waddle, Paul Gascoigne, David Platt; Gary Lineker, Peter Beardsley.

West Germany (3-5-2): Bodo Illgner; Guido Buchwald, Klaus Augenthaler, Jürgen Kohler; Thomas Berthold, Thomas Hässler, Lothar Matthäus, Olaf Thon, Andreas Brehme; Jürgen Klinsmann, Rudi Völler.

Referee: José Roberto Wright (Brazil).

Argentina's approach to knock-out football had been cynical in the extreme. After overcoming Brazil thanks to a superb piece of Maradona skill they seemed to play for penalties against Yugoslavia and won the shoot-out 3-2. They had been huge underdogs in Naples against hosts Italy in the first semi-final but fought back from a goal down through Caniggia before winning yet another shoot-out. Some Italians blamed the Neopolitans for favouring Maradona on the night in a city he had lifted from football obscurity to become Serie A champions in just a few seasons. Nevertheless it was clear that Maradona's side were there for the taking and would be without four suspended players for the final, including the superb Claudio Caniggia.

Lucky to beat Cameroon in the quarter-final, England had only really excelled in the 0–0 draw against Holland. West Germany, by contrast, were immense: destroying two very good European sides in

Yugoslavia and Holland, and easing past Czechoslovakia.

In the tunnel, Mark Wright emerged with a big plaster on his left eye, Waddle minus his mullet and Gascoigne gave Beardsley a kiss on the right cheek. West Germany looked ultra calm and businesslike, it was their eighth semi-final out of nine in the previous 20 years, England had not been this far in a tournament since 1966.

As England fans booed the West German anthem Gazza, who had attracted criticism for sticking his tongue out during the anthems, settled for easing the tip out and smiling sheepishly into the camera.

On Sunday, April 12, 2020 BBC Sport replayed England's heartbreak tie. With no football during the coronavirus pandemic, the game gripped the nation once again. Watching at home was one of England's stars of the tournament Gary Lineker who went back in time through the key moments responding to a torrent of tweets, so one can imagine how it would have been like back then if social media had existed... a torrent of attacks on the likes of Peter Shilton for a start! What would they have made of Gazza's reckless challenge and his tears?

When Lineker was England's ace goalscorer, there was no social media, but re-invented as the face of the Beeb's *Match Of The Day*, he also became one of the nation's most followed personalities on Twitter. Lineker tweeted:

If you're in the mood for feeling miserable, you could do worse than watch this.

@PaddyMcGuinness

I can't watch it! Still think we're gonna win it, only to end up losing.

@GaryLineker

What's weird about the Italia '90 semi-final is that despite being distraught, I never shed a tear at the end. Yet watching it just now, tears flowed. Getting soft in my old age.

@amylawrence71

Oh God the @GaryLineker 'have a word' moment, in the context of the whole game rather than a little clip, is properly spine tingly.

@GaryLineker

[Of Gazza] Love that crazy kid.

@GaryLineker

Knew I shouldn't have watched this Italia '90 re-run of England v West Germany semi-final. So comfortably the better side. Still heartbreaking 30 years on.

@GaryLineker

I've just scored in a World Cup semi-final. Felt great.

@GaryLineker

Feel like I'm playing again. How joyous.

Thirty years earlier back in the studio with Des Lynam was *Match of the Day* stalwart Jimmy Hill, England captain Bryan Robson, Spurs boss Terry Venables and World Cup winner Bobby Charlton on call to give his advice to Bobby Robson's side…

Cue *Nessun Dorma*, roll titles, cue Des Lynam…

"Good evening and welcome to the most momentous day for English football since 1966. Over half of the population will be watching. What the other half are doing - well, that's up to them!"

Bobby Charlton was clearly nervous: "The Germans are favourites. The responsibility to put England into the World Cup Final is on the players, and the players alone. I was more nervous in the semi-final of 1966 than the final itself. We are the underdogs but we are here and we are ready."

England kicked off in traditional white, the Germans in their green away kit. Butcher, rather than Wright, was playing as the spare man at the back. Walker was tightly marking Völler and Wright likewise on Klinsmann. England come storming out of the traps and Lineker wins a corner on the right inside 15 seconds. It's taken by Beardsley and half-cleared to the edge of the box where Gascoigne hooks the bouncing ball back whence it came with his left foot. It's a beautiful effort and, although it swerves towards the near post, Illgner leaps to his left to palm it behind. That leads to a second corner, which leads to a third. That leads to nothing but England almost get in again thirty seconds later when Beardsley, played onside by Buchwald, breaks into the box from the left. He has Lineker and Waddle in support but tries to take on Buchwald, who dispossesses him well.

"England are playing some tidy football," exclaims John Motson, no doubt shocked by their impressive start. The mood music in the build-up had been about England avoiding a hiding against the best team in the tournament but those fears were quickly allayed by England's fast start.

Minutes later Gazza cheekily Cruyff-turns away from Klinsmann on the halfway line, looking very confident and more influential than man of the tournament so far, Lothar Matthäus. The stage was set for him to show his class. Lineker was looking dangerous as BBC co-commentator Trevor Brooking says this is "easily England's best start" of the tournament. John Motson pointed out that there were three who would miss the final if they get booked: Pearce, Gascoigne and McMahon. West Germany also had three on a yellow card: Berthold, Matthäus and Klinsmann.

Then, out of the blue, Waddle strikes the bar from 40 odd yards but it wouldn't have counted as the referee had already blown for a foul by Platt a split-second earlier. Rudi Völler remains down as Karl-Heinz Riedle prepares to come on. Völler barely got a kick from Walker, but was unable to continue with a groin injury.

As the referee blows for half-time England get the breather they need following a superb first-half performance, but the Germans had gained some momentum just before the interval following a period of pressure. In the studio the BBC pundits were full of praise for Walker, with Venables describing him as 'unbeatable', much the same as the fans' song! Jimmy Hill said it was "a pleasure to see an England team give such a display in the arts and crafts of the game".

The Germans start the second half much as they finished the first, in control. "England are under siege now," observes John Motson and minutes later they win a free-kick as Pearce fouls Hässler 22 yards out. The free-kick is touched off to left-back Andy Brehme whose shot takes a vicious deflection off Paul Parker that loops high in the air and agonisingly over the stranded Shilton, who couldn't back-pedal quickly enough and ended up helping it into the net as he falls backwards.

The BBC re-run of the semi-final led to a Twitter storm of indignation at Shilton's performance, and the then veteran keeper came in for plenty of criticism for the opening goal. There might not have been social media back then, but Shilts was in for a social media storm nearly 30 years on as he found himself trending on Twitter and little of it was complimentary.

England hit a vital stage, as the Germans threaten the second they desperately need to stabilise their position. After he is fouled on the left, Gascoigne swings in a superb free-kick and Pearce, getting in front of Riedle at the near post, flicks a back-header across goal and just wide of the far post with Illgner motionless. England continue to press as Parker clatters Buchwald, bringing the first yellow card of the game. West Germany make their second substitution: Stefan Reuter replaces Hässler who hadn't recovered from the tackle from Pearce that led to Brehme's goal. Reuter is normally a right wing-back but goes into midfield.

Waddle, on the left of the box, draws a tackle from Augenthaler with a swing of the hips and then shifts the ball to his left just before being taken him down - it's a clear penalty but the referee waves play on. Waddle gets straight up but the replays show it should have been given.

Robson switches back to his preferred set up as Trevor Steven replaces Butcher and England revert to 4-4-2. Robson plans a final throw of the dice and Steve Bull starts warming up. But wait....

On 81 minutes Parker swings over a long cross towards Lineker from near the halfway line on the right. Suddenly there is indecision between the German defenders and it hits the thigh of Kohler, who was running towards his own goal, and as it bounces up Lineker knees it away from Augenthaler and Berthold before cracking an excellent left-footed shot across goal and into the far corner, it was a typically clinical finish. On the bench Robson reclines in his seat with a satisfied, probably relieved, smile to recognise Lineker's tenth World Cup goal: four this tournament, six in 1986. Having started this tournament slowly he looks really sharp against the Germans and he took that beautifully, it was a more difficult chance than it looked. With Beardsley still on, the plan to introduce Bull is aborted after the goal.

And so for the third game in a row, England are into extra time. At the break Robson rallies the team, giving tactical instructions to Paul Parker while Waddle and Bull share a laugh! England look relaxed. 'We've got another half-hour and we might have penalties,' says Des Lynam. "Are you ready for this?"

The Germans come out reinvigorated and move the ball slowly across the field from right to left with Thon eventually shifting it down the line to Brehme who curls over a wonderful first-time cross and Klinsmann, towering above Walker on the six-yard line, thumps a downward header towards goal. Shilton plunges to his right to make a superb reaction stop with both hands. It wasn't right in the corner, and someone as good in the air as Klinsmann might feel he should have done better, but it was a brilliant save. Minutes later Klinsmann is set free 12 yards from goal and in line with the left-hand post but screws his left-footed volley across goal and just wide - another chance missed.

Then on 99 minutes it happens. Gascoigne overruns the ball in midfield and lunges with typically naïve enthusiasm at Berthold, committing a clear foul although it might not have merited Berthold's reaction or that of the rest of the German camp, both on the field and from the bench. Gascoigne, realising the implications, puts his hands up in apology like a kid caught out doing something wrong. He immediately goes to apologise to Berthold but to no avail. Out comes the card. He would not feature against Argentina should England reach the final.

Gazza was wobbling. Lineker says something to him and then is visibly concerned and says 'have a word with him' to the bench. Gazza's world collapses in that instant and there was no knowing how he'd react. After that initial wobble, Gascoigne managed to refocus and perform some diligent defensive work.

Gazza: "I got the ball in the centre circle and bundled my way forward. Then, as Matthäus tried to nick it off me, I nudged the ball out of his reach, but overran it. I had to stretch as Thomas Berthold came across. I was giving it 110%. It was the World Cup semi-final and I didn't want to give them anything for free. To this day I honestly don't think I touched him, but down he went, rolling around as if in agony.

Bobby Robson gathers his men before Extra Time

I crouched down to make sure he was okay and at that stage I wasn't thinking I was in trouble. There was nothing in the challenge. Then everything turned to slow motion.

"I suppose I'd have to say the occasion got to me, but this German guy is 6ft 5in and he dives and screams like a baby. For a couple of minutes I was going around in a daze. My whole world had been shattered. I had gone out of my way to steer clear of trouble and there I was - out of the World Cup Final if we had won. I've looked at it hundreds of times and it becomes clearer and clearer that I didn't touch him. The boss had told us, any trouble pat them on the back, say you're sorry and shake hands. I did just that, even helping the bugger to his feet, gave him a smile and then I saw the ref, I held up my hands, half in surrender, half in disbelief. Then he did it. It seemed like slow motion. He took out the yellow card and with the booking I'd already received I knew at once I was out of the final if we got there. We'd been told two yellow cards and it's a one-match ban, the next match, only when I'd been told that I never thought the next match could be the World Cup Final. I thought at twenty-three I'll never get another chance. I wanted to be anywhere but on that pitch."

"I straightened up and turned to the ref," Gascoigne continued in his book *Glorious: My World, Football and Me*. "He's gone for his pocket. Suddenly I can't hear anything. The world just stops apart from the bloke in black. My eyes follow his hand, to the pocket, then out with the card. There it is, raised above my head. I looked at the crowd, I looked at Lineker, and I couldn't hold it back. At that moment I just wanted to be left alone. I didn't want to talk to anyone or see anyone. My bottom lip was like a helicopter pad. I was devastated."

"My heart sank the moment the referee took out the yellow card," Bobby Robson said later. "My heart hit my shoes. Because I realised instantly, that was the final for Paul Gascoigne - out. And that's a tragedy; for him, me, the team, the country, the whole of football. Because he was so good, and he was superb in this particular match. The bigger the game, the better he got. Gascoigne knew as well, the moment the card was produced. Because I saw his face change, from being aggressive, fighting for the ball, to realising he'd committed an error, and he'd been booked, and he knew now the final was not for him. Tears began to well into his eyes. And Gary Lineker was very clever, he saw it immediately and came as close as he could to me and said, 'watch Gazza'. He thought now his mind might just go a bit berserk, even more berserk than he had with [giving away] the free kick. And I understood it. He knew the supreme penalty he was going to have to pay for that slight indiscretion. At the time of the booking, he was probably a bit rattled. Gary Lineker knows him well and he came over to the bench and shouted at us to watch Gazza for the next five minutes."

Waddle was one of the first by his side. "Come on, Gazza, get on with it." He just kept saying, "I'm going to miss the final…"

Brooking, in commentary, "Paul Gascoigne is almost in tears. There's no need to book him there, he's got tired legs. He's shattered. It's been a gripping match and I just hope that doesn't affect his performance. All the Germany bench were up, encouraging the referee to book him. To miss the final after the tournament he has had would be a travesty."

Andreas Brehme, speaking to *the Independent* in 2010: "England had an exceptional group with Gary Lineker, Chris Waddle, Paul Gascoigne. Paul was a great player, the same as when I played against him [for Internazionale against Lazio]. He had everything – he could win the ball, he struck the ball well, he could beat his opponent in a one-on-one. Technically he was strong and tactically too."

Terry Butcher, speaking to *the Express* in 2018: "I was watching from the bench, having been taken off to bring on a more attacking player in the 70th minute. When Gazza was booked, and Gary Lineker said across to the dugout, 'Have a word', everybody had a word. The whole bench was up shouting and encouraging Gascoigne."

Lineker won 80 caps for England and returned from the 1986 World Cup with the Golden Boot and scored 243 times for a variety of clubs including Everton, Tottenham and Barcelona. But for all the goals and glory more than anything he says he is remembered for the time someone else was booked and he made a face at his manager. "Out of everything in my career, the moment people ask me about most often was when Gazza got booked in that semi-final. I could see his bottom lip was going. I think it says a lot about Bobby that it was him I turned to, to ask him to have a word. I didn't know that the moment would be caught on camera."

Robson believed that the Germans had pressured the referee into showing the card. "He flew in at the boy, upended everything, and the German bench all stood up, which unfortunately I think affected the referee. We don't allow players to do that. We say, 'Sit down, it's got nothing to do with you.' They all jumped up and it made it worse for Paul. It was only half a booking."

The Brazilian referee spoke to *The Guardian* about the incident in his first interview with a British newspaper in 2014. "Listen, there was no controversy," insisted José Roberto Wright. "The lad tackled an opponent from behind and nowadays he could even have been sent off. It was none of my business if Gascoigne already had a yellow card – my job was to apply the laws of the game. He tried to argue with me and apologise, but I told him in English that it was a bookable offence. Then I got on with the game."

In 1990 Wright was named the best referee in the World Cup by the International Federation of Football History and Statistics, and later that year named the best official on the planet by the World Referees' Federation. "I didn't see him crying or all that commotion," says Wright. "It wasn't until later that I saw footage of the game and noticed how upset he was. Years later I read that Gascoigne's tears were some kind of watershed moment in English football, that it helped people fall in love with the game once again.

"The tackle was bad, and if I hadn't booked Gascoigne I would have lost control of the game. But I must say I was surprised he got so upset about it. I've never met him again, but I'm sure now he'd agree with me about the incident."

John Barnes was naturally hugely disappointed to be watching but thought Gazza's injury might have opened the door for him should they reach the final. Barnes undoubted flair might have swung it England's way, "it was frustrating. However, I was pleased that we were there. The squad had a real feeling and desire for the team to do well even though some players were on the bench. There was a real squad mentality. Viv Anderson went to two World Cups and never got on the pitch. I don't think I would have been fit (for the final). I might have played, but I don't think I would have been fit! [*Laughs.*] I would have had three days to get fit. I don't know... It would have been up to Bobby Robson, wouldn't it? But I would definitely have been available for selection, as we say. To be honest, it would have been the wrong thing to do, but how could you turn down the chance to play in a World Cup Final? I had a lot of injuries leading up to the 1990 tournament. From the point of view of age and experience, I was a better player than in '86, but, physically, I wasn't at my best and I should have been because I was 27. I should have been in my prime. But the team itself in 1990 was a better team than '86. We had the right blend of youth and experience. The best performance was against West Germany when we lost. You have to say we were fortunate against Belgium and against Cameroon but we had a lot of experience of getting through adversity."

As it turned out Barnes was not destined to find out whether he would have made the final but Barnes' favourite World Cup story. Well, it just has to be Gazza. "My favourite is one I only found out about years later when I worked with Thomas Berthold in South Africa. Berthold was the player Gazza fouled in the semi-final and it was because of that foul and the subsequent booking that he knew he wouldn't be playing in the final, had we won. After he fouled him and Berthold was lying on the floor, Gazza went up to him and everyone thought he was rubbing him on the head to say sorry and Berthold was pushing him away. What actually happened – and Gazza told me this and Thomas confirmed it – was that after he kicked him, he saw the referee coming over and Gazza said to himself, as only Paul Gascoigne could in his own mind, that if the referee hears him screaming – and Gazza said he was screaming like a baby – if the referee hears him screaming, he's going to book me. But if he doesn't hear him screaming then maybe I won't get booked. So I'm going to squeeze his lips shut. So that's what he was trying to do. It didn't work, but it was a brave effort!"

Of the incident Bobby Robson wrote in his autobiography, "I don't know anybody who dislikes Paul Gascoigne. The affection we all felt for him added to the poignancy of his booking. As we went into the second period of extra time, I had said to Paul, 'Look, I know you can't play in the final but what you can do is make sure all the other lads can. Just concentrate on that.' This was in the heat of the battle. Now, I can appreciate how crushed Paul would have felt had we beaten the Germans that night in Turin."

From a German point of view Gascoigne had let his country down, "Had Gascoigne been German he would be *persona non grata* today," the former Liverpool and Newcastle midfielder Dietmar Hamman wrote in his book *The Didi Man.* "[After the booking] he went to pieces. The game was still tied, and a job still needed to be done, yet his first thoughts were for himself. When the game went to a penalty shoot-out Gascoigne was earmarked to take [a] penalty for England. He decided that he wasn't in the right frame of mind to take it. For Gascoigne, in that moment, it was all about him as an individual, and the way he was feeling. It was nothing to do with his duty to the team. If Gascoigne was German his behaviour would have created a national scandal, and the player would be forgotten forever. If it were possible to erase his name from the team sheet then it would be done."

There is a parallel with a German player; Gascoigne received his caution with 20 minutes of extra time to play and the scores level; Michael Ballack was booked in the 71st minute of normal time in the 2002 semi-final against South Korea with the scores level. Both knew they no longer had a chance of appearing in the final. Ballack was the midfield inspiration behind a poor Germany side's run to the final in 2002 and scored his side's winner within four minutes and celebrated without reservation.

Yet in the crucial moments before the shoot-out in Turin, most of the England manager's time was spent not with the five designated takers but with Gascoigne, coping with the midfielder's emotional disintegration.

Despite the drama and tears, England came within an inch of going ahead with the last kick of the first half of extra time when Trevor Steven's cross from the left is partially cleared, the same man leaps above Berthold to head it back towards the area. It falls to Waddle, 12 yards out on the left side of the box, and he smacks a brilliant first-time shot across Illgner and off the inside of the far post and back out. Platt stretched for the rebound but it flew off the post so quickly that he couldn't react in time.

Co-commentator Trevor Brooking observed: "Chris Waddle's shot came back off the post like a rocket, nobody could even get near it. I can't believe it, that would have given everyone a lift just before the break. A beautiful strike and the Germany keeper Bodo Ilgner could not get near it."

England kick off the second period of extra time facing the prospect of their first-ever penalty shoot-out. West Germany had been in three: losing in the final of Euro '76 but winning at the World Cup in 1982 against France and in 1986 against hosts Mexico.

With few options left Robson switches wingers so that they were playing on the 'wrong' side: Steven on the left, Waddle on the right. Gascoigne is shielding the ball down the right wing when he is kicked up in the air from behind, it was an appalling tackle and much worse than Gascoigne's on Berthold and Brehme was rightly booked. Brehme and Gascoigne shake hands and pat each other on the head. Gascoigne's response to that yellow card was unexpectedly mature. He seemed to have got over his own disappointment.

From the resulting free-kick, swung in by Waddle, Platt flicks a smart header past Illgner but he had been flagged offside a split-second earlier - it's a close call on the replay and he looks level; the Germans push up but Berthold stayed a bit deeper and was close to playing Platt onside; Platt was fractionally onside and Gascoigne fractionally off. For a blissful, glorious moment, it looked like England might be on course for a World Cup Final. Platt is involved again, arriving late in the box and leaping almost backwards to head Parker's cross over the bar from the penalty spot. John Motson reveals that Bobby Robson told him that the five penalty takers, if needed, would be Lineker, Beardsley, Gascoigne, Pearce and Platt before adding ominously, "You wouldn't want it settled on penalties. You certainly wouldn't want to lose it on penalties."

The final chance saw Buchwald place a lovely curler to the left of Shilton that bounced up on to the outside of the post. With England hanging on, the referee blows five seconds early. The players embrace warmly after a magnificent game. The mutual respect was visible.

The bond between Robson and Gascoigne was again evident as the manager comforts Gazza before the shoot-out, admitting later he'd been holding back the tears himself. The yellow card left Gazza so emotionally drained that he withdrew from the penalty shoot-out – Chris Waddle replaces him.

Lineker drills the opening spot kick confidently into the left side of the net as Illgner dives the wrong way, surely the confidence boost England needed to go on to win the shoot-out? 1-0

The first German penalty is even better, as Brehme places a shot carefully into the bottom-left corner with his right foot. Shilton dived the right way but it was a wonderfully accurate penalty, right into the side-netting. When Brehme took a penalty at the 1986 World Cup he used his left foot. 1-1

Beardsley shuffles forward nervously but executes another excellent penalty, high to Illgner's right. 2-1

Matthäus cracks his penalty low to Shilton's right. Shilton went the right way again but was getting nowhere near that. 2-2

Platt side-foots his spot kick to his left but it was at a saveable height and Illgner managed to get fingertips on it, but not a full hand on it and could only help it into the net. Platt trots back to the halfway line with a nervous smile. The pressure on England is mounting. 3-2

Again Shilton anticipates the right way and again he is nowhere near saving it as Riedle whips it high into the net. 3-3

Then Stuart Pearce, so reliable from the spot for Nottingham Forest, has his tame kick saved by Illgner. It wasn't one of his best, he blasted it almost straight down the middle but low enough so that, even though Illgner had dived to his right, he was able to save it with his feet. 3-3

England are on the brink of penalty shoot heartbreak as Thon places another accurate spot kick into the bottom-right corner. Shilton goes the right way yet again but, again, gets nowhere near it. 3-4

So it is Waddle rather than Gascoigne, who has the chance to keep England alive but smashes his penalty inches over the bar – although such was its trajectory it looked like he skied it miles over.

England's dream was over in the cruellest way after such a wonderful performance against the best team in the tournament. As Waddle sinks to his knees, Lothar Matthäus breaks away from the German celebrations to help him to his feet. Bobby Robson smiles ruefully but also proudly, gently punching the air as if to say, 'bad luck.' His campaign, which started farcically, ends in glorious failure. There are more Gazza tears as he salutes the fans.

John Motson: "Bobby Robson's dream is shattered in the coldest way possible. His England career ends sadly on the precipice of a great achievement and with it the hopes and dreams of every Englishman. Waddle belted his kick over the bar, and West Germany scored all four of their penalties. That is the sad and dramatic finish of England's World Cup adventure in Italy."

Trevor Brooking: "Words cannot express what the England players must be experiencing, over the 120 minutes before penalties they were the better side and looked sharper. They didn't get the luck when they needed it and I am so disappointed and choked for them."

Waddle struck a post in extra time, but no one will remember that, only his shocking penalty miss to hand the Germans the path to the final, a bitter end to England's first penalty shoot-out in which the Germans netted all four of their pens and England went out in tears but with pride restored.

The shoot-out loss brought a further outpouring of emotion among the English contingent. As the West Germans celebrated, Robson summed up just how close England had come as he flicked his hand as if to say 'so near'. He was full of pride, tinged with regret over what might have been. "It's a cruel situation but you have to accept it. We wish West Germany every success in the final, they are a good team. We matched them but it's over for us now, we have done well to get to the semis and can go home feeling very proud. When you get to the four best teams in the world there is not a big difference between them, all have tremendous fitness, tactical knowledge and technical ability, but it comes down to the ability of one individual to break the deadlock. It was always close."

Chris Waddle, speaking to T*he Express* in 2018 said, "The only penalty I had taken before was for Tottenham in a pre-season game. I had watched the goalkeeper very closely and noticed that he dived low. I decided to hit it hard and high. I kicked the post in anger and frustration, and the first player to speak to me was the West German captain Matthäus. He said, 'Don't worry, it's a horrible way to go out of the World Cup'. That was a magnificent gesture."

Peter Shilton said: "I'll never forget that moment when Chrissy blasted it over the bar. My stomach just dropped, it was awful. That was it. I was devastated. To make it worse myself and Stuart Pearce were both called in for a drugs test at the end of the tunnel, we never went back in to the dressing room with the lads, we only saw them about two hours later back in the hotel. By that time everyone was eating and it was like a morgue. The last thing you want at the end of a penalty shootout is to be sat in a small room opposite two German lads for an hour. To be fair, they were good lads. They were obviously very pleased but they realised how we were feeling and didn't make too much of it."

"We were transformed against Germany, hitting our best form but not getting that bit of luck all teams need," Butcher said. "The only genius Germany showed was from the penalty spot. The pressure on the takers is enormous. Walking up to the ball knowing that billions are watching. You can practice every day, put the ball exactly where you want time after time and still make a mess of the responsibility. Nothing much disturbs Stuart Pearce on the field and yet he couldn't drive his kick home. Chris Waddle strikes a great ball, but he failed, too."

Trevor Steven, speaking to *The Guardian* in 2018 said, "On the field absolute devastation emotionally. We felt so badly for those who'd not scored. I don't know how they must've felt to have that forever around their necks. When we got back into the dressing room, it was heartache, everybody consoling each other. But what can you do? It's gone. The moment has gone, you can't get it back. It's difficult to put a jar on the emotions – we were so proud of what we'd done and yet one of the biggest regrets you can have as a player is not getting to the final. We could've won it and that would have been life-changing."

Butcher remembers Pearce and Waddle being inconsolable, his heart going out to them and the Germans so clinical in the shoot-out, "Just like they were again when it came to penalties in Euro 96," he said. "All of them were ice cool."

"The Germans scored a fluky goal and then nothing," adds Mark Wright.

"We were the better team. We battered them," said Gascoigne.

"I consider ours to have been one of England's best performances in the last 25 years," said Robson.

"It's the one thing I look back on and regret," said Lineker. "It still rankles. We were within a whisker of a World Cup Final. We'd have won it too. Argentina were shot."

Outside the stadium afterwards Germany's bus drew alongside England's.

"We could hear their players singing and shouting," Butcher recalls. It's a sound he will always remember.

In a TV interview the manager conveyed his passion for his country. "I wish I was home because they tell me people are dancing in the street. Well I'd like to be home dancing in the street," he said, beaming. For all the flak he had taken, Robson had now done something no other England manager had, he'd led the side to the semi-finals of the World Cup on foreign soil.

England had saved their best performance until last, only for their luck to run out. "We hit the inside of the post, they scored a really lucky goal and we lost on a shoot-out," Lineker observed.

Trevor Steven recalls: "It was a surreal atmosphere aboard the team bus to the game. We knew that the world would be watching us, and that this was the gateway to an incredible opportunity. We all just had to hold our nerve. My mindset was still positive and after about an hour I was asked to warm up. On I came for Terry Butcher as we switched from a back three to 4-4-2 in search of an equaliser. I had to pinch myself. Soon after we were level, through Gary Lineker, and from then on it was end to end. It carried on that way through extra-time. Waddle hit the post for us. They hit the post too. Paul Gascoigne became a star of that World Cup and, in this game and up against Lothar Matthäus, he ran the show. To be on the field and feel the confidence now flowing through the team was amazing. You have to remember as well that English clubs had been banned from European competition since 1985. We hadn't played against Bayern Munich or AC Milan or Barcelona for five years – that's half a career. To be in touching distance of the final when we were nearly all playing in their back yard was a massive achievement against the odds.

"The penalties, looking out at the frenzy of excitement in the crowd and then the recognition that we'd have to take a kick, was like an out-of-body experience. Although I'd taken spot-kicks for Everton, I wasn't one of England's five takers. I was due to be sixth, though, so I had to believe I was going to take one and keep a calm head. I knew I could become the hero or the villain. Football is full of ifs, buts and maybes but this was a different level. The emotions were so intense and it's difficult to relate to now. We started the shoot-out well but then suddenly it was over, after Stuart Pearce and Waddle missed the fourth and fifth kicks. All that opportunity had gone. We were completely deflated. It could have been so different. We were the better team in the semi and I don't think there was any doubt that we believed we'd have beaten an Argentina side that wasn't very good in the final. But my overriding emotion when I look back is pride. It was the biggest stage I ever played on and, although it didn't end well, that is what being a footballer is all about."

England's wins over Belgium and Cameroon had their elements of luck. Yet, Argentina, Romania and Colombia had all been unable to draw level with Cameroon after falling behind during the tournament, but England had done so and gone on to win. But Robson desperately wanted to bow out with the greatest prize of all.

In the dressing room there were more tears, but not confined to Gazza, and regrets in silence. Silence too for the first ten minutes on the coach. Then Gary Lineker said: "It's gone, we can't bring it back." Then the singing began and even Gazza joined in, and back at the hotel it was time to drown their sorrows with a few beers, make that plenty of beers.

Gazza said, "I've been asked over and over again, would it have been worse for me if we'd won and I'd had to sit out the final. The answer is no. I wanted us to win even if I couldn't play, and maybe we could have appealed. It wasn't just me who'd lost, it was all of us, not the team, the squad, but the country, including my family. We just felt gutted, but we also couldn't let the Boss, or the journos, see how badly we were taking it deep inside."

Back at the hotel, Gazza went straight to his room at first, to phone his parents to let them know he was fine. John Motson recalls how he went back to the England team hotel to say his farewells. He observed: "Bobby Robson was in jovial mood. 'I'm not retiring, John,' he joked." Motson continued, "He was fifty-seven at the time and had already agreed to take or as coach at PSV Eindhoven. 'Come and see me in Holland', he shouted above the hubbub. Little did any of us know he still had half a career in front of him; in Holland, Portugal, Spain and back home with Newcastle United. Latterly Sir Bobby has fought cancer on five occasions. What a hero."

Motty did retire, eventually hanging up his sheepskin, and in his memoirs he wrote: "To Paul Gascoigne goes the accolade of dominating a World Cup like no other English player, the victorious 1966 team apart. He embodied the spirit and tenacity of Robson's team in Italia '90 - the nearest England has come to the final since Moore, Charlton and Hurst lifted the trophy."

There was criticism for Peter Shilton; the 40-year-old goalkeeper had made several decent saves in open play but in the shoot-out decided to delay diving until each kick had been taken and got nowhere near any of them and was widely blamed by his team-mates for England's shoot-out failure. "You should have bloody gambled," Stuart Pearce shouted in the dressing-room after the game, however he was hardly blameless himself having blazed over his spot kick.

Gascoigne would face Germany for a second and final time, in the Euro '96 semi-final. Again he was booked, and again his side lost on penalties although on this occasion he took one, and scored. He would never play in the finals of an international competition again.

★

When Sir Bobby Robson sadly passed away in 2009, one of the many tributes came from *The Guardian*'s David Lacey, "Robson could get angry but it never lasted long. His occasional spats with reporters were quickly forgotten. He was never one to hold a grudge. During the 1990 World Cup his fiercest critics were among those who gave him a farewell lunch in Sardinia. And Robson did suffer some vitriolic criticism shortly before England left for Italy.

"Following some ancient kiss-and-tell revelations in a newspaper Bert Millichip, the chairman of the Football Association, as good as told Robson his contract would not be renewed after the tournament. Robson wasted no time getting himself fixed up with PSV Eindhoven for the new season and was labelled a deserter by the more hysterical sections of the press. Yet when England returned home after losing to the Germans on penalties in the Turin semi-final a large crowd at Luton airport greeted Robson with loud cheers. He had left the country a condemned man but came back a hero of sorts."

BBC football commentator Jonathan Pearce recalls, "We first worked closely at the 1988 European Championship finals. The competition proved atrocious for England. On the field they were humbled by Ireland, the Netherlands and the Soviet Union. On the streets of Germany beer-bellied bruisers shamed the nation with acts of thuggery. The press savagely turned on the manager but not once did he duck a radio interview or briefing. When he spoke into the microphone he tried to explain the way the games had gone or what he planned to do. The answers weren't terse. They were rich in insight and passion. There were verbal blunders. Ahead of the opener against Ireland he announced that Viv Anderson was in the team. A nudge from an aide reminded him that he'd actually picked Gary Stevens! He frequently mixed up Stevens and Trevor Steven. I once heard him call Bryan Robson 'Bobby'. The mix-ups made me laugh out loud. You couldn't help but warm to the man.

"In 1990 I was one of half a dozen journalists allowed to stay in the England team hotel. With the pressure mounting day-by-day he remained scrupulously polite and welcoming. We weren't made to feel like interlopers. We were allowed to witness close up the deep affection the players felt for him.

"He'd commissioned an Italian tank to be positioned outside the gates of the hotel on Sardinia for added security. The players and journalists still managed to break out on secret drinking trips thinking he'd never know. He always found out though. His tongue would give a lash, but there was a mischievous glint in his own eyes at the telling-off. His affection for the players knew no bounds. He loved football people.

"Mick Lowes of BBC Newcastle and I got terribly drunk on the eve of the pre-World Cup friendly in Tunisia and nearly missed the plane. We hurtled into the airport lounge sweaty and hungover. Bobby glanced, raised an eyebrow, wagged a finger and told us we'd be out of the camp if it ever happened again. There was no rampaging lecture, but I never crossed him again.

"After the epic quarter-final win over Cameroon, in the England hotel perched high on dizzying cliffs, we were halfway through an interview when he suddenly disappeared in mid-answer. He literally ran off. We stood puzzled for several minutes until we heard the pitter-patter of onrushing feet. There he was reappearing down a dim corridor. He resumed the answer as if he hadn't even paused for thought. We never asked him why he'd done a runner. He never told us. It was Tommy Cooper-esque. It was typical Bobby."

CHRIS WADDLE

I wish Gazza had taken the penalty

ENGLAND
CHRIS WADDLE

I watched the re-run of our semi-final and was nervous all over again. I could only take so much and had to take a walk in the garden. Each time I watch it I think "wow, how close we came to reaching the final. How good would that have been to have got to the final!"

So much goes through your mind, how we should have won that game. There are so many 'what ifs' in life. 'What if' my shot that hit the post had gone in, and I suppose the biggest 'what if' is what if Gazza had taken the penalty instead of me?

That penalty! Well, there are moments in life, in football, and it's those moments that stick in people's heads. I imagine no one talks about the fact I hit the post in that semi-final, but they know about that penalty miss.

I was not one of the penalty takers. I had never taken a penalty in my life, but Gazza was in no fit state to take one and Bobby Robson asked if anyone fancied taking a penalty. I looked round, no one put their hands up. I was feeling confident, I really enjoyed the game, I'd hit the post. My confidence was high. I thought to myself, 'go on, then, yeh, I can do it'. I put my hand up.

Of course, looking back, I wish Gazza had taken that penalty!

I was watching the keeper as I was the last up, and he really didn't dive, so I thought I would put it to my right, his left hand corner. Then I thought, well if I hit it with power he'll never save it. I hit it sweet, well, too sweet perhaps, I couldn't have hit it any better, but it flew over, and it was a horrible way to lose the game, especially this game.

It's a lottery. I know people think it shouldn't be, that top class footballers should score from 12 yards but I've seen Maradona miss, , I've seen Lionel Messi and Ronaldo miss. They've all missed them and as well as me there has been Stuart Pearce, Gareth Southgate, David Batty, Paul Ince, the list is endless... Platini, Baggio, Even Harry Kane has missed them. It is a horrible way to define a game, but as yet no one has come up with a better solution but I'd prefer "next goal wins" to a penalty shoot-out. It was a long wait until an England team actually won a penalty shoot-out against Colombia in the World Cup in Russia.

We played that semi-final the way England should play, and we ended up a penalty away from beating Germany.

Was it really 30 years ago?

As the tournament progressed we got better, but I always thought that Germany was the big obstacle to winning it, if we could beat Germany it would be ours, that Argentina were not half the team that won it in Mexico and although no game is easy I thought we had the beating of them. Germany were an excellent team and really there was nothing between us and them…

It wasn't until 2018 in Russia before England reached another World Cup semi-final, but let's be honest it wasn't until they played Croatia that they came up against any team of note, although you thought the way they were sailing through the tournament their name was on the trophy. I have to be honest I didn't think there was the same buzz about Gareth Southgate's team in Russia as there was with our team in Italia '90. How many of Gareth's team would get into our team? I'm not sure any, maybe Harry Kane, depending on the system, but if they played 4-3-3 as they had been, then would you take Harry Kane above Gary Lineker?

PETER BEARDSLEY

"There are 55 million people watching back home... don't miss!"

ENGLAND
PETER BEARDSLEY

Perhaps my greatest memory of Italia '90 was taking a penalty in the semi-final shoot-out, it was a weird experience, yet somehow enjoyable! I knew I was taking one and it didn't worry me, even though you knew everyone was watching you back home. Somehow, though, you get less credit for scoring than you do for missing, by credit I mean it changes your life, and can make your fortune oddly enough. No one remembers the three that scored; Gary, myself and David Platt but no one will ever forget the two who missed.

When it came to the penalty shoot-out, as we waited for it to begin, I was chatting with Gary and we were in a good mood and laughing and joking as we were confident we would score. Bobby Robson pretty much knew beforehand who would be taking the penalties and in which order, Gary first and I would be second. Bobby walked past Gary and myself as we were chatting and said: "You know what you have to do, don't you?"

"No", I replied.

"Just score", Bobby said. Then he added: "There are 55 million back home watching, don't let them down!"

It was a weird sensation, everyone has their own way of dealing with such a situation, but for me I found it an enjoyable experience. It was all down to you, in front of all those England fans, and quite a few Italians, you are the only person who can do anything about it, there are no outside forces to influence how you will go about it, you are in total control.

Also there was a feeling of it wouldn't be so bad if I missed as I was going second as there would be plenty of opportunities to rectify it, as it has been proven in penalty shoot-outs with France for example so if I had to pick my fondest memory of Italia '90 then weirdly enough it would be scoring in that penalty shoot-out.

Of course it doesn't seem like 30 years ago, it's incredible how time goes so quickly; Italia '90 seems like yesterday, but they tell you when you are young to 'enjoy it, it won't last forever'. I was fortunate to already have played in one World Cup so to have played in two was amazing, even though I missed out on a couple of games. Fair enough Bobby Robson was brilliant for me, and to be fair the first game was not good and he wanted to make a change, so I couldn't argue with that. Bobby gave me my opportunity in the first place and I will always be grateful for that.

There was a great atmosphere at Italia '90, really special, we got further than any England team since '66, and further than any England team on foreign soil, and I say the atmosphere was great even though there was a lot of talk about animosity toward the media. But I knew many of the guys from Mexico '86 and I knew how much the football writers wanted us to succeed. They didn't want us to fail, I know that. There was no animosity from my point of view toward them. I knew they also had a job to do, and if they felt I shouldn't have been in the team, and said so, than that was their opinion and I had to live with that, but if it was honestly given, that was fair enough. Gazza had an issue with the press but maybe there were times that he listened to the wrong people, when you become older and more experienced, you have a different view.

SHILTON'S NIGHTMARE FAREWELL

The *Sunday Telegraph* headline summed up the Third Place Play-off - "Italy spoil farewell party for Robson". It was still England's most successful tournament on foreign soil but England missed out on bronze to the hosts in Bari due to a dodgy penalty.

Bari was 600 miles from Turin, but it must have seemed a million miles away from the extraordinary tension of a World Cup semi-final with a final at stake, to a meaningless showcase game for the bronze medal.

The *Sunday Telegraph* the day after the match barely squeezed the 'news' item onto the front page, it made a 'News In Brief' and fewer than 20 words right down at the bottom of the page with a match report later in the paper.

The *Telegraph*'s chief football writer Colin Gibson left the Morris Men, now billeted in Rome awaiting the World Cup Final, to travel along with just 100 England fans; 1,000 tickets had been allocated but few were interested. The justification for giving this game the brush off was the global interest in the World Cup Final and being on hand in Rome to preview it. But a high brow broadsheet like *The Telegraph* wanted their top man on the spot to report on the play-off.

Yet not even World Cup hosts Italy made much of an effort, and it turned out to be a stinker. Stuart Pearce looked pretty cheesed off with the squad's lacklustre attempt at the Mexican wave sat next to Dave Beasant at the end of the England bench. That look was deceptive, Pearce was proud to have been part of it all despite his penalty miss against West Germany.

Pearce wrote in one of his *Daily Mirror* columns how he had no regrets about the sheer thrill of being part of English football history: "I am always asked if Italia '90 was my biggest disappointment after we went out on penalties to the Germans in the semi-finals. It wasn't my happiest day but it's certainly one of my proudest because England showed the world we were again a football force to reckon with. We might have lost the spot-kick shoot-out but Germany didn't beat us on football. We came within a whisker of reaching the final and I maintain we deserved to. Of course, I'd love to turn the clock back and see my penalty hit the back of the net, and I am sure Chris would too. But we did everything we could during the match and in extra-time. We kept

All the England bench (bar Stuart Pearce far right) join in the fun in Bari.

the ball, showed the world we could play and there was a new respect for England after that night. We put our country back on the football map."

England faced Italy without a single player in their 30s, but one in their 40s. Two months before his 41st birthday Peter Shilton captained the side as he won his 125th and final cap. It was not a perfect farewell as a lapse of concentration with the ball at his feet allowed Roberto Baggio to nip in and fire Italy ahead after 70 minutes.

David Platt scored England's goal on the ground that would become his home. Only 12 months after nodding in the equaliser from Tony Dorigo's cross, he joined Bari from Aston Villa for £5.5m. Salvatore Schillaci was on five goals, one ahead of 1986 top scorer Gary Lineker. While England's striker could not hit the target, Toto Schillaci scored an 85th-minute penalty to seal a 2-1 win for Italy and secure himself the golden boot prize.

1990 was definitely a year for unlikely heroes; Milla, Goycoechea, Schillaci, who took over the role Gianluca Vialli was supposed to play as the host's chief goalscorer. The dimimutive striker scored six goals and took the golden boot. He scored in six different matches opening his account as a substitute against Austria and closing it with a goal against England that secured bronze medals for Italy. He never found this form again and faded quickly after the World Cup. He scored 7 times for Italy in 16 appearances, all but one of them in this tournament!

Gascoigne got involved despite being suspended following his semi-final booking. He took part in a Mexican Wave with John Barnes and

Chris Waddle on the bench! Tony Dorigo got more than he bargained for on what was only his fourth England cap. After swapping shirts with Giuseppe Bergomi, the Italy captain then asked to trade shorts and socks. Dorigo replied, "Yes, but nothing else!"

There was a big farewell party back at the hotel, where the players threw their manager into the hotel swimming pool still wearing his suit just missing a concrete wall!

For the majority of this tournament the chief football writers exclusively covering England were out in Sardinia in a top class location at the Forte Village without any of the restrictions of the alcohol limits inside the cities, mainly due to concerns over drunken fans, mainly the English. We managed to bypass the rules when we found a lovely local restaurant in Turin long after the semi-final had finished after we had filed our stories and as the establishment was empty we were served some lovely local red wine.

Now we were all in Rome, and the booze ban was being strictly adhered to, our tour leader and organiser, Colin Gibson, suggested that we meet him half way from the airport at a restaurant just outside the city limits for lunch where they would be able to serve us drinks ahead of the World Cup Final.

That is what we did, and we had a wonderful pre-match meal accompanied by wine, and we all headed back to our city centre hotel where media buses were ferrying the media and other accredited personnel to the stadium.

We disembarked from the taxi having settled the bill, but as the taxi pulled away Colin realised that he had placed all his stuff in the boot. He had been distracted when he saw someone he knew and stopped to chat, and then chatted to someone else. He is that sort of bloke, he always has time for everyone. This time it backfired badly. We all started to laugh when Colin started to chase after the taxi, yelling "Stop!" We didn't realise that his overnight bag not only contained his clothes but also his Tandy, his passport, and his World Cup Final media ticket!

When he explained in a panic what he had left in the boot, it was no longer a laughing matter. The solution seemed simple enough, rush to reception, report the problem, and get the hotel to contact the taxi company and ask the driver to return his holdall as soon as possible.

The hotel receptionist made the call, and confidently reported back that the driver would be back very quickly. We were all relieved, mostly Colin. We waited and waited and waited but nothing happened, and we asked the receptionist to call again. Again we were told the driver was on his way, the problem had been that he had picked up another fare, and the city roads were jammed with so many people going to the final, or to the fans parks or to bars to watch the match.

We waited but still nothing. We enquired again. Another call. This time the news didn't seem so convincing. The driver had gone home, probably for his dinner and would return the bag as quickly as he could.

There was nothing for it, we urged Colin to give up hope of this driver returning before the match, and suggested that the very efficient media centre would sort out the crisis and be able to facilitate a duplicate ticket. That seemed the most logical option but Colin was worried it might not happen once we reached the stadium and then the option of the driver returning had gone. On balance we persuaded him to come with us to the stadium's media centre on the last media bus left. There, of course, within a few minutes they organised a duplicate ticket.

We all made the World Cup Final just in time.

Alan Green, the BBC radio commentator, spotted Bobby Robson inside the Olympic Stadium, where he had been working for TV "gazing wistfully across the venue."

Greenie added in his memoirs, "I couldn't tell for sure, but I guessed he was thinking that it might have been England out there. That, after all, was what we'd all been thinking. I got up from my seat and walked across. 'Mr Robson, I'm Alan Green from BBC Radio Sport. I hope you don't mind me coming up, I just want to say thank you. I don't know if you appreciate just how proud you've made us all feel.' I turned and walked back to my seat. This time, he was the one who looked dumbfounded. I really regret that I came to the England scene near the end of Bobby Robson's spell in charge. Though he undoubtedly had his quirks, I'm sure I would have enjoyed being in his company. His honesty and love of the game always shone through. Given time, he might even have discovered that I was a 'foreigner' he could trust."

TONY DORIGO

It made my Italian dad so proud

Yes, it's incredible to think it all happened 30 years ago. I still think about it a lot if I am honest and wonder if it was all real, it was so incredible. The biggest thing for me was the journey that we all went on, from how it all started and how much we progressed and then coming back to the UK. God what a homecoming, it was just so unexpected. When you are locked away in the team camp for so long, concentrating on the tournament, you really have no idea what is going on back home, what they are saying about you, what people are thinking. We picked up bits and pieces, you saw some of the newspapers from time to time, but just a glance at the headlines, not much else. We were locked away in a remote hotel with an adjacent golf course to keep us amused, otherwise we were training, talking about the games, thinking about the games, we were kept away from everything else.

We had no idea that the whole of England was behind us when we were cocooned away. We had to smile when we saw the welcome at Luton airport on our return, it was ridiculous, we didn't have that feeling out there that so much emotion had been generated back home. It wasn't just football supporters either, the big surprise was how much everyone had got behind us.

Of course we all know the numbers, how many people watch a World Cup on TV, how many watch back home, but they are only numbers, it doesn't equate to the real thing, and it was incredible discovering that many, many millions more than we would have ever imagined had been watching our exploits when we touched down at Luton. Our cars were all parked up at the hotel car park there where we had left them, but to get the short distance from the airport to the hotel look about an hour and a half as our coach crawled along with so many people lining the streets.

My proudest moment at Italia '90 was playing in the third place play off in Bari. My family were out there watching all the games, but although this wasn't the game we wanted, it was the game that made my father so proud, so happy. I was born in Australia, as my mother was Australian, but my dad is Italian. So playing in the World Cup against Italy, my dad was thrilled. Bari has such happy memories for me because of that, although it might not have been the same for the other players as it was for me.

The Italian team that day was captained by none other than Guiseppe Bergomi, one of Italy's greatest ever players who played more than 500 times for Inter, and ended up with more than 80 caps for his country. He was their right wing back, so played up against me throughout the game.

I was the last to leave the pitch, I was enjoying the moment as much as I could, and as I was headed down the tunnel I spotted Bergomi about 50 yards down the tunnel waiting there. I could see a lot of the lads had gone up to him, asking to swap shirts with him, but he declined. So, I thought I wouldn't ask him, he would hardly want to swap shirts with me. But I then saw him waving at somebody. I looked behind me, thinking it was someone following me down the tunnel, but he was looking straight at me when I looked round again and he was still waving.

I said "Are you waving at me?"

"Yeah, yeah, you", he replied, "Can we swap shirts?"

I was a touch surprised to say the least, but delighted.

The he said: "Can we swap shorts and socks?"

I was glad he stopped at the shorts!

I have no idea why he wanted to swap shirts with me, the only reason I can think of is that he played up against me and felt that was an appropriate memento of that game.

We had lost the game 2-1 but my dad was smiling when he greeted me after the game. I asked him why he was so happy when we had lost. He explained that it had made his day that I got a game, and had played against Italy in the Italian World Cup. It was quite funny.

He had travelled around watching all the games, and I might have got on in the semi-final in Turin, but as it turned out I never came off the bench. In the dressing room afterwards all the players were drained, including the substitutes, there was a hollow feeling and I tried to do my bit in consoling the players, but they were inconsolable, especially Stuart Pearce who found it too much to take.

Ok, so my favourite Gazza story. Everyone has one, but of course there are so many to chose from, I've certainly got a few. We had a golf day at our team hotel sponsored by Wilson sports who made all the golf equipment and supplied us with everything; golf clubs, bags with our names on them. It might have been a big promotional day for the sponsors, but we all had a fabulous relaxing time to ease the tension before the tournament. One or two of the lads didn't play well, like John Barnes, and opted out apart from the Long Drive competition. I was paired with Gazza! Great. We were in a four ball, and sorting things out but before we knew it Gazza had placed his own ball on the first tee and hit the drive and continued to move through all the holes, racing along on the electric buggy, laughing all the way. We were left to get on with a three ball, but we never caught Gazza up.

A week before the tournament we still had our wives and girlfriends with us but, of course, Gazza was on his own, so made a nuisance of himself. When we were on the beach chilling with our partners, he was running around pouring crisps on our heads. We had to chase him out to sea, but he would swim away as fast as he could so we couldn't catch him.

But I think my favourite has to be the warm up before the biggest games of our lives against West Germany in the World Cup semi-final. I was one of the subs that day, so came out straight away for the warm up with Gazza. He immediately spotted the overhead TV camera stationed about 300 metres above the centre circle. The first thing he did in his warm up was try to hit the camera hanging down from its position high above the centre circle. The way he was lashing balls at the camera, you would think he'd end up pulling a hamstring. I looked across at the Germans warming up and thought "God, what must they think of us?" They all started laughing, but then a couple came over to join Gazza in hitting balls at the camera! One of them struck a ball high into the air, then controlled it to perfection when it came down, which made me think we would be facing some great technical players in the game. Fortunately our manager didn't see any of this otherwise he would have gone crazy. We tended to shake our heads in disbelief at what Gazza got up to, but in a way it tended to relax you, it was a laugh, and you giggled to yourself at the sight of him trying to smash the TV camera. But he didn't get near it, it was so high above the ground.

As you can imagine, being away for so long, there were quite a few bizarre incidents that took place in our hideaway team hotel. Koo Stark and Mick Hucknall of Simply Red, a big Manchester United fan, came to our hotel and we saw them cooling off by the pool, chatting to one or two of the boys. It was a pretty hot day in Sardinia and Mick took off his shirt and then his shorts and was there in his Y-fronts, really wide Y-fronts, they looked disgusting. We were hoping he didn't actually jump into the pool as it looked disgusting enough when he was dry.

On a rare day off the boys liked to pop over to the Forte Village, and

I liked the resort so much I've been back there about seven times, it's a great location especially for the kids but I wasn't in the group that went over there and ended up drinking with one or two of the journalists. Bryan Robson was one of them and the group came back from the team dinner to our hotel, and our captain was so drunk he fell asleep at the first course. It was soup and when his face landed in the soup it woke him up!

We all heard about what happened to Bryan when he came back to his hotel room – I was just a few doors away and his screams woke me up that night, it was a terrible cry of pain. He was soon off back home, there was talk of an Achilles injury but he obviously badly damaged his toe that night tripping on the porcelain or whatever happened in that hotel room.

When I was selected for the England squad for the first time for a game in Scotland, he was my room mate assigned to look after the new boy. He was a great captain of England but what a shame his World Cup ended that way.

NEIL WEBB

After seven weeks - just 25 minutes.

We were there a long time, seven weeks, and at the end of it I got about 25 minutes as a substitute in the final game, the third and fourth place play off against Italy but I was still glad to have been part of such a wonderful experience.

In fact, I was surprised I was picked in the first place. I snapped my Achilles in the Sweden match back in September and had only got back playing again in the Manchester United team for two months, so it was quite a surprise, a pleasant surprise when I was called up and picked for the final 22.

But because I was just back from injury, it was difficult to expect to start and with only five substitutes and the other seven sat on their backsides not involved, it was tough to be one of the non players, training hard every day to keep in shape as the manager said, just in case you are needed.

It was important to support everyone, though, and for that reason it was essential to keep yourself buoyant and not show your disappointment at not playing, you couldn't let people see that, they wanted people to be happy around them and share in the adventure. Once out of the group and after overcoming a tricky Cameroon, it was some adventure getting to the semi-final and nearly making the final.

I did think, though, that I would start the play off game against Italy, with Gazza suspended there was clearly a space in central midfield, and I went to see Bobby Robson to put my case why I deserved to start the game, having been so supportive without getting a kick but Steve McMahon also asked Bobby the same question. I'm sure Bobby probably tossed a coin to be honest, but at least he told me I would come off the bench and I did, probably getting 25 minutes, maybe half an hour. I hit the post so at least I had a shot on target, but 20 odd minutes was not a lot to show for the seven weeks away.

We were all told before the game that we would receive a bronze medal, so no one was quite sure why we were playing a play off.

On the flight back the captain made an announcement, "I think you are in for a bit of a surprise when we land at Luton, the amount of people there to greet you".

Our reaction was, "yeh, sure!"

When we got off the plane we couldn't believe it, it was crazy, it must have taken us hours to drive the five miles to the hotel. Gazza was joking around, the mood was great, and we realised what kind of reaction there had been back home, it was quite a shock.

What we didn't realise is Italia '90 would kick start a resurgence in football, a lot more people were taking an interest, and the effect was for the game to emerge through a very rough time.

CHRIS WOODS

We could have killed Bobby Robson in the celebrations

I n the moment you didn't realise the significance. Growing up older people would tell you 'enjoy every moment because it goes so quickly', but when you are young you fail to appreciate it or understand it at the time. When you finish playing and move into coaching then you realise exactly what they meant. It's frightening how time has gone so quickly and we are now talking about the tournament 30 years on.

It wasn't until we came back to Luton airport and saw the welcome by the fans that we realised what it meant to everyone back home, our coach ride back to the hotel was unbelievable, I wondered what on earth it would have been like had we gone onto the final or even won it. I dread to think. You live in a bubble in the camp and don't realise it was quite so important to the supporters and the effect it was having on the public in general. Euro '96 was similar, and I like to think that the nation will get behind the England team, but equally the England team needs to galvanise the nation by doing well, and give them hope.

I have to admit it was disappointing to have gone to two World Cups without getting a game, but it is still unbelievable to have been part of both squads. In '86 in Mexico I didn't really expect to play and was No 2, but by 1990 I felt on par and that was disappointing, especially as I thought I would be in the team for the third and fourth place play-off game but didn't as it turned out despite being told that I would be playing. After being picked the manager spoke to Peter Shilton, and I was told I had plenty of time and that he wanted to play. You build yourself up for the game thinking of that chance of playing then all of a sudden you are told you are not playing, it was a kick in the teeth. Still, it was great to be part of it all and to be part of two World Cups, but I would have liked it even more if I could have said that I actually played in the World Cup, not just the qualifiers.

The No 2 and No 3 keepers have an important role to play within the squad helping the outfield players who want to do some work on crosses and finishing, staying behind once Shilts has done his work, as he was strict about what he had to do and once he finished we would take over to do some extra work with the strikers and forwards.

I suppose you cannot escape not having a favourite Gazza story, and mine comes from first hand knowledge as Terry Butcher and myself roomed together in the chalet within the hotel complex that connected to the chalet occupied by Chris Waddle and Gazza. How he got into the hotel I've no idea, but Gazza's big mate at that time, Jimmy Five Bellies was in that chalet next door and we had to shout at them every night to keep the noise down as we were trying to get to sleep. I imagine security is so much tighter these days around the England camp that you can't get near them.

The final day before departing the World Cup was one for celebration at what we had achieved, and we were all round the swimming pool when the lads decided it was a good idea to throw Bobby Robson into the pool. So they picked him up and hurled him into the water. I was watching and could see Bobby was far too close to a little square area of concrete jutting out from the corner of the pool. It missed his head by no more than two or three inches. Everyone was in a jovial mood but I don't think the England manager would have kept smiling if he realised how close his head came to smashing into the side of the pool.

THE WORST WORLD CUP FINAL

Argentina became the first World Cup finalists not to score and to have not one but two players sent off. That made it sixteen players dismissed at Italia '90 more than at Mexico '86 and España '82 combined. Pedro Monzón became the first man to be sent off in a final and Dezotti followed shortly after as Argentina finished with nine men.

Monzón walked after being shown a straight red card for a reckless studs up challenge on Jurgen Klinsmann. FIFA had warned officials to enforce the rules and Monzón raised his foot during the tackle, that left Klinsmann with a six inch gash on his shin. Dezotti, already cautioned earlier, received a straight red card late in the match when he hauled down Jurgen Kohler with what *The New York Times* described as a "neck tackle right out of professional wrestling", after Kohler refused to give-up the ball in an alleged attempt to waste time. After dismissing Dezotti, Mexican referee Edgardo Codesal was surrounded and jostled by the rest of the Argentinian team.

Codesal could have sent off Maradona before the game had even started. Diego was his country's great (perhaps only) hope heading into the final, after leading Argentina to World Cup glory four years earlier beating the same opponents in the Azteca stadium 3-2. "I could have sent him off before the game started as he was swearing profusely during the national anthem," Codesal told Uruguayan network Tirando Paredes, "Later, when I decided to send off Monzón, Maradona approached me and claimed I was a thief and on the FIFA payroll. I saw Maradona do some remarkable things on the pitch and also saw that his knee had ballooned from aggressive tackling. As a player he was the best but as a person he was unpleasant and one of the worst I've gotten to know in my life."

Maradona claimed the referee did not want Argentina to win. "Our players ran hard, but then came this man who ruined everything for us," he claimed, "this man was scared that we would get to penalties. He wanted to make the Italian people happy. The black hand of this man expelled Monzón for a normal action, and later he called a penalty against us from his imagination. I have been crying for a long time. Football has been my life and I wasn't crying because we got second place, but because of the way we lost. This man didn't have any right to call that penalty."

Andres Brehme coolly converted the decisive penalty in the 85th minute to win the Germans their third title after Rudi Völler was deemed to have been brought down by Roberto Sensini. In truth it looked like the defender got the ball but there could have been no complaint about who deserved the victory on the night as the Germans seemed to be the only team trying to score.

Up in the press box the English contingent pondered how their own nation would have fared against an Argentina side that had won only two games outright to reach the final and the overwhelming conclusion was that England would have beaten them, which only served to deepen the regret. We were almost certainly a penalty shoot-out away from winning the biggest prize of all.

The final was notable only for the first red card in a World Cup Final, a dodgy penalty decision, the second red card in a World Cup Final and the Germans winning their third world title. In the process, Franz Beckenbauer wrote his name in history as the first World Cup-winning captain to go on to manage a team to victory. He became the only man to have won both silver and gold medals at the World Cup as a player (1966 and 1974) and as a coach (1986 and 1990).

In a tournament of tears the last belonged to Diego Maradona, incensed by the travesty of injustice that had befallen his side. Referee Codesal had refused to award a penalty to Germany earlier in the game but later incurred the wrath of the Argentinians by not awarding them a penalty after the German team captain Lothar Mattaus tackled Gabriel Calderon.

Argentina started the final with four players suspended and ended it with nine men on the field, overall losing over half their squad due to injury or suspension. During the match, the Argentine players were whistled and booed every time they had the ball thanks to captain Diego Maradona's controversial comments in the media and the officiating was controversial throughout the match.

Argentina had only one shot on goal, while Germany had 16 scoring chances out of 23 shots. Argentina's strategy had been to defend at all costs and reach the shoot-out, having already advanced twice in the tournament via penalties. There was a sense of football justice as Brehme, taking the place of regular penalty taker Matthäus, converted the late spot kick with a low right footed shot to the goalkeeper's right.

West Germany became the nation to have reached most World Cup finals at the time (three wins, three defeats), and avenged their defeat at the hands of Argentina in 1986. Brian Glanville dubbed it "probably the worst, most tedious, bad-tempered final in the history of the World Cup".

Brehme's penalty may have won the 1990 World Cup but it is the semi-final against England that match-winner Berhme most fondly remembers. "That semi-final was the best match of the World Cup. It was a fantastic match involving two great teams – it was the final before the final. For 120 minutes the game went one way and then the other. England had an exceptional group with Gary Lineker, Chris Waddle, Paul Gascoigne."

Along with Lothar Matthäus and Jürgen Klinsmann, Brehme was one of three Inter-based players in Beckenbauer's squad who eliminated Holland, who had three AC Milan players in Rijkaard, Van Basten and Gullit in their ranks, en route to the last four. A dead-ball specialist, he admits that his deflected free-kick past Peter Shilton in Turin "was luck, nothing more". He later converted the Germans' first penalty but played down his country's shoot-out record in World Cups. "It is about concentration. We weren't convinced we'd win – we practised in training but in front of 60,000 people in Turin it is difficult. You can get nervous and perhaps the England players were a bit nervous."

Brehme recalls the tremendous spirit between England and Germany. "It was very clean, 22 players with respect for each other." The same could not be said of the final against nine-man Argentina, decided by Brehme's right foot. "That final was horrible, Argentina didn't have a corner, they didn't create a chance on goal. We had 10 chances to score. Argentina had a terrible World Cup but a lot of luck. Would England have beaten them? Definitely, 100 per cent."

STUART PEARCE

We made the nation proud but I wanted to go straight home

STUART PEARCE

My fondest memory from Italia '90 is making the nation proud of us, so from that point of view it was fantastic that we got as far as we did in the tournament. This was my first major competition, my first major finals, and a chance to win six England caps, and in general performances we were not too bad, personally and collectively, it was a wonderful experience, and turned out to be the only World Cup I went to. I would have expected to have gone to the next one, and didn't expect England not to qualify, but it is what it is.

If you ask me which personal performance I felt was my best I would have to say it was the German game, it was as good as any of my performances.

Coming back to Luton the welcome was totally unexpected, it blew us all away, it made it such a special day, but in all honesty I really just wanted to go home.

I had missed the penalty that contributed to our semi-final defeat, so that's why my overwhelming feeling after being away for six weeks, was to get back home. I didn't see anything to celebrate. It was quite a welcome to be fair, and I don't believe there is any country in the world that would have lauded its team like that having actually lost a semi-final, rather than returning having won the World Cup.

As for that picture of me sitting on the end of the bench at the third and fourth play off not being too thrilled with everyone on the England bench doing the Mexican wave, I was representing my country and didn't think doing a Mexican wave as one of the substitutes was the done thing!

BACK HOME

On landing back at Luton airport the returning heroes seemed totally unaware of the impact they had made on the folks back home as they were saluted by thousands of fans, perhaps as many as 200,000, as they embarked on an open top bus ride around the town. It had been a rollercoaster ride; from the jeers of the opening game to the cheers of their progress through the tournament and then Gazza's tears before even more cheers as the nation thanked its football team. After a decade of grim news; falling gates, hooliganism, several football tragedies and expulsion from Europe, the public had fallen in love with football again as 'Gazzamania' took hold.

On the plane journey Gazza asked Chris Waddle, Peter Beardsley and Peter Shilton how many fans had welcomed them back from Mexico and they told him "around 10,000" so he was shocked by the turn out. "Cor, you'd think we'd won the war", he said and promptly donned a pair of false boobs presented to him at the airport.

After inching their way through the crowd, they made it back to the hotel where Gazza was reunited with his dad who then smuggled his son and Chris Waddle out of the hotel in a campervan. Fortunately no one spotted them lying on the floor as it drove off, heading back to the north-east, as the exhausted pair feel asleep on the floor. At ten that night they were given their own party at the Dunston Excelsior.

Mel Stein, who was Gazza's minder, confidante, friend and agent for more than a decade, later confirmed my role in Paul Gascoigne's rise from promising footballer to cultural icon. In his book on Gazza he wrote, "*The Sun* started Gazzamania officially with their constant use of the phrase, but Harry Harris in *The Mirror* had probably been responsible for coining the phrase almost a year before. All *The Sun* was doing, as it did so often, was reflecting public opinion." The events at Luton were yet another step along Paul's path to superstardom which unfortunately led to his demise.

Bobby Robson missed the heroes return, having stayed on for the final with Gary Lineker where they collected the Fair Play award at the

Thousands welcome back the England team at Luton airport

end, an accolade a long way off being what they had most craved but one that recognised the discipline shown by the side – something that wasn't in evidence from Argentina during the dreadful final. Further satisfaction for Robson came with the news English clubs were being readmitted to Europe, proof that the nation's hooligan problem was beginning to ease a little after rearing its ugly head so often during his reign. So by staying for the final Robson missed out on a hero's return, but he would quickly realise the affection people now felt for him. Previously he had been mocked for getting names wrong, now it was part of his appeal; he'd endured barracking during his England reign but would now be applauded; where Robson had been criticised for being too loyal to his players, soon Graham Taylor would be taking stick for discarding them too quickly; and as Taylor failed at first the 1992 Euros and then the '94 World Cup qualifiers, appreciation grew of Robson's acheivements. And it has continued to grow ever since, as England continually failed to reach the last four of major tournaments – the only exception being Euro '96 as hosts and 2018 in Russia.

Italia '90 is not universally loved by football purists due to the often poor standard of football and the negativity of finalists Argentina who snarled their way to the final via penalties and cynical play before behaving appallingly in the final itself but for English football supporters it remains revered far more than any other tournament since 1966. In many ways it was an even greater achievement than '66 because England were away from home and written off before the start yet came back from so many set backs before putting in one of the all-time

great performances against a genuinely great team in the semi-final and coming within inches of glory. It was so good there are still plays, films and books being written about it... like this one.

Then there were the peripheral memories of the period which continue to spark nostalgia for anyone old enough to remember them; *Nessun Dorma*, *World in Motion*, Gazza's tears, Des Lynam's introductions for the big games, Gary Lineker's celebration against Belgium, even Waddle and Butcher doing that silly dance on the podium in that otherwise meaningless final game - it all made for a tournament and a summer to remember. And right at the heart of it was Robert William Robson, a man who had withstood constant criticism during his England reign but was now bowing out as a national treasure.

Peter Shilton observed, "Everyone just wanted to get home but we were all blown away really by the reception we got when landing at Luton airport. There were thousands of people there to welcome us and that's when it really hit home how well we had done. We didn't win it but we went further than any other England team had done away from home and I'm very proud of that. Then when I got back to my village in Leicestershire there were 40 or 50 people waiting to clap me out of my car. They had put flags up and all sorts. I couldn't believe it."

As always with England it was black and white; for a brief period the national team were world beaters but they came within seven minutes of going out against Cameroon in the quarter-final and a minute from penalties against Belgium (who hit the woodwork three times) if either result had gone the other way the reaction at home would have been very different. Something very similar occurred in the euphoria of Euro 96; the hosts played all their games at Wembley; a great Gazza goal against the Scots and an inspiring rout of an ageing Dutch side riven with in-fighting before a penalty shoot-out win in the quarter-finals, where the Spanish had a perfectly good goal disallowed prefaced yet another brave exit to the Germans in the semis on penalties where England took the lead and came within inches of winning it. In many ways Euro'96 was a repeat of Italia '90; uplifted by the anthem *Football's Coming Home* there was a wave of nationalist pride and as for the legacy… England got to the last 16 in France in 1998 where they could consider themselves unfortunate to lose on penalties before they were dumped out at the group stage against Romania in the Euros two years later. It was the same old story!

Gary Lineker has one regret about his life in football; just how close he came to "winning the big one" with England at Italia '90 ."It's the only thing I look back on with a thought of 'if only'. It was a really strong England team with a bit more creativity than other sides we have had. We were fractions from winning the World Cup." Lineker won the Golden Boot at the 1986 World Cup and scored England's equaliser against West Germany in the 1990 semi-finals, making his return 10 goals across 2 tournaments – no other Englishman has scored more than 6 in total on the biggest stage.

Lineker described his association of eight years with Robson as "probably the key relationship I had as a player. The main memory we always shared was 1990," Lineker said. "How close we were to winning the World Cup. I've spoken to Bobby about this and he felt the same as I do. It's the one thing, looking back, that I've got a tinge of disappointment about. We were on the brink of getting to the final and I think if we had got there, we would have been strong favourites. I had this conversation with him once or twice. I remember the frustration, getting that close."

That semi-final remains the biggest England game of the past 40 years. "I think 1990 was hugely important to football in this country," Lineker said. "After that everyone became interested in football. It wasn't just working-class men it was all classes, women, kids – it returned to the family game it should be. Bobby was at the helm then and that helped to cement his popularity."

According to Lineker, the key relationship in that 1990 team was

Robson's with Gazza. "Bobby knew instinctively when to scold him and when to put an arm round his shoulder. Gazza was an emotional guy and I know he exasperated Bobby on occasions – I remember he was out playing tennis on, I think, the night before the semi-final, and Bobby had to go out and drag him off the court – but Bobby was brilliant at connecting with people.

"I've never met anyone more enthusiastic about the game, and I think that was one of his great strengths. That's why he kept going for such a long time, and one of the reasons why he was genuinely popular. He was certainly popular with the players. He got the maximum from everyone who played for him, which his record proves. He did amazingly well with Ipswich and England, was a success in Europe and he did a decent job with Newcastle, as they probably realise now.

"He expected a lot: if you were slacking, Bobby wouldn't hesitate to give you a tongue-lashing. But if you earned his trust he was fiercely loyal. I was one of the ones who benefited – he could easily have left me out in 1986 after I hadn't scored in the first two games. He did make a couple of changes before we played Poland but he stuck by me and it changed my life, really; I got a hat-trick in that game, and from then on I started scoring goals."

In 1992, two years after Graham Taylor took over from Robson as England manager, Lineker retired from international football, after famously being hauled off against Sweden in Stockholm with England a goal down and chasing the game. "I still saw him on occasions," he says of Robson. "We had dinner once or twice and I did a documentary with him a few years ago. The last time I saw him was a few months ago at a Newcastle game. He was frail then, but he sort of brushed it off, as he did. He'd just keep fighting it. He wasn't a man just to sit around and do nothing. After football, he started the Bobby Robson Foundation and the charity then became his driving force.

"Bobby managed to create a special bond with the public. He had such success as a manager, and as a player before that, but he was just such a likeable guy, a family man. It was his enthusiasm and his passion that came through. It's the combination of all those things that made him so hugely popular. When I look back at my time with England, it's a special thing, playing for your country. To play for a manager like that – who was so loyal, and gave you so many opportunities – makes you feel hugely grateful and lucky. I'm privileged, really, to have played for one of the greats."

That World Cup as a whole was a very defensive tournament,

averaging just 2.21 goals-per-game. As an attacking player, did that make it tough to play? "When you got the ball, you tried to do what you could but it was difficult. But it is about whether the team wins or not; not whether you are the star of the team. I was part of the team."

Replays showed John Barnes was clearly onside when you 'scored' against Belgium. "That is probably the most disappointing thing, because I was not offside. But, once again, we got through to the quarter-finals against Cameroon and so I was not disappointed at all. It was a fantastic World Cup."

However, the nostalgia of Italia '90, the romance of the great Gazza year, the emotion of the tears, and how he became the housewives' favourite, marked Italia '90 out as something special, and well worth revisiting. Yet it didn't turn out to be the profound benchmark in the England game it's often made out to be as England have continually failed to find consistency at the very highest level. Perhaps the fall out from Gareth Southgate's 2018 success will prove to be a real turning point.

Frozen in that moment, though, it was something to celebrate as England's players returned to a heroes' welcome from thousands at Luton airport after a journey of redemption. For football fans of a certain age, Italia '90 remains one of the most fondly remembered England tournaments in living memory; when Gazza's bottom lip started to quiver and Lineker went to console his team-mate, famously gesticulating at the England bench as the iconic tears began to fall. Penalties followed, and after Stuart Pearce's effort was saved and Chris Waddle blazed over, England, shatteringly, were out. The camera lingered on the England manager. You see Bobby Robson look down, permit himself the smallest grimace of pain, then stand up and prepare to face his shattered players.

STEVE McMAHON

I could have taken Gazza's place in the final

STEVE McMAHON

My best memory of Italia '90 was coming home, the welcome was such a pleasant surprise. We were living in a bubble within our camp, and although we had momentum we didn't realise quite how it was being perceived back home without the social media we have these days. We only realised the enormity of what everyone was feeling in the UK when we got back.

Gazza stole the public attention, and quite rightly but it was bitter-sweet for me when it all happened in the semi-final. Of course I didn't want it to happen, Gazza being booked and naturally I felt for him, but virtually straight away, as I was sitting on the bench, the realisation hit me that I could be playing in the World Cup Final. Bobby Robson picked me for the final game, the third placed play-off against Italy, so I've no doubt he would have played me in the final had we got there.

I had played in four out of the seven games, our first choice midfield player and captain had gone back home injured and you take a purely professional approach that one man's problem is another man's opportunity, and that opportunity was to have been mine. However, everyone had to feel for Gazza, and before the penalty shoot-out I was consoling him. He couldn't speak.

As for the penalty shoot-out, Shilts said he guessed right for every penalty. Fine. But he needed to have saved one or two. If you go the right away every time, then logically you have waited for the spot kick to have been struck so you know which way to go. Perhaps it would have been better to have gambled and gone the wrong away on a few occasions but when going the right way you'd save it. Of course hindsight is such a wonderful thing, and with hindsight it may have been preferable to bring on a giant of a keeper like Dave Beasant who had a knack of saving penalties as us at Liverpool had discovered in the FA Cup final!

ALL PLAYED OUT

The success of the tournament made artistic works about football more mareketable and none has been more lauded over the past 30 years than Pete Davies' account of the finals *All Played Out.*

The book blurb gave the impression this was the definitive account of Italia '90... "Once you could ignore football, avoid the back pages, turn the telly off, leave the pub. Now that's not possible because on 4th July in Turin's Stadio delli Alpi, Gazza cried, England lost and football changed forever. Pete Davies witnessed all of this at first hand. The players, the hooligans, the agents, the journalists, the fans - the full cast of football's rowdy circus. For nine months he had access to the England squad and their manager, Bobby Robson, talking to them freely about their hopes, their fears, their methods and their lives. So this is the real story, the unedited version. *All Played Out* - the first and last book to give the inside story of the greatest show on earth."

Thirty years on, Pete Davies is still best known as the author of this account of Italia '90 that has been continuously in print ever since. The book perpetuated a myth because, despite claims of unlimited access, this was far from the reality. At the time it was published I bit my lip and made no comment but 30 years later it is possible to reflect on some of the aspects of the book that would make a hardened hack's skin crawl.

He writes early in his personal account of travelling around observing the workings of the game: "Two pressman gave me a lift in their cab form the airport to the training ground in Pula." For me that just about summed up the guy's insight into what really happened beyond his very pertinent and accurate assessments of the attitudes and behaviour of the fans, the locations, and those very much on the periphery of the real story. Pete Davies asked for lifts whenever he could from the 'Morris Men'.

Steve Curry and I were great mates back then, not that anyone would have detected our fondness for one another had they watched the original *Hold The Back Page*, on Saturday nights and *Sunday*

Supplement on Sunday mornings with Jimmy Hill as we often went hammer and tong at each other during those Sky TV debates. Steve was a big Manchester United fan, a huge character, with thespian training and could be extremely opinionated. His response to Davies' request for a lift was "tell him to bugger off". My view was to give him the benefit of the doubt but to be careful what we say in his company. It was pretty transparent he wanted to listen to our chatter as he would pick up behind-the-scenes gossip for his book.

The press men saw Davies as a chancer. Let's face it, no one really thought England would excel in Italia '90 but there is always hope, and hope springs eternal mainly in England when it comes to the World Cup and the tabloids indulge in the usual jingoism that England *will* win the World Cup, ramping up fan expectation, exploiting their misplaced patriotism on the eve of the tournament, in an effort to win the tabloid circulation war, only to be eventually badly let down when those same tabloids rip into the manager and call for him to be sacked when they get knocked out.

On page 176 of *All Played Out* the reason for cadging a lift from a couple of unsuspecting journalists to Pula became clear, as he put it "The Hostess Isabella story had broken". This was a reference to a *Daily Mirror* exclusive that three players, unnamed at the time, had enjoyed a late night disco and after-hours 'nookie' with a local hostess who had subsequently been moved on from Is Molas to another hotel much further down the road. Davies reports in his book that a journalist from a respectable broadsheet told him that the freelance touting the story around tried *The Sun* first, who turned it down, but when *The Mirror* ran with the story, *The Sun* then called it "more lies" from the Robert Maxwell paper.

Davies then referenced 'The Rotters', an endearing Fleet Street nickname for news hounds, who were following Isabella all over Sardinia in search of a follow up. Davies felt sympathy for the England players who had turned on the sports journalists and gone on a 'quotes strike' as he put, and referenced Paddy Barclay saying he would join them, suggesting he disapproved before savageing Barclay for being a media rent-a-quote who was always "good for a reaction".

Davies described the article as "the biggest piece of shit yet in a long-building tunnel of press sewage. Journalists - they were all the fucking same." This was just the kind of gratuitous nonsense Davies thought the average fan would lap up, the arty farty book reviewers would enjoy, but it's like saying all football fans are hooligans.

Chapter 19 is a classic account of someone who had no idea what was really going on, when he reports that he is on a train from Milan to Bologna when he read in *Corriere dello Sport* that England's prized skipper had flown home. Meanwhile I was on Bryan Robson's early morning flight from Cagliari to Rome, where he was catching a connection back to Manchester, Davies continued his amazing insights by writing "The inflamed Achilles had not responded to Olga Stringfellow or anything else, and surgery looked likely." Clueless!

The truth was Davies had no real access, and felt his best chance of getting some snippets was to tap up proper journalists who did have access and had heard stories that they couldn't quite stand up and weren't using in their papers. But he also had a chip on his shoulder. I'd imagine his book was speculative to say the least, the advance was modest and he was clearly mixing with the elite football writers of a generation where the newspapers were flush with dosh, and all expenses meant a lavish life style. By contrast Davies was slumming it and admitted as much in his book, "I got to Bologna and found at the station that there wasn't a cheap room left in the city. I decided I'd be a commuter for the day, and go back to Milan that evening - the trip was only a couple of hours - and for the night of the game, I booked a room in a three star hotel for the unearthly sum, for me, of £40. But I thought at least I'd get a mini-bar for once in my life - it'd be like being a journalist..." Really, does this guy's travel arrangements, his mini bar, or general lack of it, and mostly two star hostels, really constitute insightful reading? Not for me.

MEL STEIN

It was open house for agents – it wouldn't happen now!

M onday 11th June 1990 seems a million light years away as I sit in my little office at home, looking out at the rain and very little else. The world has ground to a halt and we are reduced to watching replays of matches that occurred so long ago that we have forgotten the results. But it was on that June day that the World Cup began for England when they drew with the Republic of Ireland 1-1 in Cagliari with a goal by Gary Lineker equalized by Kevin Sheedy.

It's so long ago that I can't even remember if I went to that game, but two players that I represented, Chris Waddle and Paul Gascoigne certainly did. I think I may well have watched the goalless draw against Holland a couple of days later and looking back and comparing the access agents and the like got to players, compared to the security ring of steel that's cast around the current squad, I find myself open-mouthed in disbelief.

We had full access to the team hotel, the players' rooms, even the management. We could pull up a chair at Bobby Robson's table and join him for a coffee. And all the players' representatives got along; nobody was trying to poach somebody else's player and we would sit side by side in the stadia and be delighted by the success of another man's player.

We even communicated with the Press mob. Harry Harris himself, Rob Shepherd, Charlie Sale - if we told them something off the record, it stayed off the record. Of course, there were exceptions. Some of the guys were simply not to be trusted and Len Lazarus (my co-manager of Gazza) and I operated on a 'one strike and you're out' basis. If somebody let us down we simply blanked them. Or made sure we kicked them off the park in the 'friendly' matches we played against the Press,

I clearly remember the game against Belgium on 26th June in Bologna. I sat next to David Platt's representative and when the game went into the last minute of extra time (with penalties beckoning… who knew what lay ahead?) and Gazza set up a goal for Platty we actually embraced.

I was working full time as a solicitor. I never charged Gazza or Chris commission like the other guys. I just charged for my time at my usual hourly rate and I couldn't really charge for going to watch them at matches. So I had to decide between going back to Italy to watch the semi-final or rolling the dice and waiting for the final. I made a huge mistake and waited.

So on semi-final day I had tickets to see The Rolling Stones at Wembley and decided to watch the match with Len first. I think I got to Wembley in time for their encore, but it was a night that was going to change my life forever; Gazzamania was born. The next day the phone started ringing and it never stopped. We set up a company for Paul, registered his name as a trademark, signed an exclusive newspaper deal with *The Sun,* designed and printed a T-shirt with a picture of Gazza crying on the front and the logo 'Tears of a Clown' and entered into one endorsement deal after another. We even got Paul into the recording studios to sing *Fog on the Tyne* with Lindisfarne which soared into the charts. I wrote the follow up *Geordie Boy* and still get royalties to this very day.

Yes, it was a golden summer when those of us in love with English football, those of us enchanted by Waddle's magical dribbling skill, Lineker's clinical finishing in front of goal and Gazza's cheeky smile that made him every mother's son, we thought it would never end.

But, of course, it did.

DAVID PLATT

A greater mental strength and we would have won the World Cup

It's quite obvious that my fondest moment should be the goal against Belgium that effectively changed my life. But that was just a snapshot and I'd rather look back at the tournament as a whole with the benefit of 30 years experience of having played in Italy, then moving into coaching and management as well as working with the FA with the England under 21s. Looking at it, it seems quite different to how I might have perceived it at the time, living the moment with all the adrenalin surge.

Naturally, there is no mistaking that the highlight of my World Cup was that goal against Belgium, but now I can see that had we believed in ourselves more as a squad going to the World Cup in 1990 we may well have won it.

Yes, the belief was there when we played Germany in the semi-final, we believed then we would beat them, and really we should have beaten them. But for me the pertinent question is how much did we believe going into the World Cup that we would win it?

I was new to the England set up, so I don't know how the other players were thinking, but I felt, in my own mind, that not enough of us went out there thinking we were going to win this tournament, myself included, and looking back, it was that mental strength that we might have been missing from the very start. I am sure we all felt we could go there and beat teams, but we didn't really believe we could go all the way, at least not until we got to the semi-final, but was it too late by then? That belief is so important and more recognised now than it might have been 30 years ago. Having spent four years in Italy, and discovered the way the Italians prepare and how they go into major tournaments, they would go to a World Cup believing they would win it and so they did.

When I was working for the FA with the under-21s we had four slides to see what kind of individual would make it to a World Cup when they first come into the system from 12, 14 or 16, they were almost pigeon holed into whether he would be a full England international. One of the pillars is mental strength and the slide showed a 16 year-old on the floor inside the 18 year box, extending his neck to take the full

"The moment that changed my life" - David Platt
on his last-gasp goal against Belgium

force of a shot; that's bravery, courage, perhaps even stupidity, but it's not mental strength, it's not that inner belief that we *will* win a major tournament. The trouble with English football is all the negativity, that lack of mental strength that the Germans would have believing they would be winners.

Had we actually set off believing we would win Italia '90 we would have won it, it would have given us that edge. Some players might have had that belief, but I am not sure there were many. In fact, I am convinced that nobody expected us to win. We had been out of Europe for five years, we were light years behind some of the top nations in terms of diet, nutrition, training, preparation (both physical and mental), infrastructure, and it was only when I moved to Italy that I discovered that they were ten times better than we were at all of these important aspects of preparation. It took a long time for our football to evolve, mainly due to the influx of foreign players and managers into the Premier League and our clubs' success in Europe.

I don't think the journalists believed we'd win it either. They are entitled to write their opinions and what they believe, but often they would sit down together, confer and come up with the same ideas, as they didn't want to get a bollocking from their Editor if they came up with something different to everyone else!

I went to the World Cup as a squad player, and even that was happening very quickly; I came on as a substitute in November 1989, came on again in a friendly and then only made my full England debut against Brazil in March. I didn't even think I would be in the final squad even though I'd had a good season. I had no real caps, no real experience, but it's only when I had experience of coaching and management, I realise 'why wouldn't you?' pick someone like me. You know three or four players who are certainties, pick a few to mix and match and then you would want a player like myself who can play in two positions up front or midfield, and score goals from either position, I was effectively a 'two in one' player, someone who would be great to have on the bench.

The actual tournament was a blur, the first game in Cagliari, having listened to the team talk, I didn't expect to be in the team, and didn't even expect to be among the substitutes, I thought I would be in my suit watching from the stands, but I was surprised to be on the bench. Again, looking back with the benefit of experience it's a case of "Why wouldn't you?" as I gave the manager more options for different scenarios. You want at least one defender and a goalkeeper but then you want players who are flexible who might score with 10 minutes to go, and being on the bench I felt one step further forward toward the team. I never expected to get on, and didn't in the opening game but did come on against Holland and Egypt.

The happiest moment of the tournament, the best moment of my career, without doubt, was the Belgium goal, because without that goal I wouldn't have got a starting place and scored against Cameroon, there's no doubt Bobby Robson and Don Howe would have gone for Steve McMahon in midfield, and there's little doubt I wouldn't have then been in the side against Germany in a World Cup semi-final. I started out as a squad player, and ended up making my name on a global scale as a world 'star' so to speak. It catapulted me into recognition from top clubs.

The day after the Belgium game we arrived in Naples for the quarter-finals, at the foot of the stairs as I got off the plane there was an Italian TV crew wanting to interview me, speaking in Italian, but I didn't understand a word they were saying but I thought "this sort of thing doesn't happen to me!" Normally, it would be the Midlands guys John Wragg and Dave Harrison who would want to speak to me, and I had got to know them over the past 18 months because I was the only player from a Birmingham club in the England squad. Now, suddenly, I was one of the players on the world scene. Up until that Belgium goal I didn't have to deal with the 'nationals' and if I did it was still via Wraggie and Dave Harrison, who worked for the national newspapers, but were permanently centred on the Midlands. So, I was a third party in a couple of stand offs between the players and the senior journalists over various things the players were upset about, but it was inconsequential to me as I wasn't involved, and in any case, I hadn't read it, and why should I have done, as it wasn't about me.

But the senior football writers were caught up in the conflict because others on their own newspapers had created a situation that the players were not happy with. We heard of reporters going into pubs to buy supporters drinks so that they could cause mayhem in Cagliari so they would have a headline. There was clearly no discrimination, everyone was tarred with the same brush. Did that really happen? I have no way of knowing. It might well have been an urban myth. Either way, it was not helping the squad with that kind of reporting in the papers, it made the players become very insular.

It was the same with Gazza. He was part of the squad, I knew him within the football environment, he was full of energy, full of fun but in no way arrogant. But I didn't have to avoid him, as I was more than happy shutting myself off, slowing my mind down, coping with being away for so long and hotel life didn't get me down, nor was I bored, as I was concentrating on the tournament. I focused on a daily routine of training, having lunch, going back for a rest, having dinner, watching games in the evenings - repeat.

I'm asked by people I know all the time "tell me about how the manager changed the formation?" but the truth is I don't know if it is bull or whether some of the senior players lobbied Bobby Robson to persuade him to play a sweeper system.

The Belgium goal gave me the platform to launch my career, as immediately after that I was linked with Italian clubs and although I didn't move for a year, during that time it was always in the newspapers as almost a matter of fact that a couple of Italian clubs were chasing me. As we reached the World Cup semi-final, all that negativity around the camp, the battles with the newspapers, it all turned full circle. They couldn't keep writing negatively when we were playing Germany in a World Cup semi-final.

Playing in Italy I found another type of newspaper reporting, a nation with three broadsheet sport newspapers, 75% of them filled with football. It was incredible to think that before I went to the World Cup I would spend three quarters of an hour once a week with the local Midlands reporters, now in Italy it was every single day, every paper but it was easier in Italy as they had so much space to fill, they would report your every word, nothing was taken out of context. Even when I was assistant to Roberto Mancini at Manchester City and filled in at a press conference, I knew the reporters wouldn't be writing a word of my answer because it didn't fit the headline they had in mind.

Hellfire, is it really 30 years ago? How quickly time goes. I'm retired now and I look back with fond memories, and I am sharing them for a book which I feel is the right thing to do, as I did become synonymous with Italia '90, but I no longer engage with the media, now I shy away from any media involvement.

It was a well run World Cup because Italy, at that time, was the hot bed of European football, it was *the* nation for football at the time with such fervent supporters that wherever you went; the waiters, people around the hotel, no one ever shut off, they talked football all the time, in bars, coffee shops, everywhere, it was their big passion.

THE MEDIA RETURN

Soon it was time to pack up and head back to London, the show was over, but no doubt the memories would linger as this was one of the most exciting tournaments to cover as a journalist, irrespective of the standard of football. Accommodation wasn't easy to come by in Rome, but pre-tournament the media's group travel agent had booked me into a lovely spot, a grand old-fashioned five star hotel with a swimming pool, which was open to non residents albeit at a hefty price.

Rob Shepherd was *Today's* chief football writer at the time and Fleet's Street's very own Gazza as he could, on occasions, be as daft as any brush Gazza could be compared to but 'Shep', as he was universally known, was a genuine and likeable chap, even if he was an acquired taste at times. Resembling Brutus in the old Popeye cartoons, with his jutting jaw, and intimidating physique, it was usually best to have him on your side than against you, and it was a delight to be on his side! We had a strong relationship and in fact we had shared the cab from our respective homes in south London to the airport to depart for Cagliari and were the first in situ at the Forte Village; myself, Shep, Bob Driscoll of the *Daily Star*, and Alex Montgomery of *The Sun*.

Shep was actually "parachuted in" to replace Bob Harris, who suddenly moved up from *Today*, to become Sports Editor of *The Sunday Mirror*. Such was the profile of the senior football writers in that era that David Bailey was commissioned by *FourFourTwo* to portray football in a different light through his lens and as well as the usual suspects such as David Beckham, he turned his attention to the tabloid war and how that manifested itself in the competitive nature of their journalists, and used Shep and myself in a picture session in his studios.

Having arrived together in Italy what seemed a lifetime ago, "Shep" and I were booked on the same flight leaving Rome for London a couple of days after the final, so it was agreed that he would pop into my hotel, as it had the better facilities, and he had an early check out. We would then share the cost of the expensive taxi journey to the airport. Just about everything; hotels, restaurants and taxis had inflated their prices for the World Cup, as indeed they have done with every tournament irrespective of which part of the world they take place. As our flight was late afternoon, there was time for a spot of swimming and

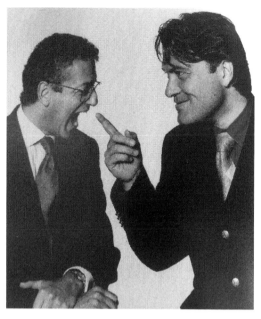

David Bailey took this picture of Today's *chief football writer Rob Shepherd and I to illustrate the ongoing tabloid war.*

sunbathing before departure. Shep arrived, dumped his suitcase in my room and changed into his pool side gear. My admission to the outdoor pool was part of the hotel package, but I put Shep's entrance fee on my extras bill, and we set about relaxing for a couple of hours as *Mirror* expenses were far more generous than *Today's*.

Loungers, towels and sun cream sorted, Shep decided on an immediate dive into the pool. Unfortunately, he forgot that he had packed his lira safely in his swimming trunk pocket as he would need it for the taxi fare. He had quite a lot of lira, as we were about to discover as it spilled out into the pool as he hit the water!

Shep went into a frenzied panic and shouted for my help to rescue his money. In I went and as he had an aversion to going underwater, I fished the cash out. We laid all the notes side by side around the pool's edge to dry out. It covered virtually the entire perimeter of the pool. Fortunately we were the only ones using it! Most people had been staying for the World Cup Final and had already checked out or were packing to prepare to leave, and generally speaking the fees were a touch steep for entry to the pool. Drying out so much lire Shep, who has a wicked sense of humour, recalls the incident when I reminded him of it, "That's what you call money laundering!"

The impact of this tournament had far-reaching consequences on English culture. For example a play based around the England v West Germany semi-final - *An Evening with Gary Lineker* - was a stage hit, and was even nominated for an Olivier Award, such was the interest created by this tournament among what were then called 'the chattering classes'. This would have seemed unthinkable on the eve of the tournament when many in the upper echelons of the FA and government believed England would be expelled from the tournament because of hooliganism.

Professor Matt Taylor, of De Montfort University's International Centre for Sports History and Culture, pointed out there had always been middle-class football fans but agrees that the 1990 World Cup was a turning point. "The social constituency of football definitely changed in the 1990s but the World Cup was one of a number of factors. The 1980s was a really low point, people forget how much of a cultural outpost football had become. In newspaper, it was very much restricted to the back pages and it represented much of what was bad about 1980s society. It was a period when there were a lot of disasters and it made people question whether the country could organise public events.

"So Italia '90 came at an opportune moment for change, along with the Taylor Report, which was quite a radical report and said football clubs had to treat their fan base as customers. It was one of a number of things that helped to position football at the forefront of English cultural life. It could have happened just for the month the tournament was on but it struck a chord. Football, amazingly, was seen as being cool and that was something that hadn't look likely to happen five or six years prior."

In the 1990s football filtered into much of England's cultural life, from Nick Hornby's book *Fever Pitch*, to Sky buying up the rights to Premier League games and satellite dishes appearing on houses all over the nation. Cambridge-educated comedian David Baddiel teamed up with fellow football fan Frank Skinner to host *Fantasy Football League*, a BBC football comedy show based loosely around a game that captivated broadsheet newspaper readers. Baddiel and Skinner's anthem *Three Lions* then reached number one before Euro '96 and again in 1998, while Gazza had a hit with *Fog On The Tyne* later in 1990.

Prof Taylor says it was "thin pickings" for football in the arts before 1990 but then "it became a topic that could be considered of interest beyond just football fans"

The cost of attending matches rose significantly in the 1990s and led to accusations that traditional working-class fans had been priced out of the game by the mushrooming corporate sector and growth in sponsorship. "What happened with Italia '90 is that football became re-imagined as a people's game again and these people were from a broader base than before," says Prof Taylor. "But there is a problem if the social base that had propped up football for so long is edged out. The pricing out of the working classes has happened and I think it's a concern for the future of football, as is the low number of young fans."

In the wake of Gazza's meltdown in Turin it became okay for men to cry – it was no longer a sign of weakness. As Gascoigne himself said,: "Once I knew I was going to miss the final you could see how heartbroken I was and I just could not stop the tears." Dr Thomas Dixon, an expert on crying and the author of *Weeping Britannia: Portrait of a Nation in Tears*, said Gazza was not the first footballer to cry, but his tears were different. "Normally sportsmen wept because they had just won something or lost something, or perhaps because they were at the end of their career," says Dr Dixon. "With Gazza it was self-pitying, out of control and in the middle of a match that he should have been trying to win. The thing that was notable was he was running up and down the pitch in tears."

Dr Dixon believed he changed attitudes. "It was a very high-profile example of what was, by then, seen as the culture of the 'new man' who shows his feelings. But he was someone who was a traditional man - a 'lad', heavy drinking - and it was an example of that meeting the 'new man' culture." He added that 1970s sportsmen who cried had prompted letters to newspapers saying they should have shown a stiff upper lip, countered by the likes of agony aunt Marje Proops saying other men should follow their example. And by the time of Gazza's tears the attitude of acceptance was far more common.

Mrs Thatcher's tears when she left Downing Street a few months after the World Cup helped establish the 1990s as an emotional decade, an image cemented with the outpouring of grief after the death of Princess Diana in 1997. Yet when Andy Murray cried after losing the Wimbledon final in 2012, columnist Toby Young referred to it as a "big girl's blouse routine".

Commentator John Motson told how the 1990 World Cup restored his faith in football after a bleak decade of hooliganism and disasters. His views had certainly mellowed after his acidic comments in his memoirs published a good few years earlier. The 74-year-old has been the voice of the beautiful game for more than 30 years, told how his love for football deserted him in the 1980s, particularly after the Hillsborough disaster. He told *Desert Island Discs,* "To be honest with you, my love for football had slightly deserted me prior to [Hillsborough] because it was a bad decade, the 80s, and hooliganism was a major part of that. We had a lot of personal injury with fans attacking each other at grounds. And we had Heysel, for different reasons obviously, and we had the fire at Bradford. The game went to an all-time low, I thought. And then the tragedy of Hillsborough. I did wonder whether football would get back on its feet after that. But I'll tell you what turned it. We had the 1990 World Cup within a year, England in the semi-final, Gazza's tears."

Motson joined the BBC in 1968 as a radio sports presenter and went on to commentate on more than 2,000 games, including World Cup and FA Cup finals. But his role changed to reporting a disaster at Hillsborough in April 1989 as he provided live coverage for the thousands of listeners who thought they were just tuning into for updates on the FA Cup semi-final game between Liverpool and Nottingham Forest. His *Desert Island Discs* included *Three Lions* by David Baddiel and Frank Skinner, *Annie's Song* by John Denver and *Abide With Me* by the Westminster Abbey Choir.

One of his most loved pieces of commentary. Gazza's Tears of Turin of course. "Oh dear. Oh dear me," Motty reasoned with the nation. "He's going to be out of the final, if England get there. Here is a moment that almost brings tears to his eyes."

In December 2007 Sir Bobby Robson received the Lifetime Achievement Award at the BBC Sports Personality of the Year awards. As he made his way to collect the accolade, the great and the good of British sport in the audience stood up to applauded the former England manager and the applause went on and on.

Gary Lineker admitted later it was the one time in his broadcasting career that emotion threatened to stop him getting his words out. If Robson was in any doubt about the esteem in which he was held by the nation, then this night confirmed just how loved he was. Millions of viewers will also say what a moving moment it was, as they saw the adored pensioner receive such an ovation.

Yet beneath that kindly and slightly eccentric image, Bobby Robson was actually a very astute tactician. Terry Butcher: "That's also what you need if you are going to react to the twists and turns of a tournament. When you go back to 1978, the [Ipswich Town] team Bobby put out for the FA Cup final was completely new: a 4-3-3 shape which he had never tried but which smothered Arsenal and clinched the trophy. With England at the 1986 World Cup, we took a point from the first two group games, so he changed the system around from a 4-3-3 to a 4-4-2 and we flourished. People say he was never a tactician. Well, I would politely and fundamentally disagree with that."

Butcher returned to the scene of England's glorious failure with two other members of the team to make a film *Return to Turin*. Butcher, Paul Parker and Gary Lineker retraced their steps two years ago. His late son Christopher once made the same journey, flying out with his mother, Butcher's wife Rita, to see the semi-final against Germany.

After arriving with Lineker and Parker at the site of Turin's Stadio delle Alpi, where the semi-final was played Butcher said "My wife was here. My son Christopher was here. He passed away last year, aged 35. It affected me because I knew he'd been there in the stadium. We lost a World Cup semi-final that year and it's not the end of the world, but losing a son is the end of the world..." An inquest into his son's death heard that he had been forced to leave the army in 2015 when experiences in Iraq and Afghanistan began to affect him. He then suffered catastrophic mental disintegration. Butcher believes the Armed Forces failed in a fundamental duty of care. "He became a victim of war," he said, "his life spiralled downwards as the demons took control of his mind. Our country has many veterans suffering from the same situation - released from the Armed Forces too early and having to rely on an overloaded NHS that is ill-equipped and underfunded to cope."

AFTER GAZZAMANIA

In the years that followed that night in Turin it was clear that England's triumphant campaign and the career of its star player had already peaked. Paul Gascoigne was frequently injured during the qualifying campaign for the 1994 World Cup in the USA and not one of the players who played that night ever graced the biggest stage again. One of England's star men, David Platt, admits "The magnitude of it didn't sink in. You're only young and you think, 'I'll have another World Cup in four years' time'. You don't realise how quickly your career comes to an end relative to World Cups."

Bobby Robson told Gascoigne on the pitch at the Stadio delle Alpi that night. "Don't worry, you've been one of the best players of the tournament. You've been magnificent. You've got your life ahead of you – this is your first." It certainly looked that way when he won the coveted BBC Sports Personality of the Year award in 1990 and was named as Tottenham's Player of the Year but Gazza soon pressed the self destruct button.

Long after Italia '90, long after Gazza retired and became a shambling tabloid figure of derision, Bobby Robson was still calling him up, checking up on him. Even at the very end, during his last public appearance at a charity match days before he died, Robson was looking out for the daft kid who almost won him the World Cup. Gazza's tribute to his father figure is simple and moving: "He made me feel safe."

Gazza had been taken on by Newcastle United at 18 and made 92 league appearances scoring 21 goals before moving to Tottenham for £2 million. He inspired Spurs to third place in the league in 1990 and followed up his Italia '90 exploits by guiding Spurs to the FA Cup final in 1991. He became a club legend during his three-year spell, winning the FA Cup and amassing 112 appearances. David Howells remembers the time Paul Gascoigne almost killed himself, falling off the roof of the East Stand trying to shoot pigeons with the groundsman's air rifle. Yet his most memorable moment in English domestic football was yet to come. During an FA Cup semi-final against sworn enemies and champions-elect Arsenal. "He destroyed their Double dream.," Howells recalls, "Gazza should not really have been playing; he was rushed back from an abdominal operation and was barely fit but, knowing he wouldn't go the distance, he tore into the match to leave Arsenal 2-0 down after

10 minutes." Gazza's awesome free kick, arrowed past David Seaman, is one of the stand out moments of many in his career. "That", said commentator Barry Davies, "is schoolboys' own stuff" he also helped set up a second for Lineker just minutes later. He was substituted after an hour, having personally destroyed an outstanding Arsenal side that lost only one league game that season. David Lacey eulogised over an "inspired display of individual, highly idiosyncratic football".

Yet a month later in the final Gazza charged about Wembley like a demented idiot and quickly ruined his career and almost ended that of Nottingham Forest's Gary Charles with a crude knee-high challenge that saw him lucky to avoid a red card but saw him leave the pitch on a stretcher with ruptured cruciate ligaments. Just like the Arsenal game Gazza was wound up but this time his energy was misdirected into an awful challenge that kept him out of football for a year.

Gazza's prolonged recovery put his big money move to Lazio on hold and became a bargaining chip in the battle for control of Spurs between Irving Scholar and Terry Venables, who eventually brought in Alan Sugar after a series of failed takeover bids. In Scholar's desperation to find a sugar daddy of his own he turned to Robert Maxwell on my advice as I felt at that time that his genuine love of football would make him an ideal partner for Scholar and *The Mirror*'s proprietor was convinced by me that his intervention would keep English football's crown jewel in England by aborting the proposed move to Lazio.

As Stein wrote in his book on Gazza, "On 9 September, the morning after the Derby game, the headlines were not so much about Paul's hat-trick as Robert Maxwell's bid for Tottenham. Paul's reaction was immediate, 'I'm not playing for that bastard. If he takes over then I'm off.' He knew the appalling way Maxwell, when owner of Derby, had treated his mentor Arthur Cox and he knew that football to him was an ego trip rather than a passion, and wanted no part of it. Harry Harris of the *Daily Mirror* phoned me on behalf of his newspaper's proprietor to ask if there was any chance of a photo of Gazza with Maxwell if the deal went through. 'No chance', was the reply.

"But Maxwell was still playing his own game, and whilst no formal proposal had been made, he was still using *The Mirror* to sway public opinion in his favour by campaigning to keep Gazza, seen as a national treasure, in the country of his birth. Harry Harris, chief football writer of *The Mirror*, was recalled from abroad." Stein is referring to how I was summoned back from Malaysia, the last port of call for a summer England tour in 1991, to help Maxwell orchestrate his final pitch to buy

Spurs. Maxwell's bid failed, Sugar took control and Venables authorised the sale of Gazza to Lazio for £5m to cover the club's debts.

Despite an injury ravaged spell in Rome, Paul's charismatic yet down-to-earth persona left an indelible impression in the Curva Nord. Yet he had become an increasingly isolated figure in the Italian capital. Lazio manager Dino Zoff was an aloof figure while Gazza's pranks and sense of humour frequently antagonised those in authority and the media. Nevertheless, a bond remained with the ultras and Gazza was invited to the headquarters of Lazio's most renowned supporter group, the Irriducibili, where he was seen chanting, joking and drinking just like a regular supporter. He received a rapturous reception when Lazio invited him to be their guest of honour at the 2012 Europa League fixture against Tottenham.

In 1996 he was signed by Glasgow Rangers and made a triumphant return - scoring in his first Old Firm game and leading the Ibrox team to a league and cup double. With his old mentor Terry Venables in charge of England at Euro '96 the tournament proved to be a personal triumph as he played a starring role in England's run to the semi-finals. Yet the build-up to the tournament had seen some controversy as England players were pictured on a 'Dentist's Chair' being plied with spirits in a Hong Kong bar which prompted more lurid headlines. Yet Venables was a father figure Paul respected and there was an acceptance from the former Spurs boss that Gazza needed to let off steam now and again, in return the Geordie produced some of his best football for his country – scoring a sensational goal against Scotland, dictating the play against the Dutch in a 4-1 win that most rated England's best performance at Wembley since 1966 and coming within an inch or so of scoring a golden goal against the Germans in extra time in the semi-final.

Later that year Paul married his girlfriend Sheryl Failes but they later divorced in 1998. It was in the midst of splitting up with his wife that Paul flew out to La Manga before the final squad selection for the 1998 World Cup in France. Yet when word reached him that Glenn Hoddle had omitted him from the final 22, Gazza went nuts smashing up the England manager's hotel room.

Extracts from David Davies' book about the tournament are highly descripitive of events leading up to the end of Gazza's World Cup dreams. "On May 15, 1998, just weeks before the start of the World Cup, Glenn Hoddle and I were flicking through the papers over breakfast. 'Oh, no, look at this' I said. One of the tabloids contained a picture of Gazza falling out of a restaurant late at night. For the first time, I believed

Glenn might leave Gazza out of his France '98 squad. I knew what a story that would be. I also understood what it would do to Gazza — break his heart.

"The story took a further twist when *The Mirror* published a picture of Paul with a kebab at 2am in Soho with the DJ Chris Evans. My phone almost melted; Glenn's face contorted with rage at dealing with another Gazza mess. He was clearly losing patience. That frustrated Gazza's friends in the squad, players like Paul Ince and Ian Wright. They felt he should be more understanding."

Back in 1990, relaxing at England's World Cup base in Sardinia before the World Cup, I noticed Gazza becoming friendly with a waiter who served him cappuccinos at all hours of the day, each laced with brandy. Graham Taylor's subsequent comments about 'refuelling' lead to some concern within the game. Eight years later he'd lost his ability to take games by the scruff of the neck and was living off his 1990 exploits as everyone wanted to buy him a pint.

Davies continued, "On May 27 we left our La Manga base to fly to Casablanca for a World Cup warm-up against Morocco. The coach was only 200 yards from the hotel when somebody shouted: 'Where's Gazza?' He hadn't reported in time. The bus turned back to collect him. It was his birthday, which might have explained why he was late. 'Maybe he's been celebrating,' someone said. 'Maybe he has been on the phone to Sheryl,' added somebody else. 'Can you go back and get Gazza?' Hoddle asked Glenn Roeder. Roeder brought Gazza to the bus. I looked at him, then glanced at a seething Hoddle. A collision course was set. Gazza was in his own world by then, his mind 1,000 miles away, distracted by events at home. When he read an article on Sheryl's 'new man', Gazza plunged into a deeper depression. His life continued to unravel.

"The day before we headed back to Morocco for a game with Belgium, he spent most of the afternoon on the phone. 'He's meant to be resting,' fumed Hoddle. Before kick-off, Gazza stood in the centre circle, again talking on his mobile. This was madness. Glenn was about to whittle down his squad and everyone was on their best behaviour — except Gazza. Glenn made up his mind not to take Gazza to France on the flight back from Morocco on the Friday evening. In the La Manga hotel bar on the Saturday night, Gazza was on the karaoke big-time. Glenn had given the players permission to have a couple of beers, a limit exceeded by Gazza. On Sunday morning, Glenn confirmed his bombshell to me on the way into breakfast.

"'Gazza's out,' he said. I nodded. I wasn't shocked. The rest of the world would be.

"When Gazza was called into Hoddle's room to hear his fate, mayhem ensued. On hearing the commotion, I ran out of my room and witnessed the carnage. Flowers and vases were strewn all over the corridor. In one corner, Gazza was being comforted by Incey and David Seaman. 'I thought he was going to hit me,' Glenn told me. Gazza had kicked a chair over and punched a lamp, showering the carpet with glass. Glenn was standing in the middle of the room, talking to John Gorman about getting the glass tidied up before the next player walked in."

Ian Wright recalled having to help the England boss tidy up his hotel room in the aftermath. Wright, who also missed out through injury, said: "Every member of the squad spoke to Hoddle in his hotel room to be individually told whether or not they had made the cut but Gascoigne heard a rumour that he was set to miss out. He stormed into Hoddle's hotel room and confronted the manager, trashing his hotel room when news of his omission was confirmed.

"I was in next. I remember when I went in and we were actually talking about me being in the squad while cleaning the room up and fixing the mattress, things had been smashed to bits! I was embarrassed because I was thinking about how the gaffer had to deal with Gazza going mad in the room. I just naturally went in and started helping tidy stuff up."

Hoddle said: "I gave him so many opportunities to get himself fit. Six or seven months before, I said, 'Look, you've got to be fitter. This is another chance, this may be your last World Cup'. But you could see he was never fit. The saddest thing I've ever had to do, was leaving Paul Gascoigne out. And that was purely because he wasn't fit, and he wouldn't have been fit for the tournament."

Hoddle described Gazza as acting like "a man possessed" repeatedly swearing, kicking over a chair and smashing a lamp. Hoddle suspected Gazza was drunk. "I thought about trying to talk to him but knew I couldn't, not while he was in this state. He would never take it in. He had snapped. He was ranting, swearing and slurring his words. He was acting like a man possessed. He seemed to be dealing with it quite well... then he stopped, turned and flew into a rage, kicking a nearby chair. It was a full-blooded volley and I was concerned because he had bare feet. The kick was so hard I thought he must have broken his foot. He was a different person now. He had snapped. I stood there and he turned as if to go again, then came back with a barrage of abuse. Physically he wasn't 100%, mentally he was all over the place."

Gary Neville recalled, "It was an extremely difficult day. We went to La Manga for a training camp and to play against Morocco and Belgium. The last two days were relaxation days but that was when Glenn Hoddle was going to announce his squad. He wasn't malicious, he wanted to do it in the right way.

"There were 28 of us and he had to get it down to 23 after these two matches. On the Saturday, a list of appointments went up on the wall in 10 minute slots. On the Saturday night everyone was panicking like crazy about their appointment. The next day, Gazza was 10th or 11th in the queue but he knew Glenn Roeder who was on the staff. Before his appointment, he saw Roeder and asked him what was happening, and Glenn looked away from him, so Gazza cottoned on that he wasn't in the squad. So Gazza ended up storming down the corridor where the meetings were and jumping the queue. The meetings were already running over, so there was already a queue of people waiting to get into this room. It was not well organised. So Gazza storms in and all hell broke lose. The tables went, he's shouting, he's screaming, he was obviously beside himself. Everyone heard it.

"Everyone was shocked. Nobody expected that Gazza would be left out. The way we looked at it, he was one of our most important players. He was coming towards the end but he was a brilliant character and nobody thought he would be left out. So the Gazza thing was going on and in the meantime the meetings started again. Phil went in and came out, and it was the most upset I've seen Phil in my life. He was absolutely devastated. I thought Phil would be in the squad. He'd actually been told two days before from one of the coaches not to worry and that he would be alright. Glenn had changed his mind the day after and the coach didn't come back to him.

"It was an absolute nightmare that day. Nicky Butt was left out, Phil was left out, Dion Dublin was left out, so that's three Manchester United players; me, Scholesy and Becks were left. We didn't used to share a room. It was Butty and Scholesy, then me and Phil. But that night I went in to Scholes' room and we were talking all night about how bad it was. I take the piss a little bit now but at the time, Butty was devastated, Phil was absolutely beside himself because he'd been told that he was in, Gazza was all over the place. It wasn't just that. In the meeting, they were given their plane tickets, so they left that day. It wasn't a great time."

Gazza returned to the home of his estranged wife Sheryl after being rushed away from the England training camp in a private jet with the other dropped players. Gazza admitted in *The Sun* that he was drunk, having joined other squad members for a drinks and karaoke session at a bar in their hotel. "Yes I was drunk. I got drunk quite quickly - I'd not had a drink in nine days." He later left the bar and had sandwiches in his room with team-mate David Seaman, then "crashed out". But he felt that he had done nothing wrong as Hoddle encouraged the squad to enjoy themselves. He said he also drank cans of lager as he played golf with his team-mates, and it was after he finished his round that Hoddle delivered his decision. Paul Ince and David Seaman led him back to his bedroom. "I gashed my knee as I kicked the door, I was crying and out of control. I didn't want to talk to anybody and I didn't want to listen to what Glenn had to say. There is nothing he could say." He couldn't sleep for days afterwards. "I wanted to be part of England's World Cup glory but he has destroyed my biggest dream." Paul Gascoigne never played for England again.

For years to come Gazza would make headlines. The headlines used to be funny – for instance when High Court judge Mr Justice Harman asked a court: "Who is Gazza? Isn't there an operetta called La Gazza Ladra?" Yet by the time of his La Manga meltdown he'd disappeared down a rabbit hole never to return. Davies said of that time, "To this day I regard Gazza as a friend but I fear for him. His public humiliations, drunk or sober, make me weep. In my last days at the FA, I sent him to Botswana to campaign against HIV-Aids. As usual, he was brilliant in public with children. Privately, his demons exhausted all of those travelling with him. I still discuss him with Terry Venables, who was called in by the Metropolitan Police earlier this year to talk some sense into his old midfielder. It's an uphill battle. As Terry says endlessly: 'Only Gazza can save Gazza.'" More recently Gazza has admitted: "I had a situation with my ex-wife so credit to Hoddle. Even though I had my rows with him, he probably made the right decision."

A few months later his former England captain and now Middlesbrough manager Bryan Robson took a massive gamble when he signed him. His first full season was a success on the pitch. He struggled for pace but his control and passing was at times sublime as Boro finished a creditable ninth but his off the field antics continued; he caused £14,000 of damage after taking the team coach for a joy ride, astounding pensioners awaiting public-transport in the sleepy village of Hurworth as he halted at bus-stops to offer them a lift before crashing to a halt just outside the training ground. Gazza hit rock bottom making a rambling drunken phone call from a deserted railway platform to Robbo in which he said he was contemplating suicide. His problems had spiralled out of control and, for the first time, he admitted that he was an alcoholic. Robson dropped everything to drive to the rescue and whisked his distraught friend off to the Priory clinic for counselling and long spells of treatment, yet incredibly he never missed a match during this turbulent spell as he used football as a theraputic tool. His final game was an infamous 4-0 St Valentine's Day massacre at the hands of Aston Villa live on Sky in February 2000 when he became increasingly frustrated during an ineffective 44 minutes before being stretchered off in tears after attempting to land a forearm smash on George Boateng left him with a broken wrist.

Former Rangers boss Walter Smith took him to Everton for a patchy spell but it was a fruitless attempt to resurrect his talent then he wound his way down the leagues via Burnley and Boston before a disastrous trip to China and then on to an abortive spell in management at non-league Kettering where he was accused of turning up to games and training under the influence but at least he beat Brian Clough's record at Leeds – he was sacked after just 39 days!

In 2008 he was detained under the Mental Health Act after strange behaviour at a hotel in Newcastle. He was sectioned again in June and rushed to hospital in September after a suspected drink and drug overdose. In 2010, he attempted to talk to his "good friend" Raoul Moat, during the gunman's armed stand-off with police. He later admitted it was his alcohol problems that led him to believe he knew Moat. He continued to battle alcoholism and mental health problems. Over the years he has faced charges including common assault, drink driving and being drunk and disorderly, resulting in numerous stints in rehab. He tried cocaine after hearing about it in rehab and ended up being sectioned. He said: "My dad took me in – it was the best thing he ever did for me."

In one of Harry Redknapp's many books the wily old football man asked a pertinent question "Where are Gazza's friends now? The advisers; the agents; the celebrity pals? How did it end up like this? The people I would want to hear from, right at the start, are his agents, his accountants, his lawyers, all the people that made fortunes from the industry that was Paul Gascoigne. What do these people actually do to help when the money stops coming in?"

A group of his old friends, including DJ Chris Evans, ex-team-mate

Gary Lineker and broadcaster Piers Morgan, chipped in to pay for his treatment at the Meadows Rehab Centre in Arizona. They covered the £13,600 first class British Airways flights for Paul and his carer. They also covered the £6,000-a-week costs for his treatment at the Meadows facility. Now Gazza has had stomach pellets inserted to prevent him from over doing the booze. Yet he remains fodder for tabloid headlines, as recently as 2018 he was cleared of assaulting a woman on a train. His father John died in 2018 aged 72 and he also suffered the loss of nephew Jay Kerrigan, 22, in 2016 – which he called the worst year of his life. He commented: "I can sit indoors and be miserable, or I can get out and just have a coffee – even that helps. I lost Jay, my dad, then had the sexual harassment case. I'm so glad the jury saw sense and I was cleared. I was panicking. If I ended up on the sex offender register, my life would have been finished. I'm glad that we went to the jury and I have turned my life around. For a year, I felt like I could do nothing, I was really stressed out about it. But I received great support."

Two months after his court appearance he left a Little Waitrose store at London's King's Cross Station with a £9 bottle of wine and was followed by a security guard and a manager before apologising and returning inside to pay for it in cash.

In a recent interview with the *Daily Mirror*, he said: "I've probably got through about £20million when you take into account royalty payments, wages, sponsorship deals. I've bought some lovely clothes, jewellery, had some great holidays, I've really enjoyed it. I gave a lot of money away to family. I'm not materialistic. If I was to wind my life back, I'd do it all again. I am happy."

It all seems a long way from Turin...

WORLD CUP FINALS 1990

Group 1

Italy 1-0 Austria
Czechoslovakia 5-1 United States
Italy 1-0 United States
Czechoslovakia 1-0 Austria
Austria 2-1 United States
Italy 2-0 Czechoslovakia

		P	W	D	L	GF	GA	GD	PTS
1	Italy (H)	3	3	0	0	4	0	+4	6
2	Czechoslovakia	3	2	0	1	6	3	+3	4
3	Austria	3	1	0	2	2	3	−1	2
4	United States	3	0	0	3	2	8	−6	0

Group 2

Cameroon 1-0 Argentina
Romania 2-0 USSR
Argentina 2-0 USSR
Cameroon 2-1 Romania
USSR 4-0 Cameroon
Argentina 1-1 Romania

		P	W	D	L	GF	GA	GD	PTS
1	Cameroon	3	2	0	1	3	5	−2	4
2	Romania	3	1	1	1	4	3	+1	3
3	Argentina	3	1	1	1	3	2	+1	3
4	Soviet Union	3	1	0	2	4	4	0	2

Group 3 results:

Brazil 2-1 Sweden
Costa Rica 1-0 Scotland
Scotland 2-1 Sweden
Brazil 1-0 Costa Rica
Costa Rica 2-1 Sweden
Brazil 1-0 Scotland

		P	W	D	L	GF	GA	GD	PTS
1	Brazil	3	3	0	0	4	1	+3	6
2	Costa Rica	3	2	0	1	3	2	+1	4
3	Scotland	3	1	0	2	2	3	−1	3
4	Sweden	3	0	0	3	3	6	−3	0

Group 4

Colombia 2-0 UAE
West Germany 4-1 Yugoslavia
Yugoslavia 1-0 Colombia
West Germany 5-1 UAE
Yugoslavia 4-1 UAE
West Germany 1-1 Colombia

	P	W	D	L	GF	GA	GD	PTS
1 West Germany	3	2	1	0	10	3	+7	5
2 Yugoslavia	3	2	0	1	6	5	+1	4
3 Colombia	3	1	1	1	3	2	+1	3
4 UAE	3	0	0	3	2	11	−9	0

Group 5

Belgium 2-0 South Korea
Uruguay 0-0 Spain
Spain 3-1 South Korea
Belgium 3-1 Uruguay
Uruguay 1-0 South Korea
Spain 2-1 Belgium

	P	W	D	L	GF	GA	GD	PTS
1 Spain	3	2	1	0	5	2	+3	5
2 Belgium	3	2	0	1	6	3	+3	4
3 Uruguay	3	1	1	1	2	3	−1	3
4 South Korea	3	0	0	3	1	6	−5	0

Group 6

England 1-1 Rep of Ireland
Holland 1-1 Egypt
England 0-0 Holland
Rep of Ireland 0-0 Egypt
England 1-0 Egypt
Rep of Ireland 1-1 Holland

	P	W	D	L	GF	GA	GD	PTS
1 England	3	1	2	0	2	1	+1	
2 Republic of Ireland	3	0	3	0	2	2	0	3
3 Netherlands	3	0	3	0	2	2	0	3
4 Egypt	3	0	2	1	1	2	−1	2

Second round

Cameroon 2-1 Colombia (aet) – Naples – 50,026
Milla (106, 108) ; Redín (115)

Czechoslovakia 4-1 Costa Rica – Bari – 47,673
Skuhravý (12, 63, 82), Kubík (75); González (54)

Argentina 1-0 Brazil – Turin – 61,381
Caniggia (80)

West Germany 2-1 Holland – Milan – 74,559
Klinsmann (51), Brehme (82); R. Koeman (89 pen)

Italy 2-0 Uruguay – Rome – 73,303
Schillaci (65), Serena (83)

Rep of Ireland 0-0 Romania (aet) – Genoa – 31,818
(Rep of Ireland win 5-4 on penalties)

Yugoslavia 2-1 Spain (aet) – Verona – 35,500
Salinas (83); Stojkovic (78, 92)

England 1-0 Belgium (aet) – Bologna – 34,520
Platt (119)

Quarter-finals

Argentina 0-0 Yugoslavia (aet) – Florence – 38,971
(Argentina win 3-2 on penalties)

Italy 1-0 Rep of Ireland – Rome – 73,303
Schillaci (38)

West Germany 1-0 Czechoslovakia – Milan – 73,347
Matthäus (25 pen)

England 3-2 Cameroon (aet) – Naples – 55,205
Platt (25), Lineker (83, 105 pens); Kundé (61 pen), Ekéké (65)

Semi-finals

Argentina 1-1 Italy (aet) – Naples – 59,978
Caniggia (67); Schillaci (17)
(Argentina win 4-3 on penalties)

West Germany 1-1 England (aet) – Turin – 62,628
Brehme (60); Lineker (80)
(West Germany win 4-3 on penalties)

3rd/4th place play-off
Italy 2-1 England – Bari – 51,426
Baggio (71), Schillaci (86 pen); Platt (81)

World Cup Final
West Germany 1-0 Argentina – Rome – 73,603
Brehme (85 pen)

Golden Boot

Salvatore Schillaci – 6

Tomáš Skuhravý – 5

Roger Milla – 4

Gary Lineker – 4

Míchel – 4

Lothar Matthäus – 4

David Platt – 3 s

Andreas Brehme – 3

Jürgen Klinsmann – 3

Rudi Völler – 3

FOOTBA11LEGENDS

F irstly, I'd like to thank my mate Harry Harris for sharing his insight and for tracking down every member of the England squad for sharing their personal recollections of the tournament.

Footba11legends Ltd trades in sports memorabilia and promotes Questions & Answer evenings with football legends. I look forward to reading the finished book which I hope that Harry can re-write history and England win The World Cup in Italy rather than West Germany!

Life seemed so simple in 1990 or at least it was for me and my mates. I was a decent sportsman at school and youth level representing Middlesbrough and Cleveland at Basketball which was no mean feat as I never grew past 5ft 8 ½ inches due no doubt to my Japanese grandfather who had moved to Great Britain in the early 1900's (more about this later).

I was sports captain for my house, year and entire school which was Brookside Comprehensive in Middlesbrough. I went on to study in Newcastle from 1982 to 1988 so watched Newcastle play if Boro games did not clash so I had watched Paul Gascoigne develop and move on to Tottenham Hotspur.

My sports teacher at Brookside was Colin Gerrad an International Basketball referee who had studied at Loughborough University - he was a great teacher, although I did not always appreciate it at the time. In 1990 I had a house in the beautiful North Yorkshire market town of Yarm on Tees and became friends with the managers of the local night clubs and bars in and around the town.

Among my favourite places at that time were The Tall Trees, MacMillan's (after Harold Macmillan 1st Earl of Stockton and Prime Minister of Great Britain 1957 to 1963), The Mall (where The Hitman and Her hosted by Pete Waterman and Michaela Strachan often took up residence), Cross Keys and the Italian restaurant Santoro and The Black Bull.

World In Motion was being played in most of the clubs as New Order were popular and a "real" band. It was hilarious years later to watch James Cordon as Smithy use John Barnes' Rap section in his team talk for comic relief with the England Squad prior to the 2010 World Cup. (My personal opinion is that Smithy should have had John Barnes do a cameo as John nailed it in 1990 and apparently still receives

requests to perform it to this day)

I was later told that ex Middlesbrough and Liverpool Legend Craig Johnston penned the Rap section and he must be some guy as he also created the Adidas Predator football boot and was a great footballer too.

Bryan Robson OBE had been in great form going into the Italia 90 tournament but the press did not give England much of a chance. I played football for the newly formed Silleck Mouldings football team in the Stockton & District League which started life in the 3rd division as newcomers to the league. (We managed consecutive promotions to reach the 1st Division if my memory serves).

Geoff Armatage was instrumental to get company backing for the team from The Directors of Silleck Mouldings. Derek Holgate Sales Director and a loveable Liverpudlian supported the team both financially and from the touch line and knew a thing about football as he was a fan of his hometown team Liverpool FC and his locally adopted Middlesbrough FC.

Geoff managed to get some great signings; Terry Richards, a prolific goal scorer who dropped down from the 1st Division where he was playing for the Cross Keys to the 3rd Division, Alistair a midfield creative and hard tackling Glasgow Rangers fan and Ian who had been released from Wolverhampton Wanderers and was built like Hot Shot Hamish from *Tiger* and *Scorcher* comics.

Ian also had a phenomenal free kick; he was brilliant, any free-kick won he would take or at least wrestle the ball off Terry in order to take. The first free-kick Ian would pick a person in the opposition wall and just smash it at them with such power that any subsequent free-kick the opposition wall would be very weakly defended. Ian was also a Steve Bull fan with his Wolverhampton Wanderers connection.

All of the Silleck Mouldings team were looking forward to the squad to be named for Italia 90 with anticipation. I was expecting Gary Pallister, who had left Middlesbrough in August 1989 to join Manchester United for a British record fee of £2.3 Million, to be named. Gary's departure to Manchester United had opened the way in the Middlesbrough team for another local lad, Nicky Mohan, who I knew well. Nicky always praised Gary for his support and interest in his personal development as a young pro at Boro.

The England squad was named, but we were missing our local hero Pallister as Mark Wright was selected. This caused a few discussions in the Black Bull with most agreeing that Gary was a better defender but not a goal threat on set pieces. We all agreed Pally should have been in the squad over a few beers (we would work them off in training).

Peter Shilton was 40 and in unbelievable form; England's number 1 and master of the art of goalkeeping, his performance against Poland in the qualifiers was out of this world. I still find it incredible how many caps Peter won considering the competition for the number 1 spot. Chris Woods and Dave Beasant were in fine form too.

As a Boro fan I took an interest in The Republic of Ireland squad under our former boss Big Jack Charlton. I had met Jack a few times as a child through a close family friend, Joe Bright, who was the Kit man at Boro for many years. Bernie Slaven, who went on to become a Boro legend, also made the Republic of Ireland's squad for Italia '90. My loyalty however was and always is with England so roll on the first game against The Republic.

The group games came and went with Paul Gascoigne playing brilliantly against the Dutch with Ruud Gullit at the time saying The Netherlands were lucky to get a draw. Mark Wright proved Bobby Robson's selection to be correct playing an excellent game as a sweeper against the Dutch and scoring the vital goal against Egypt which clinched England's qualification to the knockout phases.

This also started my friends and I to believe that England could beat anybody in a knockout game even though Bryan Robson had returned home through injury.

For the Belgium game my friends Christine Little and Andy Read hosted a night at their Yarm apartment along with a selection of Italian food and wine. After two tense hours and with us all preparing ourselves for a penalty shoot-out, Gazza plays a sublime ball and David Platt scores the last-minute goal in extra time. This is one of my all-time favourite goals and I suspect that of a few million other England fans too. It was also the start of Gazza Mania.

Fans are the same as players when it comes to superstitions so it was decided there and then that we couldn't change a winning format so the next game was back at Christine and Andy's; the magic formula worked again - Cameroon 2 England 3 - Christine's special Italian

"The Smile of a Legend"

nights were obviously the missing ingredient for English success! (Gary Lineker was always going to score from 12 yards!)

I have had the opportunity through Football Legends Ltd to meet Legends from these games and speak to them about their thoughts and feelings from their playing time. It has been fabulous arranging signing session and creating some bespoke shirts for some iconic Football Legends which are available @ football1legends watch out also for our digital magazine *FloodLight*.

I find the phrase 'legend' over used but what I believe is that everybody remembers where they watched vital important games if they were not actually at the stadium. We all have our personal favourites; mine from 1990 was Bryan Robson (Captain Marvel, Robbo). I have spoken to Bryan over the years and he told me Italia '90 was when England should have won the World Cup during his playing days. Bryan told me a great story that his son Ben as a youngster adored Gazza and would just stare at him. Bryan also told me Gazza was a phenomenally gifted and talented player which those of us just watching live as a fan may not always have appreciated. Bryan later backed up this belief by signing Paul for Boro from Glasgow Rangers.

I shared this story with Gazza at an event in Newcastle which was hosted by Steve Wraith (a top guy and Newcastle United through and through) at Number 9 Bar at St James Park. Paul went on to say he always treasured pulling on an England shirt and wished he managed to help Robbo lift the Coca Cola Cup when at Boro in the 1997/98 season.

Anyway, back to Italia 90. Bryan Robson, an inspiration and leader on the pitch, had returned home injured and as a fan I thought he

Sir Winston Churchill inspecting his regiment The Royal Scots Fusiliers and my Uncle Ken Kobayashai is the soldier in the foreground. I included this as Gary Lineker has funny story about the Sir Bobby's team talk before the Semi Final.

should have stayed. (Hopefully, I will find out why he did not in this book. I know he was working as a pundit for the BBC.) David Platt had stepped into Bryan's place and scored those important goals and now we'd got to the last four and so it was the semi-final against West Germany on 4th July 1990 and everybody was watching the game at Christine and Andy's. We played the Germans off the park that night and they knew they got lucky. Chris Waddle played one of the best games I had ever seen him play for England and was so unlucky not to score several times throughout the match. Chris is the favourite of my good friend Sophie Wetzel. In the end though perhaps we just didn't quite believe we'd win...

By the end of the tournament everyone accepted that England had a great manager in Sir Bobby Robson; he was a truly inspirational man and Sir Bobby had a team of great leaders on the pitch in Terry Butcher, Peter Shilton OBE, Gary Lineker, Stuart Pearce MBE and of course Bryan Robson OBE.

I would like to take this opportunity to thank the entire England squad of Italia 90 for some fantastic memories and Paul Gascoigne who I believe to be a national treasure not only for his performances in Italia 90 but also for my all-time favourite goal which he scored in 1996 but that's another book for Harry!

The England team came back to a great reception and rightly so after their best performance on foreign soil at that time. The feat was repeated by the current England Manager Gareth Southgate (Boro Legend) and his team in 2018

Good luck to the current England Squad when football resumes we have some fine players in Harry Kane, Jordan Henderson, Raheem Sterling and Trent Alexander Arnold.

Continue to Stay Safe and enjoy the nostalgia of Italia '90 Revisited.

Ant Verrill

@footba11legends

Printed in Great Britain
by Amazon

63509212R00173